PLEASURE BY THE BUSLOAD

Books by EMILY KIMBROUGH

OUR HEARTS WERE YOUNG AND GAY
(with Cornelia Otis Skinner)
WE FOLLOWED OUR HEARTS TO HOLLYWOOD
HOW DEAR TO MY HEART
. . . IT GIVES ME GREAT PLEASURE
THE INNOCENTS FROM INDIANA
THROUGH CHARLEY'S DOOR
FORTY PLUS AND FANCY FREE
SO NEAR AND YET SO FAR
WATER, WATER EVERYWHERE
AND A RIGHT GOOD CREW
PLEASURE BY THE BUSLOAD

PLEASURE

BY THE

BUSLOAD

by Emily Kimbrough

Drawings by
MIRCEA VASILIU

HARPER & BROTHERS • PUBLISHERS
NEW YORK

PLEASURE BY THE BUSLOAD

Copyright © 1961 by Emily Kimbrough
Printed in the United States of America

FIRST EDITION

Library of Congress catalog card number: 61-6195

To the busload with love

GINA,

SOPHY,

ALEC,

BROTHER THEODORE
and
to the bus

Foreword

In this chronicle of a trip through Portugal, I have made no mention of the country's government. The omission was intentional. I have neither the knowledge nor concern that would make such reporting authoritative, even relevant. My purpose was to share the pleasure my companions and I had from landscape and people.

Recent events, however, have brought the government to the front page wherever newspapers are printed. Therefore, lest my seeming unawareness of its existence give the impression my viewpoint of the country was that of an ostrich at bay, I insert this foreword, still about landscape and people.

Shortly after our arrival in Lisbon we were told Dr. Salazar had made known through the press his wish for all his people to have shoes. Our informant assured us we would see a response to this as we made our tour. The country people, who had always traveled the roads barefoot, would display their spirit of co-operation.

We saw that display along the roads. Bright, new pairs of shoes, the soles unscratched because they had never touched the ground, hung around the neck of the owner, or, serenely balanced, rode on the head.

This was Portuguese co-operation as we saw it, from those who heretofore had not owned footwear. Their dictator had said he wished his people to have shoes. He had not said he wished his people to *wear* them.

PLEASURE BY THE BUSLOAD

ONE

It had not been my intention to fly to Lisbon. It is never my intention to include flying when planning a trip. Flight is a last-minute expedient thrust upon me as a *faute de mieux,* and in my opinion travel by air is all *faute* and nothing *mieux* about it. Up above the world so high is the last place I would choose for twinkling like a diamond. Therefore, a travel agency, under my merciless prodding, had found a boat with an itinerary made to order for me and other cravens. The *Olympia* not only goes from New York to Portugal, it sails up the "Main Street" of Lisbon. I would disembark a few blocks from the hotel where my airborne traveling companions would be waiting for me. There is a perverse influence that presides over my travel pattern. It shoots me into the air when I think my heels are firmly dug into the aisle of a train or deck of a boat. This time it accomplished a skyward jerk by crowding speaking and other inextricable engagements around me until there was no way by which I could reach Lisbon on the appointed date except through the air.

Sophy traveled with me. Sophy is a friend of many years and the indispensable, indisputable leader, self-appointed, of any group in which I travel. "Group Leader" is a term by which she is frequently addressed. She can read maps and I cannot; she can figure out how far one place is from another, a branch of mathematics beyond my grasp. She applies herself to learning the language of whatever country is to be visited. I apply myself, too, with a serene conviction that since I absorb and retain things better by ear than by sight I can

1

pick up a language with little effort. This conviction over recent years and trips has begun to waver with my surprised discovery that while I am wrestling with the numerals one to ten in a foreign tongue Sophy and the teacher are involved in the subjunctive mood and a sizable clutch of nouns and adjectives.

We would be five when the full strength of the company assembled in Lisbon. Gina Bachauer and her husband, Alec Sherman, his brother Theodore, Sophy and I. For some months preceding the allotted day and hour of meeting at the Tivoli Hotel in Lisbon, the Shermans would have been on a tour ranging from the West Indies to a smattering of concerts in Gina's native Greece, from there to Israel, back to their house in Alec's native London for a quick change from concert clothes to cottons, and then Lisbon. Alec's brother Theodore somewhere along the way would have grasped the tail of their comet flight and come to earth at Lisbon with them. Letters might have reached Gina and Alec on their brief concert stopovers but I had seen no reason to reiterate in writing the plan shaped in my living room one winter evening when Gina and Alec were staying with me in New York—what time Gina was not at the piano on a concert stage. The five of us, Gina, her husband, her brother-in-law, Sophy and I, had dined together.

The plan had been no carefully nurtured growth from a seedling. It had sprung full-panoplied from my observation that I longed to visit Portugal. I knew very little about the country, I admitted; I did not even know many people who had gone there, but those few had sung the same tune, that they had intended to stay only a few days, and after one had changed their itinerary in order to allow longer time for seeing more of this fascinating country. "Why don't we all go in the spring?" I had proposed, and they had on the instant agreed.

"We go," Gina pronounced. "Alecmou, look in the little book." I have never heard her address her husband by his name alone. *"Mou"* is the Greek for "my." She makes one word, "Alecmou." "See the concert dates—when we are back from Israel. It will be

May I think—" she nodded decisively— "yes, it will be May. That is good for wildflowers and for me. We must see Sintra and Coimbra and Alcobaça. I have played in Portugal but not for a long time and there are many places I have not seen. I will find them for us."

I risked a side glance at Sophy. She is the one who sets the time and places. The expression on her face of total astonishment I had seen only once before, and that was years ago on the Jersey Coast when she came up from under a wave that had taken her by surprise and rolled her up on the beach.

Gina was continuing. "We must have a car. Should we take ours, Alecmou? No, it will be too long in the driving from London. We must not waste the days out of Portugal. Brother Theodore will be in London ahead of us. He can drive his car."

Brother Theodore spoke to Sophy and me: "My car," he said, "is an Austin."

When I first knew Dr. Sherman in London his familiar name was Teddy, but simultaneously with his first visit to New York the preceding winter there had appeared in shop windows and on billboards, placards announcing with startling illustration the arrival of Brother Theodore, a muscular phenomenon who would show the way to salvation through physical development. Since Dr. Sherman is short, slight, with the look and slow gentle voice of a scholar, the application of the title "Brother Theodore" by virtue of its dissimilarity was inevitable.

"It's a *baby* Austin," Brother Theodore repeated, and looked appraisingly at the group. Alec is the same height as his brother, but a little stockier. Gina's beauty partly derives from her heroic proportions in the Greek classical manner. Sophy and I diet ineffectually.

Sophy shook her head in the manner of one endeavoring to rid herself of salt water, sand and loss of breath. She spoke for the first time. "We will hire a car," she said.

Gina approved. "And Alecmou will drive," she volunteered.

Sophy breathed deeply. "If you don't mind, Gina," she said, "I will do the driving. I would count it a favor. I love to drive and frankly I'm more relaxed than when anyone else is at the wheel."

I relaxed at her words. We were both remembering, I felt sure, a story of Gina's that involved Alec whirling over a highway in Germany at some eighty-odd miles an hour, and missing by two hours the turnoff to their destination.

Alec, who is an amenable man, concurred immediately. "If you're sure it won't tire you, I'm happy to be driven."

"And I will read the map—" Gina fell in joyfully with the pattern—"and you will listen to me—which Alecmou never does. That is why once in Germany we missed a turning that I am pointing to on the map, only Alecmou will not look."

Sophy took advantage of the opening granted her. "I will arrange about the car," she offered, "and suppose," she insinuated gently, "I work with a travel agency and draw up a tentative itinerary."

"There is nothing tentative," Gina asserted, "whatever is that word. We go where you say and I find on the map—I show you places I have been—we show ourselves places we have not been— places we are not in before."

Alec inserted the information he too had visited Portugal, as an orchestra conductor, but it had been some time ago and he was not sure how much he remembered.

Gina had cut this short. "Please, Alecmou," she urged, "we will not find out now how much you have not remembered. Later. You will tell us when we are there." She sighed happily. "Now *I* am remembering," she confided, "that it will be the first time for twenty years, perhaps more, that I am as long as two weeks away from a piano." She looked at each of us searchingly. "I will ask you to do this for me. You will go ahead of me when we come to a hotel or a building and if you see a piano in a room, you will turn around quickly and say, 'Gina, do not go in there. There is nothing you would like to see.' Except, of course, a church will not have a piano," she amended. "There I will not have to stay behind to find out if the coast is clearing."

There was very little more we had added to the plan, a desultory

4

talk about clothes, not too many but enough to include medium and lightweight for a range of temperature. Sophy would let us know the hotel that would be our base and where we would meet in Lisbon. Gina and Alec had consulted, their heads together, the little book of concert engagements. Gina had looked up making a rueful moue.

"This will surprise my agent," she said, "but not Gina. The concerts I must cancel are the ones that pay. The ones I can fill are, of course, for charity."

Brother Theodore ventured to suggest if she were not quite so generous in agreeing to give charity concerts her schedule might have included a further release. "She even has ideas of her own," he amplified to Sophy and me, "in addition to the ones she is asked to give. One stormy night in London, I remember, when we were held up in traffic for a long time and she was watching the night life along the street, she said she would like very much to give a concert that would provide raincoats for streetwalkers."

Brother Theodore, Sophy and I had agreed we would continue our trip after Gina and Alec left us for the charity concerts. We would miss them acutely, but we would not cut short our exploration of Portugal. We three would continue for the whole month of May. That had been the end of the community planning and the evening.

Group Leader Jacobs took over. An itinerary began to emerge. The delivery of a drive-it-yourself car in Lisbon was guaranteed. This was not an easy accomplishment in itself because of the model Sophy had stipulated. We had been told by friends who had been to Portugal a drive-it-yourself car was not easily come by nor desirable because throughout the country, even in cities, very few English-speaking people were to be found. A Portuguese chauffeur was helpful in more ways than driving. Sophy, however, already deep in Portuguese subjunctive and conditionals, flouted a chauffeur and demanded a Volkswagen Microbus. She had used one the preceding year in Scotland, she said, and had found it a heaven-sent chariot for transporting a number of people. She had not described it further, and though I had never seen one, I was, as always, docile about her recommendations.

My only interference with the master plan had come about when I discovered my calendar would not permit me to pursue my independent course across the Atlantic by boat. Then I had encroached on Sophy's territory with an ultimatum.

"If I have to fly," I had stipulated, "I will go by one extreme or the other. Since jets are not yet going into Lisbon, there may be old-fashioned planes with berths. I will pay whatever extra is required to allow me to lie down with the covers and pillows over my head. If there are no berths I will go economy. I am not going to loll as I fly, so a difference of inches in reclining will make no difference; but I can be soothed a little by thinking about what I can buy in Portugal with the money I will have saved on the passage. I want a Portuguese rug and Portuguese tiles. If I sit up straight all night I may be able to buy one or the other. You go luxury," I had urged. "You know I don't like to talk when I'm flying. I have to listen to the motors." I had recently been told about a friend, a happy naïve traveler who on her first flight had said joyously to her husband, as they were well out over the Atlantic, "George, aren't these planes wonderful—look at those big propellers; three of them turning around and the fourth ready to turn on as a spare if needed."

"You go luxury," I had repeated to Sophy, "I will listen, do Double-Crostics and think about rugs and tiles." Sophy changed her luxury accommodation already acquired and reserved instead two places economy. I accused her of leaning toward martyrdom and she accepted this diagnosis. "It's calculated," she revealed. "I can use my self-sacrifice as blackmail when I want you to fall in with some plan of mine."

On Thursday afternoon, the twenty-eighth of April, at Idlewild, we weighed in, and over by a hundred pounds.

"Traveling economy," the man at the scales explained apologetically, and unnecessarily. "You're only allowed forty-four pounds." It was Sophy's expression, like the mournfulness of a basset hound, or perhaps my tendency, so my children contend, to tell the story of my life at the moment of any crisis, that made me babble. "It's my dictaphone. Actually this is a new traveling model and lighter than the regular one. I've been given a special attachment, too, that will let me plug it into the car we're going to have in Portugal, so I can talk notes as we travel. It weighs ten pounds."

"That leaves ninety unaccounted for," Sophy explained, as if I were mathematically that weak.

I am not sure I would have pursued a detailed recital of the other contents of my luggage—my children probably think I would have done this—but other people were immediately behind us.

We divided the excess cost between us, thereby adding a financial to a martyr's hold Sophy could exercise. We moved on to secure our seat allotment. In economy class these are not reserved at the time of purchasing the ticket. They must be secured at the airport. We were at the head of a line that formed in front of the desk where they would be assigned; but when that office opened a lofty young man consulting a chart told us all the double seats were gone, we must take places in a bank of three. There is evidently some secret society of economy seat reservers to which Sophy and I do not belong.

We went disconsolately without communication to the bar, where we each drank a bottle of beer and swallowed a pill prescribed and guaranteed by Sophy to still the rising surf in one's stomach. When, after what seemed like several days of waiting, our plane was called, we were approximately in the position of runners at the starting tape. I was the more conspicuously in that crouching position because I was carrying an extra topcoat in addition to the one I wore, a camera over one shoulder, over the other a knapsack filled with books of Double-Crostics, crossword puzzles and paperback detective stories, in one hand my ten-pound dictaphone, in the other my pocketbook of approximately the same weight. By the time an American woman bound for Europe has put into her handbag her passport, traveler's checks, address book, cosmetics and trivia, she could more lightly carry on her arm a six-months-old baby. Therefore, though the stance was for running, the pace was slower.

We arrived at the gate to find one passenger ahead of us. She was a small woman with gray hair; she was inconspicuously and well dressed, except that even seen from behind, her hat looked to be at an angle more raffish than dashing. Her tickets checked, she moved on and turned so abruptly we almost touched noses. Her cheeks were flushed, her eyes widely opened, but a little glazed; she smiled at all of us before she spoke.

"Oh," she said, "I've had so much Dramamine I'm up in the air already. I have the most 'Ithuriel' feeling." Her face saddened unexpectedly. "But do you know something?" she confided. "I haven't got a solitary soul here to kiss me good-by." Her happy smile returned. "So I'm going to kiss everybody here." I backed away in silly embarrassment, but the ticket inspectors, a young man and woman on either side of the exit, were either not so quick or not so self-conscious. Each one was enthusiastically hugged and smacked. With renewed buoyancy the happy traveler returned her wavering steps toward the plane. Again she stopped. So did the ticket tenders in the act of affirming my credentials. We crowded the doorway with Sophy coming up abreast—a captivated audience. I think none of us anticipated what the star's next turn would be. From the gate at which we clustered, a long enclosed passageway led on our right to the open airfield. I do not know what its terminus was to the left, but at a small distance from us in that direction a man stood at one of the windows that lined the passage. Perhaps he was awaiting the arrival of a passenger; he may have been only watching planes landing and taking off. He was as unobtrusive in appearance as in his purpose for being there, but he caught the dancing eye of Miss Dramamine. With finger to her lips she tiptoed down the passage until she stood behind him. She put her arms around his neck and covered his eyes with her hands. His startled jump nearly unbalanced them both, but she spoke soothingly.

"'There's no use your trying to guess who this is because you don't know me. I just want you to turn around and kiss me good-by. I'm going traveling in that big airplane over there and the Dramamine and a few other little things I've been taking have made me happy as a person could be. Except that I haven't got anybody to kiss me good-by." She moved her hands down to his shoulders, spun him around to face her and planted a hearty buss. "Now that was very sweet of you to wish me *bon voyage*," she assured the object of her transitory affection, though that object had not uttered an audible sound. Off she went in the direction from which she had swerved, singing a little tune I did not identify, and at a gait I associate with children at nursery school who are learning to skip but can only do it on one foot. The gentleman she had accosted and quitted with equal spontaneity revolved himself back to his original position and resumed his watch at a window with not so much as a look, let alone a spoken inquiry to her or her audience. Our number had increased during her farewell scene. Passengers coming up behind Sophy and me were held back with us at the threshold by the gatekeepers. Perhaps they did not wish their own view impeded; they might have reckoned that a sudden influx of people would provide for the happy traveler so generous a scope for good-by kissing our plane departure could be delayed. Whatever the reason, we were not released until the hopping skipper was out of sight. Sophy was enveloped in dour foreboding.

"Mark my words," she told me, as we walked the corridor, "that will be our seat companion."

She was not. We did not see her nor hear her voice again. I think after her exhilaration she was wafted across the Atlantic in quiet sleep.

Sophy insisted I take the seat on the aisle; the one by the window was already occupied. "You won't feel trapped," she urged. "If you get restless you can move about." I was ashamed to admit to her, because I know it is irrational, how much I dislike anyone's moving about on a plane. I am convinced this unsettles its balance and makes doubly difficult the job of the pilot to keep it from tipping. I wish everyone would sit down and stay there. I know this is irrational, because I have much the same feeling on an ocean liner. When the captain of the *Queen Elizabeth* sends word through the loudspeaker that the *Constitution* will soon be visible on the port side, I must muster all the self-control I can summon to keep from moving among the passengers with the suggestion we do not all go to the port side at the same time, but arrange ourselves in even shifts so that the spectators can be balanced by an even number on the starboard side awaiting their turn to change places.

The take-off in my estimation lasted about a day and a half. The pilot, announcing over the loudspeaker heavy traffic ahead had held us up, computed the delay at thirty minutes. During that time I reviewed my shortcomings and the inadequacy of the things accomplished in my life. I resolved to sweeten my nature to saintliness and to accomplish finer and greater things, were I permitted a longer life span. Sophy, while the engines roared and we stood still, read a newspaper, as irritating to me as the sleep of her neighbor. But in my newly promised nobility of character, I did not remonstrate.

When the stewardess, as soon as our safety belts were removed after the take-off, came to inquire if we would like to order drinks, I thought enviously of the hop-skipping traveler, wondering if I might acquire the ingredients for Euphoria. I remembered dismally such happy-making stimulants were not for me. I was morose because I had a foreboding nothing she could offer would provide the elation I coveted. The reason for my skepticism was that some twenty-five years ago I was stricken with a violent allergy to alcohol in the form of whiskey or gin or brandy. A rash of hives was the least of the plagues that swept over me within a few minutes of a few sips of a cocktail. So for nearly twenty-five years I have tasted nothing stronger alcoholically than vermouth, Dubonnet or wine.

"Have you Dubonnet?" I asked the stewardess. She not only did not have it; she had never heard of it. "White wine? I will have a small bottle and some soda." No white wine. "Very well, then, plain vermouth with ice."

10

"We have no vermouth. Our cocktails are already mixed."

She was becoming impatient and I was approaching desperation. "You have only whiskey or gin?" I was pleading for just one item of selection closer to my category.

"And vodka," she amplified.

"I will have a vodka Martini," I told her.

"My God," came fervently from Sophy, who up to this time had taken no part in the conversation.

At the stewardess' look of polite inquiry, she added with even greater fervor, "A double Scotch for me." The stewardess moved to the next bank of seats.

Sophy put to me a question she did not mean to be rhetorical. "Do you want to die?"

I considered this briefly, but reflectively. "I'm not sure; if I become unconscious that will be lovely."

"For me, too," Sophy echoed bitterly, "just lovely. How will I get you, dead or unconscious, through the customs at Lisbon?"

The vodka Martini did not make me unconscious—it did not even give me hives. When nothing happened after the first one I tried another. Over Sophy's moans, I polished off a third; then I did have a reaction. I slipped off into a blissful, dreamless sleep, that carried me over the Atlantic and through the night. When I awakened without a blemish, without even a headache, the sky was pink and there was land beneath us. I turned my head lazily to tell Sophy the miracle vodka had bestowed upon me, and saw she was asleep, but in a jerky and, it seemed to me, uncomfortable pattern. It began with her head up, progressed through its steady lowering, reached its nadir at a neck-snapping jolt, then began again. I felt sure my slumber had not been punctuated by such convulsions. With an urge to good will induced by my own miracle, I thought to bring peace to Sophy. Doubling the small pillow with which I had been provided, I pushed it under her chin, securing the immobility of her head by wedging the pillow with my elbow and, to keep the elbow and pillow firm, bracing my hand on the arm of the seat lowered between us. Then by miracle twice given I drifted off to sleep again. I wakened to a sense of turmoil and upheaval somewhere. Sitting up to ascertain the source I removed my hand from the arm of the seat. The pillow released from the brace of my elbow fell down as if thrown and I saw that Sophy was holding her throat, that she seemed to be blushing deeply, and that her eyes bulged. In considerable anxiety I asked her to speak to me. Her mouth opened and closed a few times before she spoke. Her voice, when it came, was a hoarse rasp. "I'm choking to death," she said. "Was that your idea?"

"I was trying to help you sleep more comfortably," I explained, and I was a little offended. "From the way your head jerked I thought you might snap a vertebra." Sophy's expression conveyed ingratitude; but she said nothing further until she had massaged her throat and gingerly moved her head from side to side and up and down.

"I slept like a child," I told her. "The night is over. We'll be in Lisbon within an hour."

Evidently I had tried Sophy's temper even before I applied the pillow. When she spoke after completing a treatment on her neck she revealed another grievance.

"I know you slept like a child," she corroborated bitterly. "I watched you. I thought if you were dying I'd better know it, though God knows what I could have done about it." She shuddered. "Three vodka Martinis. My God! Finally, when I'd convinced myself you were sleeping, not dying, I dropped off. It must have been nearly daylight by then. And you chose to help me sleep by ramming your elbow into my windpipe." She looked at me searchingly. "Are you planning to make a habit of vodka Martinis?"

I shook my head. "Right back to the vermouth, Dubonnet or wine," I assured her. "Vodka is for flying. Not Dramamine, not Phenobarb, just beautiful vodka Martinis, three of them."

To leave the plane we walked through the de luxe section and stopped in the aisle there to allow a passenger emerging from one of the seats to precede us. As she turned to gather up her handbag from the seat we recognized a friend from New York. In the

startled pleasure of recognition and surprise at an unexpected encounter, we exchanged the inevitable inanities of "I didn't know you were on this plane, I didn't see you get on," etc. These and a recital of our respective itineraries carried us across the field. We paused at the entrance to the customhouse. This friend was going on to Madrid, but with an hour's stopover in Lisbon she would have a little breakfast and exercise at the airport.

"It was a nice flight," she said. "I slept all the way. But then I always do," she admitted. "I take two sleeping pills." She turned to me. "Do you?"

"No," I said, smiling in happy reminiscence, "I never take sleeping pills."

13

TWO

Among the flaws in my character I acknowledge and tabulate during a wakeful night is a form of egotism. This manifests itself in the assumption that among the mail on a friend's desk is undoubtedly a letter for me. When I happen to meet a Western Union messenger entering my apartment building as I am walking out of it, I am likely to offer to take the message and save him the trouble of finding my apartment, though my address includes a number of other occupants. Encounter with a florist delivery boy or any other package delivery stimulates the same impulse. I do not receive more telegrams than my neighbors receive, flowers are rarely sent me, and except at Christmastime I do not receive surprise packages. Let a hotel page mouthing a gibberish of syllables come within my hearing and I am sure the syllables properly articulated would make "Kimbrough," though I do not remember ever in my life having been paged in hotel or restaurant.

Therefore, the surprising thing is I was startled to hear my name actually and distinctly called as Sophy and I entered the customhouse in Lisbon. Incredulous, I asked Sophy if what we were hearing didn't sound to her like a Portuguese version of Kimbrough. Sophy corroborated my hearing accuracy, and I was instantly invaded by teeth-chattering panic. At home I am not alarmed by the sight of a telegram when I do receive one, nor the announcement that the telephone call is long distance, though I know people who dread both these forms of communication. Had I been summoned by a page at home I would have followed him with equanimity. But to be called by a herald in a strange country at the instant of my arrival could only be a summons to disastrous news. Something awful had happened at home, to my children, my grandchildren, brother and his family, my stepmother in California. I listed them all and found myself returning on the next plane anguished beyond the ministrations of a dozen vodka Martinis. I managed to ask Sophy to get the message, and leaned against the nearest luggage counter for the support my knees were not giving me. I knew she understood and shared my terror, because she only patted my shoulder saying, "I'll be right back," and moved rapidly down the room. I do not know how long she was gone—I was either numb or praying.

Suddenly she was returning, smiling and revolving one hand in the air in a manner to indicate a hurrah. When she came within earshot she cupped both hands around her mouth and called, "The car; it's here." I marvel at my fortitude and that of other people with families who can leave their dear ones and set out happily on a voyage. I thought, as I eased away from the luggage counter and tested the return of strength to my knees, it was remarkable that tourists abroad were not exclusively a group of solitary individuals with no home ties. How could we others voluntarily incur such torture as had racked me?

"The carriage waits. The Volkswagen is at the door," Sophy announced as she reached me. "How about that for service?" and patted my shoulder once more understandingly. "But why on earth would they call your name? I made all the arrangements." We never learned the reason.

The customs in Lisbon is easily got through, expeditiously and courteously managed. It follows the pattern of every European country I have visited, with the exception of Yugoslavia. Discomfort there was caused by the misapprehension on the part of Yugoslavian officials that the letters in the traveling scrabble set I carried represented a code and that I was therefore a spy. My detention in Dubrovnik, however, was not of much longer duration and inconvenience than the United States Customs requires of every traveler. In Europe baggage is placed by porters on a counter.

15

There it is examined by a customs official, while the porters wait, and then carried to whatever conveyance the passenger indicates. Why does the United States require luggage from a ship to be placed on the floor of the dock? In Europe, where the examination of incoming baggage is perfunctory, the arrangement is at a convenient height; but in America, where examination of baggage can be thorough, the owner must first assemble his pieces, however heavy, then sink to his haunches to open them—disastrous to a woman's nylons—or bend down, dislodging shoulder strap handbag, camera, coat over the arm and whatever other impedimenta are personally attached.

This, however, is a digression. One day I will offer suggestions for its betterment to the United States Customs. Undoubtedly the only accomplishment derived from this will be a temporary relief of my own spleen, but I will not permit myself this therapy at the moment when I am recording the pleasure of the comfortable and courteous handling of customs at Lisbon, and my mounting excitement at the realization I was on the ground again, and the ground was in Portugal.

A young blond German was waiting for us at the door. He identified himself as the driver of the Volkswagen. He had brought it down from Düsseldorf and if we would wait but a moment he would bring it from the parking lot. I had accepted with equanimity Sophy's choice of vehicle in which we would travel; I follow submissively the criterion that Group Leader knows best; but Group Leader had not included in her description a visual picture of our carriage. I am certain I have never seen a Volkswagen Microbus; I could not have forgotten such a sight. Therefore, I was unprepared to recognize, let alone acknowledge possession of, the coach that lumbered out of the parking lot across the road and drew up beside us. I had to claim it, however, because of the blond German driver. He jumped out and came around smiling to assist the porter stow our luggage.

"Is this what we're going to travel in?" It could scarcely be anything else. "I thought it was a delivery truck."

16

"This is a Volkswagen Microbus," Sophy answered. (I had already reached that conclusion.) "I told you all about it."

No one had told me it looked as big as a trailer, and that the step from ground to floorboard was a span well over three feet, not possible to accomplish in a tight skirt except by raising it sufficiently to allow one's knee full play. I was to learn this never failed to charm the Portuguese within eyesight to a rapt scrutiny of the procedure.

Sophy climbed in beside the driver. I derived more than a little pleasure from observing that after two unsuccessful tries she achieved that position by tossing her large handbag ahead of her onto the seat and then, with both hands free, hauling herself into place, clutching the back of the seat and the edge of the windshield. I had made my entry while she was supervising the stowing of the luggage, by using as a hoist the metal rod that ran across the back of the front seat, designed to carry rugs or coats, I daresay. I was thankful that it carried me into position.

All the way in to town, and it is a drive of something over half an hour, the young German spoke on one or the other of two subjects: the inefficiency of the Portuguese system for regulating traffic —and this in some way obscure to me had made it difficult for him to find his way about—or the impossibility of a woman's handling the vehicle he was at the moment driving. He himself could drive anything equipped with a motor, but certainly a woman's capability was limited and a Volkswagen Microbus exceeded the horizon of her capability. I saw the back of Sophy's neck and her spine stiffening and wondered the driver did not sense the cold air that seemed to rise and circulate within the car. Though I attempted a distraction by pointing out the charm of the scene around us, the temperature did not rise perceptibly.

The scene was charming. The section of the city through which we passed was made up almost entirely of apartment buildings of modern and, to me, stunning design. The exteriors of the buildings were in soft colors—yellows, pinks, grays, blues. Each apartment in every building had its own balcony. If there was one not awash

17

with flowers I did not see it; flowers in hanging baskets, in window boxes along the edge, flowering vines climbing up the dividing wall that separated the adjoining balcony, splotches of bright color against the pastel of the buildings themselves.

I was not surprised when we reached the hotel to hear Sophy decline the driver's offer to accompany her on a trial spin in order to give her his every possible assistance. He conveyed in this offer of services the actual accomplishment would be irrefutable proof to her that she could not possibly handle this car; his next offer would be of himself as conductor of the tour. I was not surprised at her refusal, but the young German was dumfounded. Was there perhaps someone else who was going to give her instruction? The sweetness of her tone when she gave assurance she would need no assistance should have made that young man tremble. Blandly he informed her the car was covered by insurance, but not for its complete demolition. I have read that a cobra weaves from side to side before it strikes. Sophy swayed a little on her feet before she told him she would be responsible for damages she might cause, and she would like him to go at once. We did not see the blond young German again.

Our room at the Tivoli was not oversized, but adequately large, comfortable and with a view from its row of windows to the tree-lined esplanade of the Avenida da Liberdade below. Looking down on its broad expanse of green lawn and tree-lined paths, paved in black and white mosaics, suddenly I had no eye for a view and no energy for unpacking. I was overcome with exhaustion and the need for sleep. In spite of the useful knockout of the vodka Martinis, the actual hours of unconsciousness had not been enough to count as a night's rest. When I had wakened, I had, of course, resumed helping to fly the plane. Keeping it up in the air and bringing it down to a safe landing had been both a mental and physical strain.

On my mentioning my sudden fatigue Sophy declared herself both tired and hungry, taking pains to remind me her period of sleep had been less than mine. We ordered and ate a delicious breakfast of oranges, eggs, rolls and tea and immediately after took to our beds. When I wakened it was late afternoon and Sophy was dressed.

"I couldn't make up my mind whether to wake you or leave you," she said when she saw me rousing. "I'm going out in the car. Maybe you'd rather I went alone after what that young—" she paused— "whippersnapper said." It was obvious another term for him had first come into her mind. I was already dressing as I assured her nothing would induce me to stay behind; I had every confidence in her driving.

It was not until I had climbed in beside Sophy that I realized there was nothing but the windshield between me and space and the street far below. This was going to be like riding on a roller coaster. Why the presence of a hood in front should be soothing I do not know, unless it is a comfort to think first the bumper, then the hood must be crunched before collision reaches the passenger. I do know there is a sense of exposure, of naked vulnerability about the front seat of a car relegating its engine to the rear. I had not noticed either from my position during the ride in from the airport the wheel of this equipage was set flat like the wheel in a bus. To manipulate it Sophy assumed a somewhat crouching position with her arms and hands around its circumference as if she were holding it in maternal embrace.

We were not in the most fortuitous position for starting a first trip in a strange car. The street in front of the Tivoli Hotel is narrow and yet a trolley line runs through the center of it. Moreover, trolleys run on this line frequently. In order to be out of their way, cars are parked up over and beyond the curb. They must be brought down again when a tram is not passing and this occurs infrequently. They pass in an almost steady procession, but at a slow tempo, so slow that passengers step off and on anywhere along the block without putting the motorman to the inconvenience or exertion of stopping his vehicle. This provides, however, an additional hazard for the motorist. It is not enough to time his entry to fit a space between trolleys; he must also fit it among passengers who can unexpectedly pepper the street. Sophy made the descent without strik-

ing either trolley or passenger. We both breathed deeply after this accomplishment. Flushed with pleasure and magnanimity, Sophy asked me to say which way we should go, though, she added, in her opinion if we kept straight ahead we would probably come to the part of the city we most wanted to see.

It had been my idea to propose that very route, but to have Sophy designate it was disquieting. This is not because of contrariness on my part, but because of a peculiar trait on hers. She can read a map with such pin-point accuracy I am reduced to speechless awe and that is a very considerable reduction. But let her rely on her instincts to find her way about a city, and she will, as unerringly as a beagle on a rabbit's scent, go to its slums. If there are dark and possibly dangerous quarters in a city, Sophy will take you there. She has only to say, "I have a feeling the Ritz is off this way," to lead you without deviation to a rattletrap, probably rat-infested tenement area, whose inhabitants at the windows and pedestrians on the street eye the invasion with cold, sullen suspicion. In all the trips I have taken with Sophy as chauffeur these are the only places in which she has stalled the motor.

Understandably, then, I quailed at Sophy's suggestion we move straight ahead. At the same time, I thought the Tagus River must be somewhere in that direction, not because I had found it on a map—I have seldom found anything on a map that I was seeking— but because we had not seen it on our way in from the airport. In my simple pattern of reasoning I therefore felt it must be further on ahead of us. I decided to risk Sophy's instincts and fell in with her suggestion. We were presently in the shopping and business heart of the city. The broad esplanade we had seen from our windows terminated in a large circle, like a sunburst, narrow streets its rays. We passed on our right a building of such beauty of design and decoration I was sure it must be an art museum and marked it for a later visit. It turned out to be a railway station. Other travelers have derided its style; I defend it. On either side of us as we kept our single direction the streets rose steeply. At one intersection I saw a rise so sharp the street above it was reached by a funicular. I knew resignedly, feeling as I do about leaving the ground, let alone being airborne in a frail, swinging basket, I would not visit that quarter. Unexpectedly, we came to the end of the narrow way we had been following. At right angles to it was a broad highway and on the far side, the river Tagus.

The Tagus is wide and beautiful, the sun was on it, the water was blue. I had not expected it to be such a busy thoroughfare; it was as crowded with traffic as the highway that ran beside it. We saw ferries and freighters and fishing boats. At least I saw them. Sophy was muttering imprecations at the erratic pattern other drivers were weaving. Portuguese taxis are small and black. They scuttle like beetles on unpredictable courses at demoniac speed. I shuddered at the inevitable prospect of being in one of them. Sophy's, I knew, was the more immediate prospect of keeping her vehicle out of their way. When she had maneuvered a right turn on the highway she relaxed a little and allowed herself a frequent glance at the scene.

On the far side of the broad river, we could see sloping green meadows, trees and hills beyond. On one of these, startling white, and of great height, a statue of Christ with arms outstretched, not in crucifixion, but in benediction, blesses the city. We learned later this can be seen from many miles away in every direction, save the part of the city proper where tall buildings stand in its way. The fishing boats were our particular and immediate delight, because they are so gay. Their long prows rise far above the water and are painted with bright colors in variegated patterns. The sails slant back from the prow. Somehow they made me think of a full-breasted woman moving into the wind and lifting her skirts high.

Unexpectedly and simultaneously our attention slued to a boat of such size it was obviously a liner. She was coming from the horizon and the sea, turning up the river toward us.

I made a rapid calculation of date, and said as Sophy pointed to it, "I see it and I know what it is. That's the *Olympia* coming into port. I might have been watching this scene from its deck."

My calculations were right. When we came back an hour or so later she was coming into dock and we read her name clearly.

Meantime, we had followed the coastal highway as far out of Lisbon as Estoril. Hearing about it before coming to Portugal, I had not realized this is within a half-hour's drive from Lisbon, and I had heard of it whenever anyone spoke of a short stay in Portugal. Many people to whom I had talked about my proposed trip had told of a day's stopover between planes. These travelers had invariably driven out to Estoril, describing it invariably and somewhat monotonously as "the famous resort," famous because of its gambling casino and because a number of deposed or exiled European monarchs make it their holiday meeting ground. I would not have chosen it, but perhaps royalty likes sumptuous hotels, or possibly monarchs, active or deposed, have not so wide a selection as we lesser folk. Estoril looked to Sophy and me like Atlantic City with California vegetation. Once we had encircled it, we turned our backs and returned to Lisbon. All along our route were bathing beaches; though it was late afternoon in April with a temperature of sixty degrees, there was a considerable population on the sand and in the water. The road was fringed with palm trees; we passed groves of eucalyptus, first recognizing by a pungent and unmistakable smell they were somewhere in our vicinity. Roses spilled over stone walls and climbed up the front and to the roof of many of the houses we passed. Other houses displayed an entire façade of tiles in intricate patterns, sometimes of a single color against a white background, elsewhere in combinations of blues, greens, oranges. I had looked forward to seeing tiles in Portugal; I had read about them and seen illustrations of them in cathedrals; "*azulejos*" they are called. I had even in the back of my mind the hope of purchasing enough to cover the floor of the entrance hall in my apartment in New York. I had not anticipated seeing the whole front of a house done in tiles. By my modest dimensions, a legend portrayed in life-sized figures seems a little overboard in decoration.

By the time we had returned to the city district of the waterfront the homecoming rush hour was around us by land and by sea. I found nothing remarkable in the land traffic. It might have been

New York, Chicago, any city at the end of the day. I made this observation to Sophy. Her answer, between gritted teeth, was that if I were doing the driving, I would find plenty to remark about.

"It's not so much the speed," she explained, "as the way these cars can cut in and out—you'd think they were made of rubber the way they can be turned."

I would have liked more soothing words, something to the effect that she felt completely at home. I turned my attention to the waterfront. There, indeed, were sights to bring out words of surprise and delight. Fishing boats were docking, freighters were putting in, ferries taking on commuters going home across the river. From the freighters and fishing boats women were unloading cargo. In Italy and in Greece I have seen women carrying bundles on their heads, but it was in Portugal on that late afternoon I first saw women striding swiftly and easily down a gangplank and along the shore under a bag or more of cement, a basket big as a clothes hamper filled to overflowing with fish or fagots. I did not see a stooped back, nor any other evidence that the load was heavy. I have heard my grandmother tell of being made to walk about, when a child, with a book on her head in order to develop a straight carriage and the proper lift of her head. I do not know that a Portuguese child starts with a book and progresses in womanhood to a bag of cement, but I can assert that I have never seen anywhere such superb posture and such glorious freedom of movement. These women swung their arms rhythmically, but not conspicuously. Frequently they called some chatter to friends behind or alongside, turning their bodies effortlessly and with such precision of balance the mound on top of the head was not so much as tilted. I begged Sophy to pull to the side of the road and stop so that she could watch them.

"You've never seen anything like it," I promised, "and you're going to see what the poetry of motion really is."

Sophy assured me she would be only too delighted to exchange the view she was not enjoying for the one that was making me gasp, if only she could find a stopping place. Obviously, on this thoroughfare we could not simply draw up at the curb. It was only a minute later we saw simultaneously a kind of by-pass—a line of cars parked there, but one beautiful space. Sophy stopped the car as soon as it was possible, but even so, we were enough beyond to require backing into the place. Sophy signaled out her window she was about to do this—I sat back with tranqillity. I know Sophy is an expert driver; if a space is equivalent to the length of the car she is driving, she can back into it. Backing, however, requires going into reverse and this gear in our Volkswagen Microbus was, in precise terms, a clinker. The first time she shifted, released the clutch, and we moved forward, we both laughed at the absurdity of making such a mistake. By the fifth time, neither of us laughed, and neither could have heard the sound of laughter because of the din from the cars behind. I only looked back once. The sight was so horrifying I did not wish to repeat it, nor did I describe to Sophy what I had seen: a mass of cars behind us that seemed to stretch to the horizon and the driver of every one of them within my vision pressing his hand on the horn.

Perhaps it was just as well that Sophy's rancor at the young German had made it impossible for her to inquire about possible idiosyncrasies in our machine, let alone be given a demonstration. I doubt such knowledge would have kept her from taking the wheel, but it could have cast a cloud over the serenity we had until this moment been enjoying.

Sophy, red in the face, rose unexpectedly from her seat, as high as the steering wheel would permit. She grasped the gear shift with both hands; her purpose may have been to uproot it; but, suddenly, and as smoothly as if the car were on roller skates, we were backing. I saw her lips move—I have reason to believe from experience she was uttering a torrid invective, perhaps a shout of triumph. In the cacophony from the horns around us I could not have heard her sing the battle cry of the Valkyrie.

The blaring around us did not subside for an appreciable time. Sophy and I looked fixedly toward the river, our heads turned far enough away from the road to avoid the eye of drivers passing as they were released from bedlam. We heard phrases, however, and though I did not understand Portuguese I grasped the sentiment.

Watching the boats and their unloading restored Sophy's composure and natural color. There is a list I carry in my memory, and each recital of it brings a catch in my breath. It is titled: "The First Time I Saw"—the Eiffel Tower, Westminster Abbey, St. Peter's, the Acropolis and, now, Portuguese women, moving caryatids, their heads high, arms swinging, their skirts, swelled by many petticoats beneath, eddying a little, their strong beautiful feet setting the tempo, and the music they make wherever they go, chatter, laughter and snatches of song.

When we drove back to the Tivoli the rush hour had passed. Sophy knew exactly the route to take. Possibly a little giddy at a triumphal journey without a single false turn, she drew into the entrance of the hotel with something of a flourish and considerable of a crunching sound behind us. What she had accomplished verified the ominous sound we had heard. A front fender of a modest little car immediately behind our formidable bus was wilted. Sophy's estimate of the length of our vehicle had not done it justice. I had a feeling, and acted on it; the most tactful course for me to pursue was one that would take me away from the scene and up to our room. When Sophy joined me sometime later she had learned the car belonged to a member of the Norwegian Embassy visiting the hotel to call on the new Norwegian Ambassador who had arrived that day, and offer the services of his car until the Ambassador's own would be available. Sophy would, of course, pay the damages, but that would scarcely provide the Ambassador with a conveyance by which the young secretary had probably hoped to make character, if not advancement. Furthermore, she said, wringing her hands a little, he had been so polite, so generous about the mishap as to make her feel even more guilty than at the moment when the horrid crunch had occurred.

The "shoebag hour," for which I had made readiness, comforted her. This is a practice that by daily repetition on a number of trips has developed into something between a ceremony and an institution. I have not found traveling companions who, given the opportunity, do not prefer a drink before dinner in the quiet of someone's room to having that drink in the hotel or some other bar. Therefore, Sophy, in addition to being the courier, takes on the office of sommelier. No matter how wide the range of preferences to satisfy the taste of each member of the party, Sophy provides the ingredients. By a curious and intricate pattern of reasoning, however, she does not like to carry her stock in a valise designed for such a purpose. Although such luggage is available and has been pointed out to her, Sophy's assertion is such a piece of baggage is ostentatious and self-conscious. At such times, she reveals the depth of her roots in conservative Philadelphia. She likes, she says, to carry bottles casually. Her achievement of casualness is by way of a shoebag. The baptism of a newcomer to our travel group never fails to give him a moment's shock. Invariably his eyes widen when he sees Sophy unbuckling the straps of her shoebag, extricate from ankle straps or rubber-soled walking shoes a bottle of Scotch, one of gin, bourbon, vermouth and whatever else the individual requirements of the group demand. There is always a bottle of white wine for me. The locale of these objects is the reason the ceremony has come to be known as the "shoebag hour."

We dined at the hotel. That was in itself an experience, not because of the food, though that was excellent, if not exceptional, but by virtue of the way in which it was served. There are synonyms for countries so fixed in one's mind I would wager a parlor game word association test would almost unanimously bring such clichés as: Great Britain—roast beef; France—light wines and dancing; Italy—spaghetti; Spain—bullfights and leisure. The one Spanish word universally known, I think, is *"mañana,"* and equally universal is the picture of sunny Spain where people doze in the sun and put off any activity whenever possible until *"mañana."* I have not visited Spain, but in my ignorance I had supposed the customs and point of view between Spain and Portugal were interchangeable. I was to learn the Portuguese do not wish to interchange anything with the Spanish. They pride themselves on being unable to speak or understand the language of that country. They do not wish their bullfights to be confused with those of Spain, and *"amanhã,"* the Portuguese for *"mañana,"* is not a word they live by.

The rush-hour traffic had tilted my preconception of an oxcart tempo I would find in Portugal. Dinner that night turned it all the way upside down. I have not at a lunch counter in a railway station been served with the rapidity with which food was presented to, and taken away from, me that night, and every succeeding night. The Tivoli Hotel may hold a speed record, but other restaurants are runners-up. Sophy and I had previously been accused by traveling associates of being the fastest eaters they had ever encountered. I am frequently embarrassed at a dinner party to realize I have finished a course before others at the table have made any perceptible inroad. Dalliers at the Tivoli must go to bed hungry. I relinquished my soup spoon in order to butter a roll. The soup was immediately removed, and the next course set before me. After that I held on to my knife and fork and, at the approach of a waiter, my plate as well. When we left the dining room, perhaps thirty minutes after we had entered it, Sophy and I realized and admitted to each other we had not exchanged throughout the meal one word of conversation, and that we were both in a condition of somewhat breathless indigestion. A walk down the esplanade restored our internal equilibrium. We were relieved to discover we were walking in the company of people promenading slowly, and passing other groups sitting relaxed at small tables scattered among the trees, drinking coffee and eating water ices in leisurely fashion. There were brightly lighted booths selling refreshments along the paths, fruit juices, candy, ices, ice cream, little cakes and coffee. All these confections were attractively displayed and the booths spotlessly clean. Nevertheless, Sophy and I were too recently released from the pressure of food to be able to sample these delicacies. Instead, we left the promenade for a dazzlingly lighted motion picture house that advertised a newsreel of Princess Margaret's wedding. The words "Princess Margaret" were not difficult to extricate from the surrounding Portuguese. The theater itself, though not so big as Radio City, would match in size, or very nearly, any of the other large motion picture houses in New York. Like American audiences, this one munched; not only popcorn, but nuts and candy. The captions for the wedding were of course in Portuguese. The newsreel moved on to shots of an atomic submarine launching in New London, Connecticut. New London is not far from the place in which I spend each summer. Though I am quite accustomed to seeing abroad American motion pictures bearing captions in the language of that country, it did give me a sense of uneasy ambivalence between familiarity and strangeness to see so familiar an environment described in terms completely unintelligible to me.

As we walked back to the hotel, I tried to define my frame of mind. "I'm not homesick," I said, "but to see New London in Lisbon makes me feel—queasy."

"You haven't recovered from bolting your dinner," was Sophy's rejoinder. "Try a soda-mint."

THREE

A specific errand took us out next morning at an early hour. We wanted to get it out of the way before we began our sight-seeing. I was responsible for the necessity of this errand, but I could not perform it without Sophy's assistance. When I explained to Sophy what I required of her, she was volubly unhappy.

"I suppose I should be flattered," she told me bitterly, "but I think you're out of your mind to suppose a few weeks at the Berlitz School has taught me how to say in Portuguese to a garageman, 'This gadget I have brought is an attachment for my friend's dictaphone. It is to be placed somewhere or other under the hood of our car, and the attaching wires brought up through the dashboard in that hole for a cigarette lighter, which the Volkswagen does not provide. Then if you will provide a plug, my friend can attach her dictaphone. In this way, she can take notes as we travel, and at the same time, recharge the battery of the machine.' And for all that," Sophy concluded, "which I don't even understand in English, I know one Portuguese word—machine."

Nevertheless, she went with me. First to the Europeia Travel Bureau, two blocks from our hotel at 231 Avenida da Liberdade. We established our identity, Sophy verified arrangements for our itinerary made at the Travel Bureau in New York. We had been told the Europeia was its correspondent in Portugal, and would be expecting us. They would receive our mail and forward it to us when we were out of Lisbon.

Although my anticipation of Portugal's tempo had been immediately contradicted, my anticipation that there was not yet a tourist invasion of Portugal was vindicated by our visit to the Europeia.

There were, I think, ten people behind the counter. Each one greeted us courteously and not one in English. The only member of the personnel who could hold conversation with us had to be summoned from another department somewhere upstairs. Tourism, at least the English-speaking variety, has not flooded this country; it is as yet only a thin trickle.

The English spokesman at the Europeia was young, earnest, efficient and eager to please. The sum of these qualities, however, fell short of being equal to a dictaphone part that must be inserted in the engine of a Volkswagen. I do not blame him for saying he could not accompany us as interpreter, because he was needed at the office; no one would want his language deficiency exposed by a machine part; I was grateful for his offer as a guide, a member of the Bureau personnel, who would lead us in his car to the Volkswagen headquarters. Our guide was young, handsome; he drove a dashing little sports car; he could not speak a word in any language but Portuguese. Still, he knew the streets of Lisbon, and led us in the Volkswagen through a labyrinth of them to a large garage.

Once there, Sophy and I were on our own, except for the physical presence of our guide, and that was omnipresent. Allowing for a difference of some 130 pounds, 3 feet, and perhaps 25 years, he could have been my five-year-old grandson, Alexander, who, watching his father work on the family car, directs the proceedings. Our six-foot boy first placed himself between me and the two mechanics who came to inquire our needs. After a dramatic recitative he stepped aside and presented me, pointing to my apparatus, the "thing" to be attached, that I held in one hand, the case holding my dictaphone in the other. Setting these down on the floor, I took from my bag a sheet of paper on which was typed—by a member of the Dictaphone Corporation in New York after consultation with Columbia University:

(Attach this to wire at end of "cigarette lighter" fitting.)
LIGAR AO TERMINAL POLO DA BATARIA
QUE NAO ESTA LIGADO A TERRA (CHASSIS)

Portuguese Alexander took the paper from my hand, read it over several times, furrowing his brow, then read it aloud.

The mechanics listened attentively, and made no comment. One of them held out his hand for the paper, and read it to himself, moving his lips; passed it to his companion, who had already read it over his friend's shoulder. They looked at each other and simultaneously raised their shoulders in a mighty shrug.

Sophy moved forward, placing herself directly in front of the two experts and nudging our boy gently to one side. She began a pantomime, and as she developed it, I thought of Marcel Marceau as a fellow artist. She held spellbound an audience that grew from two mechanics to eight or so. They came from behind and under cars. Their enlightenment, however, was in inverse ratio to their rapt attention. When she demonstrated with an imaginary cigarette the impossibility of lighting one in the hole in the dashboard where a cigarette lighter might have been, and where instead she wished the wire to go, one man advanced from the group and politely offered her a cigarette from his pack, and a light. When she tried herself to place the object I had brought under the hood, shrugging her shoulders and making other gestures of feminine incompetence about how to attach it, she provoked a gale of laughter and a tolerant demonstration that the engine in our car obviously had all its parts, and did not need the extra one she was endeavoring to supply. At the moment I was wishing fervently I had made a present of the wretched thing to the man at the airport who had assessed the cost of my extra weight, she erupted a flow of Portuguese. What she said I have no idea, of course, nor could she remember afterward. I cannot believe the gift of mechanical vocabulary was suddenly bestowed upon her. Nevertheless, the effect of the words she strung together was in itself a miracle. The men nodded, they babbled, they gave one another delighted whacks on the back. They bade us leave everything to them. The car would be ready for us, "thing" installed, that afternoon.

Our boy from the Travel Bureau, leaving reluctantly, deposited us at Sophy's request in the shopping heart of the city at the Rossio.

This is a square framed by hotels, cafés and shops. From there we explored on foot, pausing frequently to enjoy sounds as well as sights. Women, moving rapidly, with wide trays on their heads, called their wares—fish, vegetables, whatever, each was identified by a half-melody chanted loud, the notes exactly the same at each repetition. We walked up one street, as far as it seemed interesting, took a cross street, came down the next parallel, looking in shop windows and at the passers-by. There were many things in Portugal about which I began to speculate that morning, and to which I never had answers, because I did not know anyone to ask, and because I did not know how to say the questions. In the whole of Portugal, or as much of it as I traveled in the month I was there, I saw only one baby coach—hundreds of babies at a conservative estimate, but except at one open-air dance festival in Tomar, every infant was literally a babe in arms. In that Catholic country I never saw nuns or priests on city streets or village roads. Where were they? I think, all told, I did not see in cities or towns more than twenty women or girls wearing dresses of colored material—only black. Yet in Lisbon, I saw more shops selling fabric than any other merchandise, their windows filled with bright-colored, gaily patterned materials, lovely in texture and design. There were woolens, beautifully woven from heavy, coarse tweed to fine and thin stuff as delicate as silk, all in colors. I saw no black material displayed anywhere. Who wears colors in the cities, I cannot say. The only way I saw them used was in brilliant scarves and shawls. I did not see in Lisbon a woman driving a car, nor Portuguese women lunching together in a restaurant. During the whole of our motoring through the country I counted three women, other than Sophy, at the wheel of a car. Whether it is unconventional for a woman to drive, or only unfashionable, I do not know, any more than I can say whether a Portuguese woman considers it boring to lunch with one or more other women, or something that is not, by convention, permitted.

Sophy and I lunched at the Restaurant Tavares on the Rua de Misericordia. We found the restaurant a delight in both décor and food. It is in the grand and the Baroque style. The food was glorious, the service given in style and not at the express speed of the Tivoli.

Revived, we visited the Coach Museum. This is in Belém. Belém is called, in the guidebooks, a suburb of Lisbon. I do not know what marks the boundaries of Lisbon; I would have counted the museum within them, on the west side of the city. Certainly it is easily reached, and well worth an excursion. Originally a riding school, it now houses a double row of carriages of dazzling luxuriance, gilded, painted without, velvet- or satin-upholstered within, monumentally heavy and probably monstrously uncomfortable. The guide takes sly pleasure in revealing a detail of discomfort—a *pot de chambre* beneath a hinged lid in the seat. Next door to the museum is one of the residences of the President of Portugal. It is graceful, has style, and is pink.

Good food, I have discovered, and enough of it to induce a somnolent feeling of well-being, decreases proportionately my apprehension about steep and narrow ways to high places. Admitting it with defiant embarrassment to Sophy, I suggested as soon as we had recovered our Volkswagen we visit the Castle of St. George. The castle is so high above the city it is visible from almost every quarter of it. Therefore, I had seen it from almost every street we had walked along, and been uncomfortably aware of what was necessarily involved in obtaining a closer view.

We took a taxi to the garage. The car was ready, a mechanic told us, leading the way.

Other members of the corps were waiting beside the car. At the sight of our approach, one of them, with the dignity of a university president bestowing academic awards, handed to me the "thing," the appliance from the Dictaphone Corporation. He made a speech of presentation, illustrated in pantomime by his associates. By translating shoulders raised, eyes rolled, Volkswagen patted enthusiastically, I understood. In their expert opinion there was not the slightest reason to install this silly appendage I had brought. The machine had all its parts, was running smoothly—a chorus of sounds like a cat purring put across this message—she should not be disturbed.

"You're licked," was Sophy's translation, muttered in my ear.

I hope I gave them something of the style and flourish of their presentation. At least I gave back the gadget, with the hope—in pantomime—they would accept it as a souvenir of America.

They accepted the gift—and a cash token of esteem—assisted us up the cliff to the front seat of the Volkswagen, waved us off once more.

"Counting from the cost at Idlewild—" Sophy began, as we drove away.

"Just don't count," I urged. "Change the subject."

The approach to the Castle of St. George is as steep as I had anticipated, but it has another quality that is charmingly distracting. The streets and alleys by which the top is reached are scarcely touched sixteenth- and seventeenth-century. This section seems to have escaped the terrible earthquake of 1755. The passages are so narrow, not only is it, as Gina would say, "out of question" for two cars to pass; even pedestrians must duck into the nearest doorway at the approach of our bus. The same sort of ducking for safety is maneuvered by whichever of two cars coming face to face is nearer an intersection. That driver backs into the intersection until the other one has gone by. All along each of these ways flowers drip over balconies, birds in cages sing, young women in doorways play with their babies. (In Italy I would have seen them nurse their babies. I never saw this in Portugal.) Old women on campstools in the sun sew or knit, turning their bodies to profiles against the walls of the dwelling as a car brushes their skirts.

The guidebook says on June 13, June 24 and June 29, the feast days of St. Anthony, St. John and St. Peter, the patron saints of Lisbon, the inhabitants of this quarter restore these little streets to the days of their youth. Small orchestras make music for dancers. Everyone is in costume. Lighted by bonfires on every street, the young blades show off by jumping through the flames. Everywhere there are little stands dispensing food and wine.

37

Following the arrow that marks the route, we came to the top by a pattern of scallops, curving, winding, backing when necessary, resuming, and at last turned off the engine on a broad, tree-lined esplanade enclosed by a wall high and broad enough for me to lean upon without too great giddiness, and look down on a superb panorama of Lisbon, the Tagus River and the hills of Sintra beyond. Children played around and behind us. People went into and came from a church that marked the inner boundary of this broad terrace, the women and children quickly putting on at the threshold a lace head scarf before entering. I noticed for the first time, though I was to see it throughout Portugal, even the very small children, and even those shabbily dressed, possessed a head covering for church of exquisite lace.

Only the battlements of the castle remain, soft yellow in color. It is suitable the battlements should persist since the castle was built on the site of a fortress captured from the Moors with the help of English Crusaders. The Moorish fortress in its earlier turn was on the site of a stronghold of the Visigoths. Walking among and around the walls along flower- and tree-bordered paths I was smiling to myself at the charming paradox created by mingling a park with a grim fortress when a hideous, anguished scream directly behind me froze every muscle and vein, and the hair on my head. The park was undoubtedly a camouflage; there must be fearful places beneath where even at this date prisoners were confined and tortured. People strolled past me unconcerned. Children played along the paths undiverted by the cry of souls in agony. I might have imagined the whole thing, but I heard it again. I whirled on my heel to investigate, protest, run away, I was not sure what, only that the Portuguese were an insensitive, uncivilized, barbaric people. Turning with this vague purpose and fury in mind, I came very nearly face to face with the "screaming victims of torture": two of the most beautiful white peacocks I have ever seen. Sophy had wandered away on a divergent path, but at the instant of my introduction to the peacocks, she loped into view in long running strides, her face white.

We returned to the city through the same narrow street we had previously climbed, since that is the only route. I can assert this with no qualms of inaccuracy because at my insistence Sophy tried every other outlet. Each one either brought us to a dead end or wound us back to the familiar narrow way. All the ways were narrow, and it was not this characteristic to which I objected. What made me close my eyes for a good part of the time and endeavor to imbed my feet in the floorboard was the special effect from going downhill. With nothing between us and the road beneath but a wide pane of windshield, I might have been on a shoot-the-shoots at Coney Island—an excursion I did not care for even in my childhood, when I was bolder than I am now. Leveled off at last into the city proper, we were immediately in a swarm of city traffic—mostly taxis darting like water bugs around and at us. This induces a nervousness in Sophy that manifests itself by a form of entreaty with which she softly addresses the Deity. Contrariwise I am then relaxed. The aspects of motoring I dislike are going up or down or fast. I do not in the least mind heavy traffic, because it checks our rate of progress more effectively than my pleading ever achieves.

Back at the hotel I settled at my dictaphone to chronicle notes of what we had done and seen. After a few minutes of talk it occurred to me to listen to what I had said, in order to make sure the machine was working properly. I pushed the levers indicated on the diagram pasted in the lid of the dictaphone case. I waited. Not a sound emerged. I pressed the speaking and lifting device—that is one instrument—close to my ear; not a whisper breathed from it. I called urgently to Sophy, who was doing a little laundering in the bathroom. I urged her to listen in the ambivalent hope perhaps I had lost my hearing. Sophy assured me my senses were intact. I was quixotically enraged that the deficiency should be in the machine. Pointing out how much I had paid in excess weight for a gadget, how much at a garage to have the silly thing installed, left behind as useless at a garage, and now the machine itself might as well be abandoned. Sophy gave me dubious comfort by pointing out how much more expensive it would be in the long run had I lost my hearing. She added a more practical help by reminding me of a list in the sheaf of papers provided by the Dictaphone Company of their branch offices all over the world. Within ten minutes we were on our way to the one in Portugal.

The Lisbon office of the Dictaphone Corporation bears little resemblance to its resplendent headquarters in New York. It is, in fact, so inconspicuously located we passed its doorway several times before identifying it. Then we climbed a narrow, dark flight of stairs, knocked on a door at the head, and were immediately, on entering, at the counter of a receptionist, clerk, telephone operator, sales force, all in the person of a young woman who spoke not a word of anything but Portuguese. I placed my dictaphone case on the counter, opened it, gave a vivid demonstration of its deficiency only to realize at the end of my spirited performance she had not only failed to understand, she had not even given me her attention. Wide-eyed, she was regarding my machine. Suddenly she swept it up in her arms, cradling tenderly the awkward thing, and disappeared down a corridor. Sophy and I looked at each other in dismay and then at the solid counter obviously with the same idea in mind, because Sophy said, "I could make a stirrup and give you a leg over."

If the young woman thought I had brought her a present it behooved me to track her and disabuse her of that idea. At the moment I was crouching for the leg up, she reappeared without the machine. She beckoned me to follow and swung open one end of the counter. Sophy did not come with us. In a small room at the end of hall six men in a closed circle stood with their backs to me. There was not enough space for me to cross the threshold, but peeking from side to side I corroborated my surmise that in the center of the circle on a table rested my dictaphone. By bending down and leaning precariously forward on tiptoe I could see among their moving arms every man had his hands on some portion of my machine, turning buttons, pressing; not one portion of the exposed mechanism was untouched. At the moment of this horrifying discovery I was jolted backward by a man in the group who shifted his position. He turned around impatiently and, catching sight of me as the obstacle into which he had careened, indicated with polite authority my place was on the other side of the door in the hall. At the instant I saw myself a child again one Christmas morning, standing wistfully beside my brother on the threshold of a bathroom in my grandfather's house, bidden by my father to come no further into the room. Our quarantine permitted an unimpeded area in the room in which he, my grandfather, and my two uncles gathered around the tub, could play with a submarine and a mechanical diving doll, presents Brother and I had just received. We had stood in the doorway wailing because we could not see, and because we were afraid our toys were going to be broken. I thought in the doorway of the Lisbon branch of the Dictaphone Corporation I might wail. I did not need a knowledge of Portuguese to realize I had provided for the lads a plaything that was giving them more fun than any toy Santa Claus had ever brought. They had certainly not seen a dictaphone before. Perhaps their fathers had told them of a machine with revolving cylinders that recorded speech and transmitted it back again. The model with cylinders was discarded some ten years or so ago. How the Dictaphone Corporation had enrolled this gleeful corps as its official representatives, including them in its imposing printed list of world-wide branches, I did not know, and at the moment cared far less. My preoccupation was with getting into and never letting out of my hands again my treasure. An hour before I had been so exasperated I had been ready to give it to the hotel chambermaid. Now seeing it under such attack I only wanted to restore it to my sheltering arms, even if it never spoke back to me. While I stood helpless, but planning a head-on tackle, above the gibbering of Portuguese, it spoke.

My voice rose and reverberated with an amplitude that must have carried to the far corners of the building, perhaps to the street below. "Arrived Lisbon 10:30 A.M., paged in airport by young German waiting with Microbus." The volume produced also a quality of fervor. I might have been Billy Graham exhorting a congregation in Madison Square Garden, or a political candidate making a plea for election by way of a sound truck along a city street. One of the young mischiefs in his happy exploration had pushed from "silent" to "vocal" a tiny lever in a niche at the back of the machine, as I discovered later. I had forgotten its existence, though finding it again I remembered it had been included in the demonstration of this new traveling model. At the moment, paradoxically, I did not care that my treasure was functioning as it should. I was brimming with malevolent satisfaction at the retribution I could not have brought physically or by protesting, entreating speech. They would not have understood a word. At the instant my voice had begun to roll every hand had left the dictaphone as if burnt—every mouth stopped chattering—every figure stood frozen. They did not know this voice was recounting the trip from airport to hotel, the charm of hanging baskets of flowers, the reminder to myself of trivia along the way. By its resonant timbre, the voice could have been God announcing Judgment Day. It even brought Sophy on the run from the outer office. She may have been calling as she ran; I only heard her when she put her face close to mine and shouted, "My God, what a playback—and you thought it didn't work—can't you turn it down?"

I could. I remembered both the position of the switch and how to regulate the volume. I could see in my mind's eye the demonstrator pointing it out to me. I had simultaneously the uncomfortable recollection of how bored I had become by that time with his lengthy explanation, saying to myself I had used this machine for years, I did not need to be treated like a novice. This little button I had forgotten was allowing the citizenry of Lisbon within a considerable area to hear what I had been doing in their city, those of them who could understand English.

My immediate audience, evidently dazed by this cacophony, had involuntarily to a man stepped back a pace or two. I was able to insert my arm in the space they yielded and turn off the sound. I knew now I could regulate the volume by an old familiar button on the front of the instrument. I had overpowering evidence, too, that the busy fingers of the eager boys had not damaged the machine. I smiled happily round the circle and said, *"Muito obrigado."* No one spoke. No one so much as made a gesture of reluctance when I took the machine into my arms again. I am happy in my conviction it had scared the living daylights out of them.

FOUR

Gina, Alec and Brother Theodore were to arrive on Wednesday, the fourth of May. The date was encircled on both my calendar and mind, but the hour of their coming was not so vividly fixed, because I had lost within a few moments of receiving it a note from Alec giving me the data about their plane. I was able to withhold from Sophy my unhappy lapse from efficiency only because of a delicious dinner following my harassing *brouhaha* with the Dictaphone gentlemen. The next day, the third, had been occupied by the purchase of a rug for my dining room in New York and a delightful and distracting excursion to Sintra.

The dinner, thanks to the Negresco restaurant, had soothed us. Apart from a shared love of travel, Sophy's and my congeniality includes a mutual enjoyment of good food. While we are eating it, and afterward, a sense of beneficence mellows for a time my native acerbity. Stuffed crab at the Negresco should sweeten the meanest nature. The restaurant is at 39 Rua do Jardim do Regedor. It is not large, the night we were there it was not crowded, I cannot think why—a neon-lighted, white-tiled café not far off showed through its plate-glass façade a welter of steaming diners—and the service is, as Gina would say, "everything what you can imagine that is good."

Next morning we set out for my rug, a reiterated item on my "To Do" list. My daughter Alis takes with her on any trip two notebooks, one labeled "To Do," the other "To See." With its accomplishment she checks off each entry as if she were embarked on Christmas shopping. My "To See" list was long. The "To Do" items were not numerous, but not simple either. The list read: "rug, tiles and three hand-knitted natural coarse wool sweaters, made originally for fishermen." The sweaters were for Sophy's daughter, Charlton, and her two children, to be worn for skiing. Charlton had known better, she had asserted openly, than to entrust this undertaking to her mother. Sophy is an impatient shopper. All three of us knew she would never track down, even for her daughter, a fisherman's wife who knitted, neither was she interested in a rug for herself because of the involvement of having it made. Nevertheless she generously offered to go with me in case I needed her help in Portuguese. I was prepared with the address of the shop where a rug might be ordered and the name of its proprietor. The name of the establishment was formidable, but that of its owner reassuringly British.

We found the place without difficulty. To save time I refused Sophy's offer to say the name aloud in Portuguese and showed to the taxi driver instead the letterhead: "Sociedade Ingléza Decorações E Antiguidades, Lda."; the address 26 Rua da Emenda, Lisbon.

The owner of this intricacy of syllables is Lady Blanche Elles. She is a decorator with exquisite taste and sound knowledge of periods and craftsmanship in furniture and textiles. She has for her clients' selection a wide assortment in photographs of rug designs, and color samples in yarn. She is charming, helpful with suggestions and efficient. When pattern and colors have been decided and the measurements carefully checked and recorded, she places the order at a convent where, under the supervision of the Sister head of the workroom, the nuns weave rugs. I have been told that rug-weaving is also the occupation of women in prison, but to order one from this source involves visiting the prison, placing the order direct, and Sophy, eager as she was to demonstrate her Portuguese, had quailed at such an undertaking. Lady Elles was a delightful and reassuring intermediary. As we left, she told me I might expect delivery in between three and four months' time, and she proved as accurate in this as in her transmission of measurements.

At noon we were on our way to Sintra. Sintra is little more than

45

an hour's drive from Lisbon. By the blur of the cars that passed us, I estimate the Portuguese make the trip in something around forty-five minutes. We dawdled, enjoying the soft landscape and we stopped for more than an hour to visit the palace at Queluz.

As palaces go, this one is small, *parva sed apta*. It is eighteenth-century Rococo, delicate pink in color and in design a central block with a graceful semicircular wing at either end. The flower gardens are magnificent, the topiary gardens the finest I have seen. Both are punctuated by sculptured figures. Long alleys are hidden between luxuriant and meticulously clipped hedges that rise twice and more the height of a man. In one garden there is a playful anachronism of a Dutch canal. At least the canal itself seems Dutch, because in lieu of a bank on either side there rises a high wall of tiled panels (*azulejos*), in white and delft blue. Done as seascapes, these walls seem to come from below the water. The canal itself is of sufficient length to permit boating and I daresay this was an after-dinner diversion for the court.

The rooms in the palace are not large by palace standards; indeed, even to the eyes of a city-apartment-dweller some of them are small. I have been told by a visitor to Windsor Castle that the services of a guard are required to bring a guest from bedroom to drawing room. There is no such labyrinth at Queluz; one chamber leads directly into the next. I counted each more exquisite than the one I had quitted, until I came to the Music Room. This, for me, had the greatest charm of all. Its shape is long and somewhat narrow. Perhaps the actual length is exaggerated to the eye because of the smallness of the rooms leading to it. The crystal chandeliers are brilliant. The furniture is beautiful. What communicated to me a special charm was a semicircle of delicate candlesticks, each holding a taper. These are the footlights that rim the edge of a dais on which a piano is placed. Musicians have entertained guests by concert and by accompaniment to the dance, because this Music Room is also the Ballroom. Musicians play here now. The palace of Queluz is not like the cook about whom Saki wrote, "She was a good cook as cooks go, and as cooks go, she went." Queluz was a good, beautiful palace, and never went. It is today a beautiful guest house for distinguished visitors. Queen Elizabeth and Prince Philip had been in temporary residence there. Within a few days of our modest tourist visit, President Eisenhower was to be an official guest. The tapers on the dais would be lighted.

Around Queluz the landscape becomes bleak and stony and then a very few miles beyond we were almost oppressed by thick, luxuriant, tropical, damp vegetation. We did not realize at the moment we exclaimed almost with uneasiness at such a dramatic change we were only at the beginning of such ejaculations. By their repetition during the following weeks of our journey through the country, they would have sounded on a playing record as if the needle had stuck. I have never been in a country in which the landscape changes so frequently, and so abruptly, from plains to mountains with barren rocky sides, to vine-covered hills, to lush pastures, stark ominous cliffs, to softly rounded coves and sandy beaches. Let someone ask me what the country of Portugal looks like, and I will either moan with despair, trying to answer, or say it looks like every kind of landscape I have ever seen, all crowded together.

It is not necessary to take a car in order to reach Sintra. Its distance from Lisbon is actually twenty-six kilometers. A direct train goes from the Rossio station. From Estoril and Cascais there are buses. The traveler can choose one of two routes, direct and short from Estoril, or the more leisurely way (I refer to the route itself, not the tempo of a Portuguese driver) that takes about an hour and a half, and winds about the country through magnificent scenery.

Sintra is actually three villages on three separate levels, and boasts also three castles. On the topmost level, the walls, all that remain, of a Moorish stronghold can be seen standing out sharp against the horizon. We did not visit it. At Sophy's instigation, certainly not mine, we drove almost as high up, to Pena Castle, hairpin turns and all. The dazzling masses of color on either side replaced my usual height giddiness with a happy intoxication. There were waterfalls of purple bougainvillaea, carpets of geraniums, splatters of blue plumbago, through dark fern, mimosa like shimmering sunlight and, close to the ground, flowers I could not identify. When I left the car and crouched down over them, endeavoring to isolate from the solid mass some whose names I might know, a lizard about eighteen inches long ran over my hand. I did not care to identify him, and returned briskly to the car.

The view from the Castle of Pena is what one expects from a height, a vast area of landscape and a far-off circumference. I do not understand why sight-seers reaching a summit gasp their astonishment at the spread of the world below them. The only unexpected vista I have ever encountered was from the brink of the Grand Canyon. Furthermore, when I look at, say a river, I like to discern its color in sunlight and in shadow, the stones perhaps just beneath its surface, a prick here and there at evening on its smooth top, like testing a cake with a straw, when fish are coming up for a snap at a gnat from the shivering congregation of them just above the surface. I like to hear the little crackle of twig or leaves along the bank where a bird or small animal is moving. I like the smell of water and damp soil. My heart does not with rapture fill when under the guidance of someone's forefinger I bring my eyes to what might be a length of string, and am told with awe that I am looking at the something or other river. But for those who like it, there is vista aplenty from the battlements of the Castle of Pena. Pena was a royal summer residence until October, 1910, when Manuel was deposed, and fled for his life. (Later, at Bussaco, we were told it was from that summer residence the King fled.)

Pena Palace itself is a combination of Scottish Baronial and Moorish styles, an incongruous association geographically, and architecturally. It was built in 1840, but the site was that of a monastery centuries earlier. All that is left of the monastery are the cloister and some of the chapel, whose altar was made in 1532. The furnishing of the castle is for the most part mid-nineteenth century, uncomfortable to use, I am sure, and not comforting to the eye.

Sophy's *modus operandi* in travel is twofold: (1) to return from a destination by a road other than the one by which it was reached,

and (2) to find a road other travelers do not use. We followed both of these rules, and became almost hopelessly lost in a tangle of by-ways and woods, so tangled that when we finally and unexpectedly reached an exit and the main road, we had acquired unknowingly the limb of a tree, not a sapling either. Its twigs and leaves were entwined in a rear wheel; its trunk was a trailer. The custodian of the gate at which we unexpectedly emerged was far from un-knowing about our souvenir. He sharply called our attention to it, and remonstrated with such vehement pantomime I had no doubt we were facing a fine or imprisonment, probably both, and mut-tered to Sophy, "You and your unfrequented back roads." However, he passed a sentence only of making us detach the evidence of our innocent vandalism while he supervised, glowering and with arms folded.

Once on a road other people might use I persuaded Sophy not to yield again to the temptation of a wayward path, and just this once go straight to our destination, the Seteais. A straight road is a misleading term in Portugal. Sophy in spirit is related to all road builders in Portugal, down through the ages. They share a com-mon dislike of the straightaway. They achieve contentment by fitful curves and capricious sidetracks. I, too, like a curving road, except of a hairpin pattern. My point of difference with Sophy is that I take them as they come; I do not have to go out of my way to find them.

We found the hotel with no difficulty. It is set back, but clearly visible from the well-marked road. The Seteais is one of the love-liest hotels in all of Portugal. Seteais means "seven 'ahs' of pleas-ure." I might have enjoyed the hotel because of the charm of the name alone, but there is far more for enjoyment. At one time the palace of the Marquis of Marialva, it is now under the same management as the Tivoli Hotel in Lisbon. Under this ownership it has maintained the style, the elegance and exquisite taste it must have had originally, and has added modern comfort, even luxury. The floor coverings are woven, like the rug I had or-dered, in delicate colors and design. Much of the furniture is genuinely period, the rest so well copied as to be indistinguishable from the original. There are, I think, only about thirty bedrooms. It is advisable to make reservations well in advance. Our rooms were charming, looking out over the garden.

In spite of our errantry through the woods, we were in time for lunch. We ate very well, and this was a double satisfaction to me in itself, and by way of providing a distraction when Sophy asked what time Alec had said in his letter to me we should meet them at the airport. I had searched for the letter, but I had a clear and uncomfortable feeling it would not come under my hand again, at least not before the arrival of the plane. By a skittish swerve to the topic of the delicate flavor of Portuguese fish, I was able to touch only lightly on the matter of the plane's arrival with the assurance it was written down somewhere—and that much was true.

After lunch we explored the countryside again. Once more I was able to slide out from under Sophy's persistent endeavor to pin me down to the plane's arrival. I quoted Byron: "Harried crags, by toppling convent crowned," and added: "From peak to peak, the rattling crags among, leaps the live thunder," then: "There is pleasure in the pathless woods, there is a rapture on the lonely shore." Sophy turned her attention from the road to look at me with some anxiety. "I'm sure you know," I said wickedly, "I'm quoting Byron's *Childe Harold's Pilgrimage*. He wrote some of it here. He called Sintra a 'glorious Eden.'" This offensive pedantry on my part served its purpose beyond my immediate hope. It not only distracted Sophy from the timetable, it struck her dumb. I saw no reason to proclaim the fact I had my information and one of the lines from a guidebook.

The roads on which we traveled did seem to be closely lined by "pathless woods," though we both knew from the guidebook actually they are part of the acreage of beautifully tended and handsome estates. This is Lisbon's most fashionable suburb. It is, at least historically, the royal seat, though Estoril has come to be designated as such. But royalty in the person of John I was in palatial residence in Sintra at the end of the fourteenth century. By the eighteenth century English men of letters were writing of the beauty of the place. The poet Southey visited it in 1795 and wrote that Sintra was "the most blessed spot on the habitable globe." Some years before that William Beckford, eighteenth-century essayist and novelist, wrote rapturously of the place in his *Letters*.

The road we followed gave us tantalizing visual nibbles at the sea at unexpected turns, not enough vista to make a good-sized bite, but a sliver of blue in the distance, the more vivid because of the dark, glossy vegetation in our foreground.

When the narrow steep road suddenly widened on one side into a car park, we stopped, of course, and climbed down from our bus. From an attendant at a wide gate and from our guidebook we learned we were at the entrance to the Quinta de Monserrate, and that the grounds were open to the public. The grounds turned out to be an amazing, in size and variety, botanical garden. The garden was laid out by that same William Beckford whose prose was as lush as the planting. Slender, steep paths pass waterfalls and grottoes, over little bridges farther down than I felt it necessary to go, with an eye to the rigorous return climb. Instead, we returned to the car, and from there back to the lower village of Sintra. We visited the Royal Palace and lingered because its interior is far more rewarding than that of Pena. The palace itself was begun in the fourteenth century and completed by Manuel the Great.

Manueline, as a term of identification, was a word I had already heard more than any other during this short time in Portugal. Lady Elles, learning we were going to the Seteais Hotel in Sintra, had said, "Be sure to see a small drawing room there, because it is perfect of the best Manueline." This was only one of the times beyond counting I had heard the word. I knew from photographs and places I had actually seen that "Manueline" denoted an exuberant, lavish, intoxicated Baroque, and this is exactly to my taste. (I bridle at the definition in some dictionaries, that Baroque is "anything so extravagantly ornamented as to be in bad taste.") I can be awed by austerity of line but my senses caper at the sight of generous, full-blown ornament that is genuine, not superimposed. Therefore,

I had a happy smile for Manueline, but it had taken a bit of tracking for me to put together the bits of data and set the whole in its proper frame.

King Manuel I (1495-1521) was also called King Manuel the Fortunate, because in his reign the Portugal treasury was so filled with gold it overflowed into a great splash of magnificent building. He owed this dazzling opulence to a dedicated ascetic who was his great-great-uncle, Henry the Navigator. He was not a king, only a prince, the third son of John I and his English wife, Philippa of Lancaster, daughter of old John of Gaunt. Called by one writer "the greatest and most mysterious of the Portuguese," Henry the Navigator, scholar, recluse, from his tower on the bleak gray cape of Sagres, plotted courses and sent out voyaging expeditions that found sources of a river of gold. As a result of their discoveries and conquests, it emptied into Portugal. This was Portugal's Colonial Empire. From it came cargoes of spices, silks—as Gina would say, "everything what you can imagine"—to make a country rich.

Of course this made for extravagance in a way of living, and in the habitations themselves. I am sure the reason Manueline is both a distinctive and an enduring style is because of its basic honesty, its firm substance. This was no false front put up for show, to trick the viewer into an assumption of prosperity. The prosperity came first, heaped up in the cellars, and finally bursting out over the façade of every house and public building. The form of this exuberance is the combination of full-seasoned Gothic and warmed-over Moorish.

The Royal Palace at Sintra is accounted one of the best examples of the Manueline period. Its *azulejos* (I had by this time tossed over my shoulder into oblivion the simple word "tiles") are of wide variety, since they date from the fifteenth century well through the nineteenth. All of them are interesting, most of them colorfully charming. They are the reason the kitchen must be visited. The room is enormous, with great cone-shaped chimneys above the raised open hearth. Delicate gray *azulejos* cover the walls well up over half the height of the room. We were to see later at Alcobaça a kitchen like this with *azulejos* in pale blue. There is exquisite interior décor, beautiful pieces in the furnishing, excellent pictures and charming murals. The "Magpie" is the pride of the guides, and it is amusing, but with nothing like the beauty of other rooms. Painted magpies cover the ceiling. Supposedly this decoration was done after Don João I was caught kissing one of the ladies-in-waiting to the Queen. Each magpie holds in its beak a scroll that bears the motto of Don João, *"Por Bem,"* an equivalent of *"Honi Soit,* etc." The monarch used the magpies as symbols of gossip. The suggestion was that a friendly kiss had been grossly exaggerated by court gossips and distressed his Queen, the English Philippa of Lancaster.

At the completion of our tour of the palace I insisted the day was now over. Sophy's admission, however, that the shoebag stock was in a lamentable state of depletion restored me instantly to aggressive vigor. We would not return to the hotel, was my declaration, without a bottle of white wine. Accordingly, in the lower village of Sintra, we left our bus, exploring with pleasure and some fatigue its shops and winding streets. We peeked into the Church of St. Martinho; it is behind the Hotel Central. We found a terrace with stone benches and knelt on them to look down over roofs and little gardens in jigsaw puzzle irregularity—to a plain and, beyond, a horizon of blue sea. Happily, too, for me, and for Sophy's peace of mind, we found a wineshop. With a replenished store under either arm, we came back to the bus and finally to our hotel.

FIVE

"I would like to stop at Cabo da Roca on the way back," Sophy said at breakfast next morning. I jumped guiltily, because I was spreading a second roll with delicious jam. At the beginning of our trip I had urged her to help me discipline myself to fruit and *café au lait* in the morning. I knew the temptation of crisp European rolls with sweet butter and lovely marmalade or jam. At the moment I had thought her absorbed in her favorite reading, map or guidebook. I asked her what the Cabo da Roca was, and she told me a lighthouse. This seemed to me innocuous as long as we were not required to climb to the top of it. I know now she had seen me at my rolls and chosen that instant for her proposal. The morning was clear, warm and sunny. From a window at which we ate in our bedroom, we could see garden, green meadows and the blue sea beyond.

An earnest discussion about the selection of wine with the sommelier at dinner the night before had brought into the conversation a couple at an adjoining table. They were the first Americans with whom we had spoken, and, so far as I know, even seen in Portugal. The conversation had continued after the decision about wine to an exchange of names—they were Mr. and Mrs. Hamlet, from Pawling, New York—then to a suggestion they drive back to Lisbon with us since they had no car. As the four of us were leaving the dining room I heard unmistakably my own name called. Startled, I whirled about, and found myself facing William Wirtz, a friend from Philadelphia, whom I had not seen in years. We talked a few minutes.

When I rejoined the others, I told them knowingly how familiar this pattern was; I was sure they had experienced it, too. The moment you came to Europe you ran into neighbors and friends you seldom saw at home. This was only the beginning, I said. In the whole of Portugal I visited, I saw just one other face I had ever seen before.

An aspect of the familiar pattern for Americans abroad did fall into place as soon as the Hamlets, Sophy and I were in the bus. We discussed prices. What would be deplorable except in a burst of confidence to an intimate at home becomes abroad an absorbing topic. I do not know the price of anything in the wardrobes of my close friends, but I know what Mrs. Hamlet paid for the shoes she bought in Italy, the handbag she was carrying, the engaging little hat she was wearing. She had from me the address of Lady Elles and the approximate price for a rug. We compared with eagerness our hotel bills, purring with satisfaction that a place of such luxurious surroundings as the Seteais should have cost less than ten dollars per person for room and three meals.

We drove again over the road that wound past beautiful places with their wooded fringes, pointed out to the Hamlets the Monserrate Gardens, and discovered, though we had overlooked it the day before, a footpath across from the entrance to the garden. We had read of this approach up through thick woods to the Capuchos or Cork Convent, that it was founded in 1560 and is so small there are only twelve cells. These are cut from rock, but furnished and even roofed with cork. What marble is to Greece, cork is to Portugal, a material most easily come by and widely used. Byron had written of a hermit who had lived in a cave near this convent. We only marked the path, however; we did not follow it.

Cabo da Roca was our first stop. We left the bus, walked across bleak, barren ground to the edge of the *cabo*, which is a cape, and were on the spot that is the western extremity of the whole of the European Continent. A good deal of the whole of it seemed to me to be within our range of vision. The panorama of sea and coastline, so vast it stretched the eyes, was superb. The drop from the point on which we stood to the sea below, in my opinion, would cause the knees of a mountain goat to tremble. And yet, while I shuddered my way backward until I could not see over the rim, the others talked unconcernedly, pointed out landmarks and finally curled their toes over the edge in order to see immediately below. Had they plunged down I would not have known it, because at that sight I sagged to the ground, put my head in my lap, and my hands over my ears. The Hamlets roused me with polite concern, but Sophy assured them it was only an idiosyncrasy, not a seizure; heights made me dizzy and sick at my stomach. Since I was at the moment endeavoring to hold my breakfast, I could only give a wan smile of corroboration. I knew, then, Sophy had known at breakfast from the guidebook what that view and drop would be.

From Cabo the way was new to us, and is beautiful. It winds through a forest heavy with the scent of pine and the trees themselves, to the coast along a shore where the water, blue as an aquamarine, danced in the sunlight that day. We paused at Cascais, that is pronounced "cash-cash." The Portuguese, I was discovering, can insinuate the "sh" sound into nearly every syllable, whatever its spelling. "Cash-cash" is a little fishing town with a swimming beach, much frequented by people from Lisbon. Further on at Estoril we sat on a terrace at the beach, and had an ice while we watched a few swimmers and a great many children playing on the sand. We resumed our way along what is rightly called the sunshine coast, until we came to Belém. There we stopped.

Though I had scoffed at the identification of Belém as a suburb, in the history of Portugal Belém is very much a place in itself. Vasco da Gama, on his great voyage of discovery, sailed from Belém. An inscription reads: "Here the ships were built that found new lands and seas and took over the world in the name of Portugal." The Tower of Belém on the shore—at high tide it is an island—was built by King Manuel in 1520. It looks like a confectioner's imaginative delineation of a fortress in layer-cake tiers and icing on top. Its purpose was to guard the river, but it also served as a landmark to returning voyagers with their cargoes of gold and ivory, spices and silks. It is appropriate the riches they brought should find expression in a church close to the point of their departure and return. This is the church, the convent and cloister of Jerónimos— and it is equally fitting that each spring it is from here the blessing of the fleet is conducted, a service in the church and from there a stately procession across to the shore. It is pathetically anticlimactic to admit for accuracy that today the fleet, blessed, sets out on a voyage to discover codfish.

What Phidias was to the Golden Age of Pericles, Boytac was to the Golden Age of Manuel. Boytac was the artist, architect, overseer of public works. His hallmark is "the twisted pillar," massive stone supports as pliantly entwined as saltwater taffy at Atlantic City. In the nave of Jerónimos there is a grove of pillars, some broad and square, some broad, round and fluted, others as slender as saplings, all tall, reaching so high into the convoluted vaults above, the sight-seer's head must rest on the back of his neck in order to follow them. Almost every inch is carved, twisted or both. The tomb of Manuel rests on the back of a stone elephant. There are flowers and foliage, ships and other symbols of the sea.

Lady Elles had told me whenever I saw an example of Manueline architecture to look for the "armillary sphere"—and it is not difficult to find. It is a globe, representing the world, of course; this is banded diagonally by a slender ring—the armilla, a Latin word meaning "bracelet." The significance of its slanting placement around the globe is that it represents the diagonal course followed by Magellan when he circled the world.

A gasp in unison just inside the doors of this cathedral was an involuntary response to the impact of the height, the space, the rhythm in the vast nave before us. Immediately then, and involuntarily, we separated, each making his own zigzag tour. We came together in a search for the cloisters. Each admitted unsuccessful sorties that had landed us across an archway into a modern building whose contents held no interest, or in the other direction to small rooms at one side or the other of the altar, obviously retiring rooms for church officials and certainly not for investigation by sight-seers.

Each admitted also to having waved away with some austerity the proffered services of a guide; the same guide, it turned out, had presented himself to our separate members. When as a body we sought him out with some chagrin, we were greeted by delighted smiles of welcome and satisfaction that we were at last seeing things his way. We would never have found by ourselves the little tucked-away access to the cloisters. I thanked a beneficent Providence and a forgiving guide for humbling my arrogant preference for finding things myself, because I have not seen many things in all my life so beautiful to me as the cloisters of Jerónimos. I have never before seen a cloisters of two stories. Here the enclosure, grass-covered, is fringed by two levels of arches, each one of individual design, and each etched as delicately in involved patterns as if the artist had been a lacemaker. There is a stairway to the first level and another to the top that is a broad, unroofed terrace. From here, and it is obviously not high, or I would not be able to speak familiarly of this vantage point, the arches on the other side of the green court-yard below make a lovely sight. With the stubbornness that so often accompanies ignorance, I continue to call the open space in the center of the cloisters the enclosure or courtyard. Some of the guide-books refer to this area as the garth. I had to look up the meaning of the word, and am still skittish about using it familiarly.

We parted from the Hamlets when we left the church. At our urging, they were going to visit the Coach Museum we had already seen. We reminded them to pause on their way to enjoy its next-door neighbor, the eighteenth-century palace in delicate pink that is a residence of the President of Portugal.

All afternoon I tried alternately to evade and to distract Sophy from queries about the plane bringing Gina, Alec and Brother Theodore. I wanted to search again desperately for Alec's letter. Had I lost the only diamond ring I possess I would not have been more agitated. This was the day to which we had looked forward for so long, and by my own carelessness I had flattened the pleasure of it. My alternative purpose was to scuttle down the street to our travel agency to learn the arrival time of all planes from London.

I have made a considerable number of trips with Sophy; the pattern has always been that we go our separate ways except for the hours when we are in transit confined within car, train, boat or plane. She is a will-o'-the-wisp. She likes to set off early in the morning, guidebook and maps under the arm. She may agree to a meeting place for lunch. Frequently she is not seen again until the "shoebag hour." This pattern is mutually satisfactory. I am pokier than she. I am a dawdling, not a brisk sight-seer. My attention is caught by trivia that do not attract her eye. Therefore, at the end of the day over our shoebag refreshment we exchange travel notes, discovering that except for basic landmarks we might have been exploring separate cities.

Not that afternoon, however. When I proposed with skillful casualness I might go for an exploring stroll Sophy magnanimously insisted she go with me, lest I have difficulty with the language, adding there was much she wanted to see, too. I relinquished that plan with convincing reluctance, saying I was seriously behind with my laundry. Sophy acquiesced eagerly; her conscience prompted her, she said, to write letters. I made a brief dash for liberty, but even this was not easily accomplished, and restricted. When I announced my intention of going downstairs to the desk to purchase stamps, Sophy assured me she had more than enough and would be happy to give me what I required. My virtuous response was I would not dream of permitting such a thing, borrowing stamps was an unforgivable imposition, because one was so likely to forget to return them. Sophy's answer was, she had never before observed such meticulousness on my part.

Nevertheless, I did make my escape to the desk. I inquired of the concierge what time planes arrived from London. With no hesitation he answered there was only one, and it came in in the morning. Obviously this was preposterous. I told him so. If the plane had come in the morning, our friends would be with us. Therefore, it must come at another time; certainly there must be more than one. I asked him to telephone the travel agency, since I dared not risk even so time-consuming an interval as a gallop to that source of information. The concierge assured me he knew as much as, if not more than, any travel agency about arrivals and departures, and that a telephone call would be a very foolish thing. I returned to our room, remembering halfway I had not purchased the stamps. Returning to rectify that, I found the concierge about to telephone our room. He was going to tell me, he said, because of my insistence he had telephoned the travel bureau, and discovered corroboration of his information to me. My irritation at his Olympian superiority was washed away by my profound gratitude I had intercepted the call.

Sophy was writing her letters when I returned. As I came in, she asked if I would mind looking up in my calendar the date we had tentatively set for being in Paris. By this time I was so nervous that at the sound of footsteps in the corridor outside I dropped the engagement book *cum* calendar I had just taken from my bag. I was sure the footsteps heralded the arrival of our friends. The footsteps passed by, I stooped over, picked up the little book. It had opened as it fell, opened to this very day, the fourth of May. The only entry on the page was ringed by a circle in red. It read, "Gina, Alec, Brother T. arrive 6:30," and the flight number was included. I had entered this memorandum, then thrown away Alec's letter. It all came back to me.

"By the way," I said to Sophy, as I turned the pages on toward the Paris date, and hoped my voice did not betray the lilt of a lark behind it, "What time do you think we ought to leave? The plane gets in at six-thirty." Sophy continued writing her letters, "I know," was her answer. "I had a postcard from Alec this morning, when we got back from Sintra, confirming the flight. I'd say leave about five-thirty to allow extra time. Is that about what you had in mind?"

Please God she will never know about what was in my mind.

SIX

The meeting at the airport between the travelers and our vehicle is a moment I treasure. Concisely and precisely, they like to died.

"What is that?" Gina asked, and pointed at the Microbus. It was lumbering out from the parking lot directly toward us at the door of the airport.

"It's called a Microbus," was Brother Theodore's contribution.

As the juggernaut loomed closer, Gina clasped her hands across her bosom, her large handbag dangling from one wrist. "Alecmou," she directed, "you see what it is so high up in front of that dragon? It is Sophy." She looked from Brother T. to me, imploringly. "This is our traveling carriage? And how I am going to ascend into it— we have perhaps a guide from the Alps with a rope?"

This was a pertinent suggestion. Gina's physical proportions are in direct ratio to her stature as an artist, both heroic size. Sophy and I had exchanged misgivings about Gina's compatibility with the measurements of the Volkswagen in distance from the ground and breadth of entranceway. We had agreed the only possible solution was to allow the situation to resolve itself at the moment and point of convergence. The moment was temporarily delayed by the somewhat breathless arrival in our midst of friends who had come to meet the Shermans, but had missed them at the airport gate. Gina introduced us. "Emily," she said, "these are our very dear friends, Mr. and Mrs. Davis," and to them, "You see the lady up there in that *wagon-lit,* she is our dear friend Sophy Jacobs, and she is going to conduct that equipage on our trip." Sophy had brought the Volkswagen to a stop and leaned down from the driver's seat. Mr. and Mrs. Davis acknowledged the introduction with cordiality, clouded by a kind of mist of abstraction. Their concentration seemed to be rather on her automobile than her person.

"You are going to motor through Portugal in that bus?" Mrs. Davis echoed. Redundant as the question was, it served to explain her abstraction. Sophy answered the question with vigorous reassurance of how comfortable it would be, how practical by allowing each of us an uninterrupted view, and ample space for our luggage. Mr. and Mrs. Davis seemed to me not wholly won over to an acceptance of the Volkswagen's superiority. They changed the subject, inviting us all to come with them to their house in Sintra at least for a few days. Although we knew they owned one of the beautiful and historic places in Sintra, we had to explain our itinerary with reservations made in advance would not permit this tempting deviation. The sadness of the Davises, that the Shermans were being swept away from them, was the more acute, I think, because of their anxiety over their beloved Gina consigned to such an ignoble vehicle. Their love and reverence of Gina as friend and artist led their imaginations, I think, to a golden chariot from the Museum of Coaches as the only fitting carrier.

Immediately on their departure, our party, now complete, converged on the stowing of luggage and persons. The luggage was easily fitted into the back, and Gina as easily into the front. Sophy and I had not counted on the application of one of her great qualities as an artist to this practical maneuver. Her strength is as the strength of ten, because with a heart as pure as Sir Galahad's she has also Herculean muscles. Once she had selected a place on which she could clamp her formidable grip, she soared up and into the front seat. Half-turning there, she leaned over the back, right arm stretched down to the open doorway of the second row of seats.

"Would you like I should pull you up?" she inquired politely of the rest of us.

By the time we were out of the driveway at the airport, the new contingent was congratulating Sophy on her choice of conveyance. How easily the luggage had gone in with plenty of room to spare

for Sophy's and mine, how comfortable the seats were, how delicious that no one would ever have to be a middleman, only two to a seat, and one left over to loll.

"And presently I will take both my hands from the dashboard," Gina interpolated with apologetic candor, "because I will be sure I am not falling through the windshield onto my face in the street. I do not care that there is no machinery in the front of me," she amplified. "It is just the emptiness out there that I am resisting, but soon I will not."

Such a torrent of praise washing away all the misgivings that had weighed on Sophy must have left her light in the head. It is the only way to account for her sudden and unannounced decision to find a short cut to the Tivoli Hotel. As well as I know her leaning from a highway toward a road that branches, I would not have expected her to quit a thoroughfare that would bring us to our destination. We were not on a reconnaissance tour. But that is exactly what she did. Within a very few minutes from the airport we were on narrow, badly paved streets. I recognized the neighborhood. I have been in its counterpart in many cities, when I have traveled with Sophy. I knew her unerring instinct had brought us to the slums. Sophy was blithe.

"I have a feeling," she said more than once, "the next turn will bring us in sight of our hotel."

There was eventually a next turn that brought us with irrevocable finality to an end of Sophy's meandering. It was a dead end crossed by a railway embankment. A corps of men was working on it.

I leaned from my window, tempted to blow happy kisses to the laborers, who, already surprised at our appearance, had stopped their work to look us over.

"Without those men," I told the Shermans, "Sophy would have been up that embankment and over the tracks, or at least had a go at it."

"*Tiens,*" was Gina's comment, "*quel courage, quel chauffeur.*"

Sophy said nothing. She backed the bus, turned it, and in subdued silence retraced more or less our wavering course. Still without comment, she did bring us, after one of a great many turns, in sight of the Tivoli Hotel. Sophy's and my invitation to the "shoebag hour" received a puzzled acceptance. Brother Theodore, with a scholar's pleasure in the unfamiliar, savored the phrase.

"I think," he surmised, "they have an ingenious piece of American luggage. To examine all its pockets and secret hiding places, each one with a zipper, I'm sure will require an hour."

Gina's interpretation took a more personal turn. "I think," she asserted, "they have bought us the Portuguese *espadrilles* for the walking and the seeing sights. They will be in very bright colors and I shall wear them with *grand plaisir,* but," she added anxiously, "you will remember Alecmou has very small feet—he must not lose his *espadrilles* by falling off them."

Alec's acceptance was characteristically unspeculated, and buoyant. "I shall be ready for it in fifteen minutes," he said.

The disclosure of the shoebag rite was a success. The eyes of the guests widened as Sophy lifted bottle after bottle, disengaging a shoe from each.

"You see," Brother Theodore insisted, "I was right. It is an American gadget with concealed surprises. Even without the help of zippers."

Alec's pleasure was in the content more than the container. He congratulated Sophy fervently on her selection of Scotch.

Gina was, perhaps, the most pleased. "Thanks to God," she declared, "it is not the *espadrilles*. I do not care for them. They are broad and flat, and I am waddling in them."

"Then you are a consummate liar," I told her, and she accepted the compliment graciously.

"Now, Alecmou," she asserted, "I will become a drinker. Yes," she reiterated at his look of startled inquiry. "Every night on the tour wherever we are I will drink from a shoebag."

"Scotch?" Sophy inquired as Alec stared.

"No, no, darling," Gina told her. "One finger across of white wine and then to the top of the glass with soda and ice. That will not make me too light in the head, Alecmou."

Alec was reassured. "I really didn't know what to expect," he told us.

"You can expect now," Gina retorted, "the story of our trip from London to Lisbon. Alec groaned, and returned for comfort to his Scotch. "Yes," Gina repeated, "you are going to hear, my dears, the story of our trip, because drinking, *on dit,* unties the tongue and mine is already longing to be very loose." She took a first sip of her teaspoon of wine.

"It begins weeks ago in Israel, when I say, 'Alecmou, you think it is sensible that you make the reservations for our flying to Lisbon?' He tells me I am always in agitation about something, which of course is not so. And will I please allow him to take care of this as he takes care of all our tickets, and this indeed is so. Then I am quiet, but not for long. Then I say, 'Alecmou, you have the reservations for our flight to Lisbon?' And now he is very British haughty milord with me. 'You do not know, Gina,' he tells me, like I am perhaps three years old, 'that this is not what we call the season for going to Portugal. No one is going at this time of year. I have no need to write from here. When we come back to London, I will go to the airline office, select the plane we will take, and book our seats. That is all. Many English go to Portugal, and I happen to know when they go.' "

Alec interrupted. "Do you think, Sophy, I could have another Scotch?"

Gina continued after a complacent smile at Alec. "See how I'm getting below his skin. So now he needs a little more Scotch. So we are back in London and only once do I say, 'The reservations to Lisbon, Alecmou.' 'I have it on my calendar,' he tells me, 'to go tomorrow.' And, my dears, what a day on the calendar that is. I am working at the piano and in comes my Alecmou. He is very red in the face. His coat is flying all over him. 'Stop, Gina,' he says, and certainly I am stopping. 'There is something preposterous that has happened. Everyone is going to Lisbon. There is not a place on any plane. I have never heard of such a thing. It's ridiculous. But I have been everywhere. Even our own agent can't get us bookings. It's mad, really it is.' And that is what I am, mad. I do not say one word, but I am thinking everything what you can imagine. Finally I speak. 'Alecmou,' I tell him, 'I am going to Lisbon. All these months I am dreaming about this. You will find us a plane, or a balloon, I have not the time for a ship.' He goes away. And I am back at my piano, but I am playing everything what you can imagine that has the thunder and lightning in it. Brother Theodore comes in to find out what is the matter. I cannot hear him for the music, and he cannot hear me, and I do not stop. But I am yelling, 'There are no seats for Lisbon, but Alec will find them, or I keel him.' Perhaps Brother Theodore is hearing that because he goes quickly from the room. So now at the end of the day Alec is returning. Very happy, very British milord again. 'We have the seats, Gina,' he tells me. 'Good,' I say and we are friends again. But he does not tell me where those seats are taking us. Do you know, my dears, where we have been today? Certainly we leave London very early. And can you imagine where we go next? Paris, and after that Amsterdam, and then Zurich. Yes, my dears, that is how we are flying today to Lisbon."

Alec spoke in a small voice, "We're here, darling. Why don't you have your drink?" Gina took a sip and a deep breath.

"And now I am telling you how he is making the mends."

"Amends," Alec murmured.

Gina's eyes narrowed. "No, Alecmou," she said, "it is not Amen—I am not yet finished. In Zurich we wait one hour, two hours, by now I do not care, I think we have been traveling many days. Alec and Brother Theodore leave the plane—I sit—they come back and Alec puts down on my lap the packages and packages of *chocolat* and this is what he says to me. 'There you are, darling. I know how you love the Swiss *chocolat* more than anything so I bring you to Switzerland so I can get you the Swiss *chocolat*.' Can you imagine? And so, my dears, with the Swiss *chocolat* that is how we are in Lisbon. I say, 'Thanks God for the shoebag hour.' And thanks God we are in any case here. I drink to your health."

Sophy and I exchanged a look that the plan for the evening we had had in mind could certainly under the circumstances not be broached. We had not realized the resilience of the Shermans.

"Now then," Alec demanded, setting down his empty glass with finality, "what are the plans for the evening?"

"Aren't you tired?" I asked, and this was a pusillanimous expression on my part for the faintness I felt at even hearing about the trip they had made.

"Tired?" Gina echoed. "There is nothing tiring about it, just time. And the doing nothing. Now I want to be doing something quick."

Brother Theodore's amplification was characteristic. "We ate a good many of the chocolates," he said. "Sugar, you know, makes for energy."

69

"Well, then," Sophy began, "Emily and I had thought it would be fun to go for dinner where there is Fado singing, and then afterward to another place that is recommended for the singing, but I'm sure that would be too much."

"Not at all, not at all," Gina declared. "We go now."

Restaurant Folclore, at Rua Nova da Trinidade, where we dined, has singers in picturesque costume and a series of specialty acts. We admitted to one another, however, the presence of an impresario with an introductory patter for each artist or group made it more of a production than the spontaneous music we were seeking. We found it at O Faia Restaurante—Bar Regional, that is, at Number 54 Rua da Barrota—"Open All Night—English Spoken." The street is narrow and hidden away, but the taxi driver knew it and so evidently did a great many other people. The place was crowded when we entered at about eleven. We were to find in our month in Portugal little evidence of the American tourist, but here there was a goodly number of British. We were aware of them, because they talked and laughed throughout the time we were there, not even allowing themselves a pause while the singing was going on. Certainly this is not a characteristic indigenous to the British; I have encountered this behavior pattern among all nationalities and it is one I do not understand. Why do these people go to the expense and inconvenience of visiting a restaurant whose specialty is the performance it offers, and then pay not the slightest attention while it is being given? Why do they not stay comfortably at home where they can more easily hear one another and where they are not subjected to interruption of any sort?

Nevertheless, we did hear Fado singing given in a simple, unpretentious manner. We delighted in the music itself, and the way in which it was presented. There were three singers, one man and two women. They did not make an entrance for a number—they were there at all times, moving about separately, assisting wherever service was required for a customer. Their only preparation for a number was to take their places by the doorway, the one who was to give the solo a little ahead of the other two. At the moment before the song began, each of the two women put around her shoulders a small black shawl holding the crossed ends with one hand against her breast. Each was dressed in a simple skirt with full-sleeved white blouse. The verse would be sung by the soloist standing in front, the two in the background joined the chorus.

Fado, though the folk music of Portugal, is not, as in other countries, gay music—it is a lament. It can be sentimental—it is always sad. There is a saying that you must open your ear to let in Fado, but once you have let it in it will stay with you for your life. Accompaniment is always on the guitar. I know of only one singer who has carried the Fado outside Portugal to be known in other world centers. That is Amalia Rodrigues. She became an immediate success in Paris and later in New York, and her records are available everywhere. Her voice is reedy, and yet passionate. The Portuguese, endeavoring to explain the quality they demand in the Fado singer, insist it must have nothing to do with a trained voice. There must never be a suspicion of *bel canto*—only sadness and passion. William and Elizabeth Younger in their excellent book, *Blue Moon in Portugal,* attribute the origin of Fado to the slums of Lisbon. They say it was based on the singing of Portuguese peasants, but made sophisticated by the Brazilian Fado, and this in turn had come from an African dance. They also quote the legend of the black shawl that is requisite for a woman when she sings Fado. I heard this legend from other sources as well—that it is a symbol of mourning for the death of Maria Severa, who was the most widely known of all the Fadistas. She was a child of the slums of Lisbon, daughter of a tavern keeper known as "the bearded lady." Maria had a series of passionate and violent love affairs, but died, not of love, but of overeating.

Alec succumbed to the charms and salesmanship of another member of the O Faia personnel, and we were sympathetic to his enthusiasm. She was not young, she was not pretty, but she had charm that was a bit of magic, conveying warmth, hospitality, humor, quick understanding and no little seductiveness; all this without the knowledge of a single word of English. Alec purchased from her a

71

tiny doll in peasant costume for each of us, and before we left, a second round of them. At our departure we found her behind the counter in the cloakroom. Evidently the personnel of O Faia have interchangeable occupations; the singers were clearing our table for the newcomers entering as we departed.

Next morning, Sophy and I left the hotel early for a shopping expedition, deciding the Shermans, considering their preceding twenty-four hours, would certainly wish no contact with the world outside their rooms before noon.

On the drive in from Sintra, during exchange of addresses Mrs. Hamlet had given us the Fabrica de Porcelana da Vista Allegre, Number 19 Rua Ivenef, a shop where she had found lovely china. This was our first objective. Sophy wanted an after-dinner coffee set for her daughter. She found it. The only difficulty was in the selection, since the assortment was both varied and exquisite. There was no difficulty about having it shipped directly to New York, and when it arrived Sophy found it in perfect condition. The cost, including the shipping, was thirty-five dollars.

The next objective was on my "To Do" list. Of the two things I had fixed in my mind and budget to buy for myself in Portugal, a rug for my dining room was in the making. Tiles for the floor of my entrance hall had not been checked off. The tiles, Lady Elles had told us helpfully, might be found at a place called Souso Baptista on the Praca do Municipa, Numbers 29 and 30. Just outside the porcelain shop we hailed by happy accident a taxi driver who heeded my plea for slow driving and the pantomime of my apprehensions with not only an attentive ear, but a face contorted with distressed sympathy. He put his dear understanding into his driving. I was of a mind, I told Sophy, to engage him for the entire month in Portgual. I would drive alone with him, I proposed, behind the Microbus. Expanding my vista of a happy life behind such a driver, I said I might take him back to America. Sophy with characteristic practicality suggested I compromise by keeping him for the whole morning. He took us to the establishment that manufactures and sells tiles. It is large, peopled by a considerable staff.

Salesmen and executives sit in open, glass-partitioned offices, secretaries in outer cubicles. Workmen wearing overalls could be seen beyond the center aisle that parted the executive offices, in a section that looked like a working greenhouse behind the sales department of a florist. From executive to workman there was not an individual who spoke a language other than Portuguese.

This was a moment in which Sophy scaled an Alpine peak of accomplishment, justifying the weeks of study at the Berlitz School. I doubt that in its comprehensive system the vocabulary for dimensions of a room, patterns and colors of tiles, and shipments to America had been covered, but Sophy encompassed them all. Not only that, but before the eyes of everyone in the Souso Baptista—one by one they had formed a circle around us—she translated into meters the measurements in feet and inches I had brought. It was a brilliant display. My congratulations were no more fervent than the hand clasp of each member of her audience. Upon our entrance they had set up a smiling, courteous barricade at which Sophy had flung herself and her Portuguese. We made our exit down a triumphal aisle from work plant to front door, followed by waves of the hand, and bows on either side, and at the door parted from an escort, who by authority and dress must have been the president. With some reluctance and considerable abashment I append the note that some 800 pounds of tile cost $10. Its shipment to America was $85. Its transportation from dock to my apartment $53, and the cost of laying it in New York $150. When I skip over this appended memorandum, I refer to the purchase as my Portuguese bargain.

We visited one or two other shops, but made no further purchases and, principally because of my reluctance to part with the taxi driver, visited the Espiritu Fantof, of which we had been told by a friend in America—though it is not mentioned in many of the guidebooks. It is a magnificent old house. We wandered delightedly through a series of furnished rooms, some decorated in old *azulejos*, others with exquisitely painted ceilings and walls, and then came suddenly, on the walls of farther rooms, upon a collection of modern

73

tapestry which was not to our liking. We were more interested in the making of the tapestries themselves, that we discovered was being carried on by young women in an atelier on the top floor. They giggled self-consciously at the sight of us, and evidently, from their exchanged looks, passed a few remarks about us. Nevertheless, there seemed to be no objection to our watching and we remained some little time. When we rejoined my dear taxi driver, it was a little past noon, and reluctantly, back at the hotel, I let him go.

At the desk waiting for our key, we speculated on the possibility of the Shermans being awake and ready to receive. With the key was delivered a collection of telephone and personally written messages that ranged in tone from perplexity to indignation. "Where are you?"—"Your telephone does not answer"—"Please come at once!"—"There are people waiting to see you."

There were indeed. In Gina's and Alec's suite we found the Greek Ambassador to Portugal and his wife; the Swiss Ambassador with his; two or three other individuals whose names and occupations we never learned, all gathered round a table on which there was a bountiful array of little cakes, and Gina's Swiss *chocolat*. And we had wondered if the Shermans had as yet roused sufficiently to have their morning coffee.

"Other peoples," Gina told us reproachfully, "have been here and gone away. They could not wait. They wanted so much to meet our friends and traveling companions. Why did you not let us know you go out? Either we would not let you go or we go with you."

The guests departed shortly and while good-bys were being said at the door to Gina and Alec, Brother T. spread before me on the table a fan of pamphlets.

"I collected these this morning," he explained. "I think you may find them useful."

Had I known, as they say in detective stories, this was a clue to his similarity to a squirrel, I would have quailed. At the end of the month in Portugal, I shipped from Lisbon to my New York address twelve pounds of pamphlets.

SEVEN

We lunched at the Imperio Hotel, 17 Rua de Rodrigues Sampaio. I have never seen displayed, nor eaten, so wide a variety and so delicious hors d'oeuvres as is the specialty of that hotel—and my memory of such matters is infallible. It is a mistake to order anything to follow. Alec had stayed in the hotel years before and so warned us not to give the waiter an order for a lunch, but wait until after the hors d'oeuvres. There is no "after the hors d'oeuvres" except perhaps fruit and coffee. We began with an *apéritif* of a glass of port. We were learning that at midday, though we were not in the habit, any of us, of drinking at all at that hour, a glass of port was not only a delightful beginning to a meal, but an experience in taste. I had tasted port before. I think my impression of the drink, as much from English novels as from my own experience, was that it is a heavy wine, usually passed round the table only to the gentlemen, after the ladies have left the dining room. It is nothing of the kind in Portugal. As a matter of fact, it is very nearly everything in texture, bouquet, taste and color. It can be light, delicate, pale pale yellow, a little thin, perhaps even a little sharp. Or it can be smooth, deeper in color, a little heavier in body, and again it will be a dark amber, full-bodied, a bit sweet. It is always delicious, though certainly we had preferences. We were never able irrevocably to identify the ones to our particular liking, because each place we visited had its own favorites and served them exclusively. Even when we asked for, and were served, a particular brand we had noted down as exactly suiting our taste, we would find the brand differed according to the locale. In spite of this variation we never found a port we did not like.

As we were savoring the last drop of our *apéritifs* our waiter began rolling to the table two-tiered carts filled with cold hors d'oeuvres. I think he wheeled for our inspection three of these carts, as if choice from one were not difficult enough among such succulence. Alec urged us to be restrained, because he said there would follow a second course of hors d'oeuvres, this time hot. Gina's method of choosing was unquestionably the best. She took for herself tidbits omitted by the others, waiting to serve herself until she saw what was on the other plates. Then having filled her own, she took samples from all the others. "In this way," she explained, "I will know what is best for all of us to order next time."

We walked the short distance back to our hotel, regretting there was not a wider space between them, in order to work off a little of the glorious hors d'oeuvre banquet with which we were sated. Gina paused at the window of a porcelain shop.

"Alecmou," she said, pointing, "there is something so beautiful I think we must have."

I saw a shudder convulse his shoulders as he followed Gina's finger. She had set her eye and heart on an exquisite group of figurines so fragile as to look the equivalent in porcelain of spun glass. "Gina," Alec urged desperately, his voice shaking a little. "I cannot carry such a package as that with me all through Portugal, and certainly they could not ship anything so delicate."

Gina waited a moment in thought, then she patted Alec's arm. "We will buy it when we come back here," she told him, "before we go and then you will have only to carry it to England, and that way you will not take me home by Zurich and Amsterdam and Paris. Not when you are holding the package all the time we are traveling."

Azeitão, the first stop on our itinerary, is about an hour's distance from Lisbon, and this includes the ride on the ferry that crosses the Tagus. We left Lisbon at about three in the afternoon. The unfortunate traveler who has only a few hours' stopover in Lisbon should include a ferry crossing and back. The view of the city is magnificent, the river traffic seen at close quarters a delight. Fishing boats were on either side of us, so that we could see in detail their brightly painted high prows and hoisted nets strung like washing between poles, swinging back and forth in slow rhythm, drying in the air. Alec, Sophy and I took photographs, a little hampered by Gina's eager indication of where to focus. "Are you getting in the very center that beautiful square that makes it look a little like Venice? And you must tilt your camera so you will see how the city goes through that wonderful St. George Castle on the very top. But do not tip it so much that you will not get the city below as well."

One or two of my pictures with a diagonal streak from top to bottom I might think were light-struck if I did not know this was Gina's forefinger.

It was Brother Theodore, of course, who, moving unobtrusively about the boat, discovered the woman sitting on her haunches on the deck munching sunflower seeds. He brought us to her without attracting her attention. He wanted us to see what dignity she had, even in that position. She might have been sitting in a high-back chair, a lady in her drawing room, the railing providing the high back. She was not leaning against it, nor was she stooped in craven beggar fashion. Her shoulders were straight, her head up. She was looking out toward the river with lively interest; one cupped hand held the sunflower seeds, with the other delicately she selected one at a time. When she became aware we were standing near, and observing her, she acknowledged us with a slight bow and smile. Her aquiline nose was high-bridged, her eyes black and wide-set. A black shawl covered her head and came close around her face, throwing into sharp relief the nobility of her features. We indicated a request to photograph her. She raised her eyebrows and smiled quizzically, at the same time indicating her tolerance of such foolishness. Our embarrassment at offering her money in return for her permission lacked the poise with which she accepted our donation.

The drive to Azeitão—we learned it must be pronounced as if a clothespin were clamped on the nose—is through gently rolling green country. We found our destination without difficulty.

A sign beside tall gates reads "QUINTA DOS TORRES." We drove down a long avenue of trees. On our right as we approached the house we saw, from our height, over the top of a wall, a few people having tea at tables beside a pool large enough to be counted a small lake. Swans were on the water, white pigeons flew in and out a gazebo in the center. The avenue widened into a courtyard. We stopped the car in front of a lofty iron gate that was closed. On the far side of it, the high wall of dusty yellow stone we had followed continued, allowing us no glimpse of what the house itself would be. I was the first one out of the car, since I had been sitting in the middle tier on the side toward the house.

As I walked toward the gate I saw there was a window beside the entrance way, not high above the ground, and I could make out beyond it the outlines of a room. Evidently the wall, or at least part of it, was the house itself. A young girl appeared at the window. She was in a maid's uniform and called out a greeting. She was young, pretty and gay. I noticed again how attractive a Portuguese domestic's uniform is. I had seen a few like it worn by women who had come into a shop when Sophy and I were buying material for the shoebag. The distinguishing feature of the uniform is its moderately high collar, covered by another collar of crisp white embroidery, repeated on the cuffs. I realized now the women in the store must have been maids from surrounding houses shopping for their mistresses.

When the maid I had seen pushed open the gate, another maid followed, a porter behind them. The maids went immediately to the back of the car where Alec and Brother T. were unloading our bags. The porter paused at the gate, indicating to us to come through that way. In spite of protests from the men in our party, the maids, who were small, gathered up as many bags as they could carry—they encompassed a considerable number—and indicated they would return for the rest. They did not permit us to burden ourselves with so much as our coats, cameras and the other incidentals that always fill up a car on tour. When they had gone ahead

vasiliu

of us through the gate, Alec paused at the entrance. The porter stood waiting.

Secure in the knowledge that no one of the welcoming committee spoke English, Alec addressed his women. "I do hope you'll take good note," he urged. "I always find it makes a very good impression if one assumes the customs of a country one is visiting. Obviously, the custom here is that women carry the burdens. The men lead the way." With this, turning, he preceded us through the entrance.

We found ourselves in a small enclosed court with a high arched roof overhead. On either side a doorway at the head of a pair of steps evidently led to wings of the house. There were birds in cages in this little court, mostly budgereegahs, some I could not identify. They were all chirping, twittering. The cages hung from hooks in the wall; there were so many of them they reached almost up to the arched roof. Directly facing the entrance gate was an opening that led further toward the interior. We walked under this open arch and were in a patio that was of such size two modest houses, I think, might have found room there. A beautiful fountain marked the center and off to the right at the far end I saw a covered terrace furnished in comfortable outdoor chairs. A woman was sitting on one of these. I hesitated a moment, expecting some indication she was our hostess, but she gave no sign of recognition of our arrival, except to call back two terriers who had cavorted toward us, barking but wagging their tails. Our guides had gone to the left: we followed them to the far end of the patio and another roofed, but open arch. Two steps led to a door on either side. We went first through the one on the right, into a charming double bedroom with a fireplace, comfortable chairs on either side, beyond it a window with a long, cushioned seat below. A maid showed us the bath, then she took us out again through the arch into the apartment on the other side. This included a single room and beyond it, down a short corridor, another charming double chamber like the one we had seen, with a fireplace, a window seat, a view of an orchard and beyond it a green hill. This was obviously an apartment for the Shermans. Sophy and I returned to the room across the arch.

Once the luggage was sorted out, we began to unpack, a maid hovering over us and permitting us to do little more than indicate what things we wished removed. By the time the bags were stowed away, Sophy and I were purring with contentment. The maid left, taking with her what things she thought should be pressed. We went over to compare with the Shermans our bliss. We found Gina equally ecstatic.

"Is it not beautiful, my dears?" she exclaimed. "Everything that is here and the maids, too."

The men seemed to me unresponsive, but I put that down to masculine indifference to the picturesque and only observed that undoubtedly the men saw nothing remarkable in the service, since they were anticipating the same from us. Even this failed to bring a retort, and again I wondered a little.

Brother T. diverted me by inviting Sophy and me to inspect his room, which he said had two rather special and utterly delightful features. We agreed with his appraisal. One feature was the location of the tub in an alcove parallel with his bed and only a few feet from it, but withdrawn by means of a delicate blue curtain. It looked as if instead of hooks and racks in a clothes closet the tub had been installed there. I think one could have leaned out of bed, opened the curtain and turned on the tap, but I neglected to ask Brother T. to verify this. The other feature was a diminutive oil lamp, placed in a little niche in the small closed room that contained the washbasin and the WC, as the label on the door read. The lamp was of a sort that burned in a nursery in our grandmother's time, and was evidently to guide sleep-laden footsteps in the night.

By the time we had finished our exploration it had got on, as Alec pointed out, for the "shoebag hour." We promptly gathered in Sophy's and my room. Sophy cleverly found that when she pulled a cord hanging between the beds a bell jangled in the patio. This summoned a maid. When she arrived Sophy exhibited even greater acumen by requesting in Portuguese ice and glasses. The maid clapped her hands in astonished understanding and ran from the room. When she returned bearing a large tray on which were glasses and ice, she was followed by two other maids, each carrying in either hand a lamp. They set down two in our room, moved with the others to go across the way, pausing to indicate they would return with still another. When all three had gone, Gina clapped her hands.

"I am happy like that little maid," she said. "How could it be more charming? Now we have lovely soft lamps. *Quelle atmosphère.*"

Then Brother Theodore spoke. "It is beautiful atmosphere," he agreed. "The only difficulty, Gina darling, is there is no electricity in it. I saw that when we came to the room and I pointed it out to Alec."

"So," Gina interrupted. "This is what makes for the charm. You are so insensitive. You must always have the mechanic."

"No," Brother T. assured her, "I love the charm, but you will not be insensitive to the beards Alec and I will show you by the morning or even right now. We have only electric razors, and there is no electricity."

There is no electricity in any part of the Quinta dos Torres. It is all charm and oil lamps that burn flatteringly for women. They do not take care of men's beards.

The beards were taken care of next morning in the garage in the village of Setúbal, eleven miles away. The proprietor, after his first surprise, was graciousness itself, leading the way for the two gentlemen with the flourish of a host to the back of the establishment. Either he did not wish to expose them to the public gaze, or there were no electrical fixtures in the front office. He indicated an outlet in the wall.

The men, borrowing mirrors from our handbags, propped them up on cars, and presently added the hum of their razors to the sounds of the mechanics at their repair jobs. Had the proprietor's purpose been to spare the Shermans from the public gaze, he need not have bothered to take them so far from the street. Somehow the word got out. Perhaps one of the garagemen slipped away to tell of the unusual episode that was breaking the monotony of the day.

However the word was conveyed, the street very rapidly moved into the garage, and, enthralled, the populace of a wide range in age watched the spectacle.

Gina, Sophy and I, not wishing to deprive others of the view by taking up room, retreated to the street when the crowd began to come in. I was looking at a little church just beyond us, and thinking how pretty its spire looked against the sky when I saw something hover over it, and then settle down on what I realized was a nest. I clutched my companion.

"Look," I said, "up on that spire. If I'm not mad, there's a stork on her nest."

At that instant the other parent floated languorously through the air, circled the spire and, dropping its long legs, came to a landing close beside the nest, and then, just as the storybook pictures show, tucked one leg up underneath its feathers.

"I don't know why it should be so incongruous," I said, after we had been silently watching, "but somehow there does seem to me a ridiculous divergence between the two men in there buzzing away with an electric razor and out here storks roosting on a church spire."

When the men had emerged and the crowd more or less dispersed, we expressed our gratitude to the garage proprietor by buying petrol; he had refused to accept any money from the shavers. It was decided among us, as we drove off, that Sophy would endeavor to gauge the supply of petrol to insure the need for refueling whenever it was necessary for the men to shave. Sophy protested this was a little difficult to calculate, but we told her that was nonsense—it only required a little planning. We would all help.

"I wish to God I'd kept quiet," was her answer.

"Now, darlings," Gina said, as we moved off all in place in the bus, "I will tell you how our day is beginning. And it is not a good beginning, because Alecmou put his feet into it."

Alec protested. "I was only trying to help you—sitting stark-naked entertaining a caller."

"Only to the waist," Gina corrected. "And besides, how is one to know there is a caller when she is at the window? From the outside looking in with her arms on the window sills, and the window is open, of course, and I am at my dressing table beside it, and also I am naked only to the waist, because I am arranging my hair. Let me continue. So I am sitting at my dressing table arranging my hair comfortably, and there is suddenly a 'Good morning' beside me. I am startled. I look to pull something around my shoulder, but there is nothing to pull and so I say 'Good morning,' and look and there is a lady at the window beside me, and so she leans over and crosses her arms on the—how you say, Alecmou—"

"Sill," Alec supplied.

"Seal," Gina echoed. " 'Are you comfortable?' the lady asks. And I say very, and I want to say I am not so comfortable at this moment, but I think it is not polite, and then Alec speak. And what does he say—"

"I said," Alec broke in, " 'What a beautiful, charming place this is.' "

"That is not all," Gina prompted. "Continue."

"Well," Alec admitted, "Then I said, 'Was it at one time a private house?' I was only trying to make conversation to help Gina."

"And how you help me," Gina asserted. "If, my dears, you could see her. She take her hands off the what, Alecmou—"

"Sill," Alec replied.

"Seal," Gina echoed. "She stand up very straight, her eyes are flashing like the lightning, as she say, 'It *is* a private house, *now,* sir.' And she go. So now, dears, we are in the disgrace. And Alec with his beard, too."

"Should I go back now," Alec inquired, "without my beard and explain since we are paying, I thought it permissible to call it not so private a house as it might once have been?"

"No," Gina decided. "We continue without the beard. Tonight, Alecmou, you will be charming. Now we will see Setúbal."

The guidebooks we had consulted had not given us a particular objective in Setúbal. We had learned it was on the Sado, is important in the sardine-canning industry and produces salt. This we verified almost immediately because we saw the tall white mounds. But for the rest, it seemed a busy town considerably torn up by construction going on throughout, and widening of roads. At a dead end we had reached by way of Sophy's insistence she was taking us on a short cut, though to what she admitted she did not know, we turned round with some difficulty, since the route she had chosen was narrower than the other streets. As she was maneuvering the bus, a young man spoke from the sidewalk, and asked in English if he might help us.

We gratefully took him aboard and he led us out to a promontory beach where we might see the sardine canneries. The landscape was bleak, arid. Visitors, he said, were not admitted to the canneries. I was more relieved than reconciled; I had not anticipated joyously an indoor call on millions of sardines. Alec was almost irreconcilable. Since childhood, he insisted, he had nursed a dream of seeing how sardines got so tightly into a tin.

The place I should have liked to visit is Troia. This is a buried city on a promontory across the river from Setúbal. It can be reached by a ferry in summertime but we were too early in the season. The city or town existed in Roman, even in Phoenician, times. I am told—and this is why I should like to see it—at low tide foundations of Roman villas emerge above the sand, and from time to time visitors have found valuable coins and pottery.

On the return inland, our charming guide told us the town was being improved, and many new buildings erected. He was sorry we should see it at this stage. When we urged him not to give us so much of his time, he assured us ruefully his time was not occupied. He was a recently graduated lawyer from the University of Coimbra, he had only begun his practice, therefore, he had considerable leisure. He spoke English haltingly, but with a surprisingly wide vocabulary and accuracy of construction—particularly surprising when he answered our query of where he had learned it by saying he had taught himself. He was as deprecatory about his town as he was about his accomplishment. Setúbal, he said, had been called by a Portuguese poet, "an ugly morsel set in a silver dish." He mournfully besought us to drive on to Évora. After reiterated instructions for finding the main road, he said good-by. Refusing our urgent invitation to be driven back to our original place of meeting, he walked away, a sad young man. I thought about him often, commiserating with his melancholy, until one day I read in one of Brother T.'s pamphlets, "A man who is happy is not a Portuguese."

Sophy's short cuts have taken me over stubble fields in Louisiana, because in the dusk she did not know the road had stopped; into the slums of Amsterdam, with the assertion this was the quickest way to the best hotel; to other unlikely places beyond counting. But once in a while, enough times to give her confidence to pursue her wayward course, she either achieves a short cut or brings her passengers to something wonderful they might otherwise have missed. We saw the Church of Jesus because Sophy was sure there was a quicker way to meet the route to Évora than the one the young man had indicated.

At the sight of the little church we stopped our protests, and Sophy put on the brakes. We knew we were seeing something that must be looked into. We were seeing a church built by the great Manueline architect, Boytac. I read, later, money for it had been provided in 1494 by the nurse of Manuel I. Either the position was highly paid or that nurse had special sources of income.

The slender pillars in the nave are stone twisted and coiled like rope. The result is a delicacy and sense of fragility that makes stone seem an improbable medium of construction for such design. We left the little church reluctantly.

Évora has been called the cradle of the Portuguese classical movement. In that cradle is represented almost every era of architectural history. Chronologically, a delicate Roman temple of Diane comes first. This seemingly fragile piece dates from the end of the second or beginning of the third century. Beginning geographically at the outskirts of the city, that is, just outside the city walls, there is one of the most extraordinary churches I have ever seen, because it is turreted and has battlements as if it were a fortress. Contradicting this belligerent aspect, there is a large, hospitable square porch at one end. This is the Church of St. Bras and the date of its construction is around 1482. The interior is almost equally startling by reason of bright green and white *azulejos* in a diamond pattern that cover the entire nave, a little reminiscent of a modern bathroom.

Just inside the city walls is the Church of St. Francisco. This is of unmistakably Moorish Gothic architecture.

Évora itself is a town of narrow, steep streets, dominated by the cathedral or *"sé"* built just after the turn of the thirteenth century. Twin towers rise on either side of an arched porch, fraternal rather than identical twins, since they are strikingly dissimilar in design. We climbed streets—one does not stroll them—breathlessly not only because they are so steep, but because the sun was very hot. In the environs of the temple of Diana, we saw students of the University of Évora sitting in the open windows of what were apparently their living quarters. They were interested in us, too, because it was obvious we were the subject of conversation called across from window to window. Insofar as we saw, we were the only tourists in the town. We looked in shop windows down a long arcade because the shade of its roof was welcome. This arcade extended along one full side of the town's center square. Facing it the other side was filled with open-air cafés, and these in turn were filled entirely with men. We saw no women. Some of the men sat at little tables, others lounged against the walls. Among the standees we saw several shepherds. Their occupation could not be mistaken; evidence of it in that heat brought beads to my forehead. They wore what looked to be the entire skin of a sheep, front and back, fleece out, minus only the head. The opening created by this severance permitted the wearer to put on the garment like a tunic, over his own head. To generate further heat, he added sheepskin chaps, fleece side out. These were dark brown, the tunics were unwashed-sheep-white. To bring the blood to a boil I should think, they wore long, heavy, knitted wool stocking caps, green, black or red; the end, brought over a shoulder, was ornamented by a pompon. Nearly all of them I saw carried a long staff.

A little side street between two of the open-air cafés bore a small sign reading RESTAURANT GIRALDO. It is not large, but it is immaculate and we found the food excellent. Facing me at the table a sign on the wall read, "Se Fi Core Satisféito Recommende—nos" and indeed I can heartily give a recommendation as having been well satisfied. Gina took a scallopine of veal and found it delicious. The rest of us had the regular lunch—a substantial and delicious vegetable soup, excellent very fresh fish, a sort of pilaf with veal, chicken and livers mixed in it, and finally cheese and fruit. We prefaced the meal with the inevitable glass of port. Between pantomime and Sophy's Portuguese, we had no difficulty, though not a word of English was spoken. Certainly we were finding that old, and to me distasteful, American slogan, "You'll always find someone who speaks English, so why learn another language?" does not prevail in Portugal. Almost no English is spoken.

After lunch, we explored again on foot, delighting in the sights, but feeling the effects of heat on weary feet. I think it was the hottest day we knew in Portugal, or perhaps we were more aware of temperature because of the hillside streets to climb and descend.

On the way back to Azeitão we saw storks again, this time nesting so close to the road Alec and I felt sure we could get photographs. At our excited request Sophy immediately stopped the car. Alec and I, with our equipment, bounded out, rushed across the road, and at the instant of our focusing saw the storks settle down, distributing their legs in some fashion that permitted them to snuggle into their feathers, and roost so flat to their perch as to make them impossible to distinguish in the camera. I was annoyed. Alec was provoked to expostulation. He called to them in a series of explosive syllables he must have thought sounded like Portuguese. They had sufficient English overtones for me to understand he was urging the birds to get up on their feet, to be more co-operative, to pay attention to the camera, look into it.

At a moment when he paused for breath, and perhaps further composition and arrangement of syllables, I heard another sound. Turning I saw a young girl leaning against the trunk of a tree laughing helplessly, and in no time she was joined by a considerable group. They were not making fun of us; they were enjoying an absurd situation. I was to find this spontaneous enjoyment far more typical than "One who is happy is not a Portuguese."

More than compensating for our failure with the storks, a group of women rice workers permitted photographs. The sight of them was as unexpected as the birds had been. We saw—I think Brother T. was the first to point a finger—a group, like a flock rising up in the middle of a water-covered area. We knew it was a rice paddy. Sophy stopped the car. It took a minute or two to identify the objects as people, a little more time to know they were women accompanied by one man, an overseer. They waded laboriously through the water and mire beneath. When they were almost at the road we realized most of them were young, all of them wore bright bandannas, and all of them from boots halfway up their skirts and thighs were black with caked mud. They were chattering

89

EIGHT

Dinner on the night of our return from Évora was punctuated by a message for me to telephone Mrs. Scoville. For all my ability to comply with this request I might have been told to convey or receive a message in Morse code. I knew Mrs. Scoville, but my only involvement with a Portuguese telephone had been by way of a pitiful optimism that in Europe I could talk more readily and less expensively to my daughter who lives in Holland than was possible from New York.

The switchboard operator at the Tivoli Hotel in Lisbon had been my liaison officer. I had been unable, vocally, to make her understand "Scheveningen, the Netherlands," though at the moment of the first try Sophy, emerging from an elevator two corridors away from my room, reported she had heard my efforts. I wrote the two names on a piece of paper and carried them downstairs to the directress of the switchboard. Two days later a note was delivered to my room. It was written on the back of my memorandum, and it read, "Portugal does not find these places." It was signed "Telephone." I had not lifted a receiver again. Services at the Tivoli are obtained by pressing on a panel the button next to a picture of a waiter carrying a tray, a chambermaid with a broom, down a considerable list. One does not call for room service. I did not call for anything.

At the Quinta dos Torres I endeavored to convey all of this to a maid who brought the message. I pointed to myself, I drew down the corners of my mouth, and I said, "No good." The maid made it clear to me that nothing of my vivid performance had got through to her. A tall, handsome woman stepped into the doorway behind her.

"I will help you," she said in perfect English. "Come with me."

Before I could push mine back from the table Alec had leaped from his chair and assisted me to rise by squatting down to a curious crouching position behind me. I turned in some bewilderment to look down at him.

"That's the lady I insulted this morning," he muttered. "Don't you remember? 'This *is* a private house.'"

"Alecmou," Gina said reasonably. "You go to the garage to shave but you cannot go under the table to eat. Even if it is a private house that you do not know."

"I was trying to think of something to say," Alec explained, "only not while she was looking at me."

As I left the room I heard Brother T.'s suggestion that Alec write down a few phrases and try them out.

I found my guide at a telephone in a corridor adjoining the dining room. At the sight of me she extended the receiver.

"Here is Mrs. Scoville," she said.

As I took her place at the instrument I wondered if it would be unsuitable for me to ask the owner of a private house if she would know, and could teach the local operators, the locality of Scheveningen in the Netherlands, but Mrs. Scoville was speaking. She was asking our group to come to dinner on the following night. I accepted for all of us, and thanked her for the flowers and the note we had found from her on our return from Évora that afternoon.

"I came to call," she explained, "and welcome you, but you are so energetic you had already left on some excursion."

"We left early," I began, "because the men had to shave."

At that instant we were cut off. Since my guide had departed, and I had no knowledge of how to re-establish a connection, I daresay I left Mrs. Scoville bemused, but I had at least accepted the dinner invitation for all of us.

Sophy and I had met and lunched with Mrs. Herbert Scoville in New York some weeks before, through the introduction of a mutual friend. Mrs. Scoville, an American, has lived in Portugal many months of the year for more than thirty seasons. During these years she has restored the Quinta da Bacalbõa to one of the most beautiful places in the whole of Portugal. She and her husband had purchased what was then a ruin, with the object of restoration and the achievement of a lovely place in which to live part of each year. At Mr. Scoville's death, she has continued the work, consulting scholars, but in the end relying upon her own indefatigable and knowledgeable research until now she and the Quinta da Bacalbõa are a mecca for other scholars from very nearly all parts of the world.

When I reported to my companions the invitation, and my acceptance, the only comment, other than a general happy acquiescence, was Brother T.'s observation that two visits to the shaving garage were indicated, one in the morning before the day's excursion, and a later one—the owner bribed to keep his establishment open— in order to be freshly groomed before a party. Gina, Sophy and I left them still at the table in academic discussion as to the advisability of bathing and changing before or after a visit to the garage.

The excursion next morning—and this was Saturday, the seventh of May—was directed toward the Corniche Coast Drive. We had read and heard much of its beauty. No one had thought to write or tell me of its height. Our way led through Setúbal. We were by now becoming familiar with the village, since during the wait outside the garage, Sophy, Gina and I had walked about, watched the storks on the church and discovered the shops in the village. That morning in one of these shops Gina found for herself, Sophy and me wide-brimmed, flat-crowned, straw sun hats that were charming, and had an added feature to recommend them, because of a prevalent breeze: scarlet tape with which to tie them under the chin. Charming as they were, they were dimmed by the spectacular purchase she made for Alec. We were waiting at the car when she brought it from the shop.

"Alecmou," she said as she came toward us holding her hands behind her back, "you remember how all the way back in New York you say you will be the banker?"

Alec regarded her dubiously. "I do," he said. "But I was a little carried away that evening."

"No," Gina interrupted. "Now you will be the banker, and it will not be carried away." She drew from behind her back a straw basket of natural color, superimposed by a vivid design in reds, greens and purples. Brother T., Sophy and I regarded the object with something approaching stupefaction, but Alec was immediately delighted. He seized it from her hands, turned it round and round with exclamations of pleasure.

"Of course, I can be a banker with this. No switching from pocket to pocket—that's what I was afraid of. I just put all our money in this, and you see it has a lock and a key."

"That is just what I'm thinking of, Alecmou, and I buy it." Gina amplified. "You lock it and also you do not lose it because

this is something one will see no matter where it is put down."

"True, true," Brother T. murmured.

"And, of course," Alec continued, "if I should put it down, which I shan't do, because I shall not let it out of my hand—but if I should, one of you, or all of you, will certainly see it immediately and then the money will not be lost."

"And you see," Gina added happily, "I look very carefully at the cracks. There are none. This is so tight because they know how to weave well, these Portuguese. Not the least coin what you can imagine will slip through. So apart of Alec losing the whole thing, and this I do not think is possible because we shall all see it, nothing can be lost."

Evidently Sophy and I entertained the same idea, that to comment on the bizarre appearance of the receptacle would be irrelevant. Neither of us said anything as we resumed our places in the Volkswagen, Alec happily swinging by its handle in the center of the lid his new bank.

"Now, my darlings," Gina began as we moved along, "I will tell you other things I am thinking. I am thinking what each of us will be since Alecmou is now the banker. I will be the map reader, because I am sitting here with Sophy in the front. But for the most because I am the map reader *par excellence*. No one, I think, can read a map so quick and so fine as me. And no kind of reading makes me more happier. Is that not so, Alecmou?"

Alec alone on the last tier of seats was at the moment gleefully emptying the contents of his pockets into the straw basket. Gina repeated her question a little more sharply.

"Well, I'm pretty good at maps myself," Alec answered. But it lacked a tone of conviction, explained an instant later by his ejaculation at what had evidently been distracting him. "Oh, I say," he said. "Do you know, I've emptied both pockets into the bank. Now I had in one what I was going to put into our general pot whenever we decided who was to hold it. And in the other I had the money for any purchases Gina and I make. Only part of that was set aside as Gina's particularly. But I really don't know which was

Gina's and I can't seem to think what the actual amount was in either pocket."

I heard Sophy at the wheel. *"Ça commence,"* she muttered.

Gina had twisted round in the front seat to look full at Alec, her eyes wide with incredulity.

"I am not caring about the pot," she told him. "I am not caring about your money. But I am caring about mine. Very much I am caring about mine, that you do not know how much it is. I will tell you how much it is. It is two hundred dollars. And first you will put it into the English money that you put all our money for this trip into when we start—though I did not know then we start by way of France, the Holland, the Switzerland, but no matter. Then you will put it into the Portuguese money and then you will take from that bank there—" she pointed dramatically—"what it is in the Portuguese money."

Alec soothed her, urging her to take up map-reading, and allow him peace and quiet to work out by a variety of mathematical processes, which he enumerated, a separation and classification of funds.

Gina, mollified, transferred her attention to Brother Theodore.

"Now, Brother Theodoremou," she directed, "I know what will be exactly the role for you. You will be the reader. Not the map reader. Because only I must do that. But all the other kinds. The guidebooks, the travel folders that you are collecting, everything what you can imagine that says about a place we are coming to that I shall read to you from the map, you will read to us from your books and papers of what they say that it is."

Brother Theodore was at the moment so immersed in reading from a pamphlet he had drawn from his pocket he did not hear Gina's allotment of the job until she repeated it. He looked up, blinking a little at the interruption.

"Why, yes, Gina," he assured her, "I shall be glad to do that. I'm doing it anyway," he added, a little apologetically.

Gina assured him she knew that, but pointed out that his reading was only a here-and-there kind. She wished it to be continuous, loud, very plain for everyone to hear, and: "Slowly, slowly, like a prayer."

When these stipulations were established she turned again toward the front, sighing contentedly.

"Now everyone is occupied," she said. "Sophy is our driver, so certainly she is in the major key of occupation, except for me, since certainly she would drive foolishly if I did not tell her on the map where we are."

I ventured to point out I had been given no allotment. Gina brushed aside this oversight.

"You will talk," she said. "Except when Brother Theodore is reading. And sometimes you are writing down what you see in your little book, but mostly you are talking so we are all occupied."

The drive along the Corniche Coast is a winding thread through a tapestry of such brilliance in color and pattern as to make the traveler following its curves and loops constantly lose and catch his breath at the splendor around him. It made this traveler lose, and have difficulty catching, her breath again at the height of the narrow, winding thread. Actually, no one but a craven like me would have so much as a twinge of misgiving about the road, and even I, after a gasp or two, and a fist clenched round and imbedded in a rod across the back of the front seat, presumably for rugs, had to admit I felt no sense of peril. The road is well built up on either side and the view is dazzling. Here I could not express a disgruntled opinion that I like to be on a level with the things at which I am looking, because on the left we saw not a sliver of water to be identified from Gina's map as a river, but below us, like a fan unfolded from its handle that is a strip of land called Troia, the deep aquamarine sea as far as the eye could stretch. It was so far below us its surf gave the appearance of little creases in a fabric. Between us and this almost blinding blue the terraced ground was so studded with wildflowers as to make a blur of bright colors.

At the highest point we identified below us on the left the Convent Novo and Brother Reader told us from a guidebook this was founded around the middle of the sixteenth century by St. Peter of Alcántara, who had been a friend of St. Theresa and spent some years in the convent. Permission to visit it, he read, may be obtained in Lisbon at 116 Rua da Estola, Politecnica. But since we had not obtained right of entry, we were well content to enjoy the contrast of its whitewashed building against the sea and the flowers. Here and there irregularly placed houses perched out over the terraced formation of the land, unobtrusive in spite of their position, because of the luxuriant foliage of their surrounding.

Simultaneously we began talking about an aspect of this growth that startled us. We agreed we had not seen anything like the extraordinary cleavage our road seemed to make between two distinct types of vegetation. To our left, toward the sea, we might have been looking on the Mediterranean from the coast in southern Italy. There were palm trees and fruit trees of hot southern climate. On our right were forest and undergrowth, harsh and rough, such as grows in a northern climate zone. There were wildflowers here, too, carpeting the ground, but they were nothing like the spill of color on our left, which was the southern slope. On either side of the road were wide masses of cornflower blue running continuously, the flowers themselves of far greater size than the wildflowers we know. Later we learned these were the blue pimpernels, the more vivid on our right because of the gray-green scrub immediately behind this broad border.

Not more than three kilometers beyond the convent, Sophy discovered a road leading off to the left, and inasmuch as she promised she did not look on it as a short cut to anywhere, we allowed her to follow it. It brought us steeply down to the shore, and a village we discovered with some difficulty called Portinho da Arrábida. This is evidently a little summer place. A row of cottages follows the curve of a bay there. We moaned that we had not brought our bathing suits when we saw a few people in the water; others were water-skiing behind motor launches. We walked along the shore, picking up bright pebbles and marveling at the clarity of the water. Even at considerable depth, as we could gauge from the mooring posts stuck at intervals, we could see clearly each ripple of sand and tiny pebble on the sea bed.

Our walk took us to what had appeared to be an old fort, now transformed to a small inn or *estalagem*. An *"estalagem,"* we were learning, is an inn that is under private ownership. A *"pousada"* is one established and supervised by the government. There are many of these latter, and each one we visited we found excellent in location, service and food. We did not eat at this *estalagem,* however. At the moment we left our car, we had seen hanging out over the water a tiny restaurant that looked irresistibly beckoning. Retracing our way from the *estalagem,* we paused at the entreaties of two men, each trundling a hand cart on which were displayed shellcraft for sale. Sophy has a coating of sales resistance that amounts to a suit of armor, but Gina and I are putty at the sight of souvenirs. Each of us bought a dozen fluted shells larger than I had seen before, in which could be both cooked and served sea food *en coquille*. During the remainder of the trip in the back of the Volkswagen they rattled, an incessant reminder of our lack of sales resistance. Nevertheless, Gina carried hers all the way to her house in Greece. I, thankfully, turned mine over to my daughter in Holland, and was made uncomfortable by her gratitude.

While we were busy with our purchases, and not watching, Alec bought a large conch shell, the sort fishermen use as a foghorn. We were profoundly relieved to discover him incapable of using it, though his efforts caused both cheeks and eyes to bulge and Gina to warn vehemently if he did not cease his efforts he would at that moment fall down dead at her feet in a stroke.

The waiter who welcomed us on the threshold of the restaurant, which we discovered was called Estella do Portinho, was a scant five feet in height, all of them drawn together into an exclamation point of welcome, gratitude that we should have chosen his place, and assurance of his ability to prove how right our selection had been. He led us to a wide veranda that leaned out over the water. It was roofed in latticework with flowering vines dripping down between the slats. Several tables were set with immaculate white tablecloths, but we were the only guests. We asked timidly if it would be possible for us to have lobster, indicating our realization this was a preposterous request when we had given no word of our coming. Indignation stretched our host to a full five feet. What manner of place did we consider this if we could not order and obtain lobster merely by asking for it? I cannot explain how this was conveyed in pantomime. A shrug of his shoulders, his arms stretched wide, palms turned out, eyebrows lifted, the eyes rolled heavenward, a shake of the head at the absurdity of our assumption brought us vividly through every step of his response to the final ingratiating bow, sweep of the hand toward the table, indicating, by head tilted back, that if we would content ourselves here for a few moments with an *apéritif* we should have everything we desired.

A bottle of port was brought to the table, and a plate of little biscuits. We sat on the veranda railing to feel the sun, watch the water, and the water skiers on it, and therefore saw immediately below us a boy, the handsomest I think I saw in Portugal—and that was indeed handsome—pull away in a rowboat from the foot of a flight of stairs leading from the veranda to the water. Our host stood on the bottom step calling exhortations to the boy until they were mutually out of hearing. We watched the young boatman reach his objective, pull something from the water and return. When he had reached the steps again he tied up his boat. For a minute with his back to us he stooped over, and then with a quick turn, almost like a ballet dancer's, faced us, one foot on the steps, the other in the boat, laughing aloud with pleasure at the treasure he had brought us. He held high in either hand the biggest lobster I had ever seen, or even imagined could exist. Close on our applause at the sight, we murmured to one another doubts that anything of such bulk could be tender. But we must not show such doubts, Gina urged.

"It will be necessary to chew much, but very very quietly."

We watched a young girl, who might have been by her appearance a sister to the lobster boy, come from inside the restaurant at his hail. She carried a large pot and a dipper. He helped her fill the pot with sea water, and gave her the lobsters to carry, which she took unflinching, to my profound admiration; he carried the filled pot. This was obviously where and how the lobsters would be

cooked. When he took them back from the girl we asked if we might photograph him with such specimens. He was charmed, but we could not persuade Gina to pose in such proximity to the waving claws as even to be included within the camera's focus.

Perhaps one day I shall taste lobster as succulent and tender as those giants. I dream about this occasionally, but without conviction of its fulfillment. Our host, major-domo and waiter removed the meat with dexterous carving, piled it high on a platter, and brought, in separate containers, a variety of sauces. We had bread, cheese and wine, too, and a little fruit for dessert. Olympus and Valhalla could not have set a better table. When the bill was presented, we discovered the price of the meal was determined by the amount of lobster consumed. I shall remember for a long time with something between shame and pride our consumption totaled fifteen pounds. The assessment for this gastronomic debauch was less than two dollars apiece.

There is only one road down, and steeply down, into Praia do Portinho. Therefore unalterably the only way out is to climb that precipitate way. I had made the ascent with both hands imbedded in the rail in front of me, and eyes closed. By reason of this defense mechanism, I had missed the view. I told my companions I would walk up. I wished to enjoy the landscape slowly, and also to offset the languor and poundage induced by the meal we had just had. This ruse deceived no one and I knew it. But consistently generous over my idiosyncrasy, they suggested only that I start a little ahead of them, and meet them at the top of the slope. Slope they called it. Though I walked slowly and did enjoy the view, my breathing was audibly effortful when I climbed into the car. No one mentioned that either. They are dear friends.

There is a road that branches inward from the coast. We followed it. Sophy had read in a guidebook of a cape called Cabo do Espichel. She did not know what we would find there. She had seen the name in a guidebook, but she could not remember which book it was. She remembered only the name, the general location, and its identification as providing a superb view. Gina, from the front seat, promptly instructed Reader Theodore to search among the literature he carried for some further description. He protested a little that such research would deny him so much as a passing glance at the landscape. Gina promised if the rest of us saw anything remarkable, we would at once call his attention to it. She further directed his attention to Alec. Alec had taken for himself the entire back seat. He had spread over it the contents of his cash basket, and of his pockets. He held odd bits of paper and a pencil, was checking and adding figures, muttering what might have been an incantation.

"You see," Gina said, "Alecmou does not look either. And that is a great pity. But now he is the financier, so he will not see anything."

Brother Theodore murmured his discontent was not because of a wish to outdo Brother Alec in looking; but he is the most amiable of men, and resigned himself to his book.

Almost immediately we left the coast, we were again, those of us who were looking, astounded at the abrupt change of scene from rich Mediterranean tropical surroundings to a wide, flat heath brightly carpeted with low-growing wildflowers. We roused the scholars sharply to look at windmills, the first we had seen in Portugal. We were to find them a common sight, but we never lost our pleasure in their beauty. They are like the windmills of Greece. The circle that rotates is very large, divided in segments like spokes of a wheel, each segment rigged with sails. These are furled when the mill is not operating. All those within our sight, however extensive the area we traveled, were in motion or furled at precisely the same hours in the day, at rest in the morning—that is, during the morning hours that we were on the road—set in motion at five in the afternoon. Furled or unfurled, they were uniformly beautiful against the horizon.

The Financier and the Reader were not disturbed again until Gina called, "Do not find anything more, Teddy—" up to that point Reader had vouchsafed nothing whatever—"Certainly we are now on a cap."

"Cape," Alec echoed automatically.

"No matter," said Gina, "we arrive at whatever it is. Have you the candy? I see shildren."

This was the first mention I had heard of sweets and I did not know why they were introduced at the moment of our bumpy passage over a narrow and rocky dirt road, banked on either side and at wide intervals by small cottages. However, Alec understood the request and the association. He drew from a coat pocket a large, filled paper bag, handed it to me in the middle seat, and I in turn passed it ahead to Gina.

"Now, Sophy," Gina requested, "slowly, slowly, slowly. This we do always in Greece. Going along shildren we throw sweets. It is a happy surprise for them. You will see. Here are shildren."

There were two ragged little boys coming toward us, perhaps five and seven years old. As we came abreast of them Gina leaned out her window and simultaneously with Alec from the back seat called loudly, "Kara-*mell*-es, kara-*mell*-es."

Gina tossed from the bag some candies wrapped in bright-colored papers. Sophy and I, new to this procedure, jumped visibly, but no more visibly than the little boys. Astounded by this barrage of sound and missiles, they not only jumped, they collided, and in their haste to retrieve, fell on their backs.

Gina viewed this equably.

"You will see," she told us. "It is like that in the beginning. Then they will find what hit them and eat it with *grand plaisir*."

Sophy increased the speed. When I looked out the back window the two little boys were on their feet and stuffing their mouths.

Gina had been right, too—that we were on the "cap." She is unquestionably a brilliant geographer, both by map and extrasensory perception. Some half-mile beyond the last of the cottages, the road ended at a group of gray stone buildings. We drove under an arch and found ourselves in a vast courtyard enclosed on two sides by a long row of low, yet two-story dwellings like dormitories, the first floor resting on wide round arches. The far end of the courtyard was enclosed by a church. At first sight we thought the whole place deserted and a ruin, but as we looked we saw a man come into

104

the courtyard leading a donkey. He called out as he approached, and from one of the first-floor doorways a woman carrying a baby, with a small girl and a boy at her skirt, came to meet him. The man took the baby, held it high for a moment, hugged it and then placed it on the donkey's back. He supported the baby with one hand, reached down, scooped up the little girl with the other arm, placed her behind the baby, evidently told her to put both arms around her little brother or sister, because she did. He took the donkey's bridle; the mother walked at one side, also giving a supporting arm to the baby, the little boy followed behind. They left the courtyard. Evidently, we said, people live in these ruins. The arched entrances had no doors. Each one disclosed a single, windowless room.

We could find no entrance to the church, but to one side we saw an open archway. We walked under it, and came out on a flower-filled meadow, at its far edge a magnificent view of the sea. We sat or strolled about there for nearly an hour. When we returned to the car we saw an old man sitting in a doorway and two women talking in the quadrangle. Evidently some people, gypsies perhaps, were in residence. The old man raised his arm to us as we left.

Sophy, who does not talk much when she is driving, called out suddenly, "What on earth has happened here? Look at all those people. Do you think there's been an accident?"

"Not at all, not at all," Gina reassured her complacently. "No accident—it is the candy."

I leaned far to the side. From the middle seat directly behind Gina, it was not easy to see the road immediately in front, but now I saw at either edge of the narrow dirt road a line of people waiting, and coming toward the fringe of the road on the run children of all sizes and ages, women, some carrying babies, no men. Either they were at work or bedridden. As we drew near, every hand was outstretched.

"Not too slowly, slowly," Gina begged of Sophy. "There is not so much candy for that." She quickly divided her remaining store with Alec and as our cortege passed the cheering populace, they threw all that was left from either side of the car. This time, too, the recipients jumped, but not backward.

"Now, shildren," Gina began as we left the *cabo* and came in sight of a crossroad; "I am looking at the map and counting so I can tell you if we go to the left for twelve kilometers, we will come to Sesimbra. It is on our way back to our *quinta* and Azeitão, so we are not going too round the mulberry bush. Sesimbra is big on the map, so it must be something. And Reader will tell us what it is." She looked over her shoulders darkly at Brother Theodore. "I think you must learn to read a little better," she suggested.

Shaking his head in admission of defeat, Reader gathered up once more the accumulation of pamphlets he had put between us on the seats. Gina turned a little further, addressing herself to Alec.

"And now, Alecmou," she entreated, "you will please stop counting the money. We are not coming to Portugal—" she paused dramatically, lowering her eyebrows—"by way of France, Switzerland and everything what you can imagine—so that you can count money, like a man in a box bureau."

"Office," Alec corrected mechanically. "Box office."

"Box office," Gina repeated vehemently. "And now I am thinking, what is happening with my box office?" She turned back to include the rest of us in her appeal. "I shall tell you what he does with my box office. It is good he is our banker. That is what he does with money. He banks it. Now I tell you. He promises for every concert I play he gives me twenty dollars for myself. The rest he is managing. Is this not *raisonnable?*" Considering the fees her concert agent has hinted to me Gina commands, I assured Gina I for one considered it thoroughly *raisonnable*. Gina nodded.

"So you see—" her voice rising triumphantly—"even though that is how it is, he has not paid. Fifteen, twenty, I am lost in the count of the concerts. He is in the rear."

"Arrears," came a murmur from the back seat.

This diverted Gina's attention. She turned again to face her beloved. "So now I will tell you what I think to do to someone who

106

is in a rear. I will change my profession. I will go to one that is very old. It requires no playing at the piano—no practicing. Only some walking. Very little walking for me, I am sure. I will have triumph in that profession."

I took a quick look over my shoulder at Alec. He was regarding Gina mournfully.

Gina was transported by her vision of conquest—her black eyes were dancing. "I shall have triumph," she repeated. Instantly she glowered again at Alec. "And there," she affirmed, "the money will be paid to me immediately." A melancholy thought destroyed her dream. She sighed deeply. "No use," she said sadly. "I am remembering now it is understood even in that business there are entrepreneurs. Continue your counting, Alecmou. I tell you when we are seeing something."

Brother Theodore spoke, his voice trembling a little with the shock of discovery. "I have found Sesimbra," he said, "in a guidebook."

"Ah ha," Gina applauded. "Then we prepurr ourselves to listen. Put away the counting, Alecmou. Emily, please do not write the notes. Sophy, you are attending?"

"I am," Sophy assured her, "and I am also, in case you care, following the road you neglected to point out to me. Fortunately I saw a sign with 'Sesimbra' on it."

"Speaking of signs," I queried, "I wish, Reader Theodore, you'd look up a place called 'Paragem.' It seems to me everywhere on every road we've driven I've seen signs to Paragem. Where is it?"

"It's the Portuguese word for bus," Sophy said. "When you saw people standing beside those signs what did you think they were doing—thumbing a ride to Paragem?"

"Now we are all prepurred," Gina announced. "Emily will not speak again—for at least a little while."

Reader Theodore began. "It wasn't too easy to find," he explained apologetically. "Sydney Clark only says, 'Sesimbra is a small fishing town, nestled under the sea cliff and reached by a path between the hills with a castle now almost entirely rebuilt, crowning a summit on the right; the town itself has some lovely buildings, and the early Fort of Misericordia's Chapel and the parish church with a courtyard in front containing unusual painted decoration,' and then a little more about the church. 'The beach crammed with fishing boats lies to the right of the seventeenth-century Fort of St. Teodosio, which was built against the pirates who infested this coast at that time.' "

"Ah ha," was Gina's comment, as if the discovery were her own. "So it is a fishing town with a castle. We go."

"Whose castle?" I inquired.

"I'm sorry," Reader told me, "it doesn't say."

I can say now, corroborated by the others, Sesimbra is a charming little town. High, tree-topped cliffs overhang like bushy eyebrows a wide white beach; a narrow cobbled street fringes this, and is, in turn, fringed by a row of little shops and cafés, pressed so tightly together as to be a reminder that sardines and their packing make the foremost industry in Portugal. When we had walked the length of this street, and back, looking up at the deep and always narrow byways, we sat down at a table on an awninged terrace in front of one of the little cafés. The terrace itself was so little it could hold only our group of five. The ubiquitous Coca-Cola was available and also bottled lemon squash. As we quenched our thirst, we watched women walking across the beach in long easy strides, their arms swinging, and piled on their heads a pyramid of flat, wooden trays. They carried these to the water's edge, arranging them in rows. I felt myself irresistibly swaying a little to the beautiful rhythm of their arms and limbs and full skirts. Several of them passed so close their skirts brushed against me. I forced myself to look at their feet, realizing I had hitherto deliberately focused my sight above that level, dreading, I suppose, to mar the beauty of their carriage and motion by the ugliness their feet must show. Women who walk over all manner of surfaces, through all manner of dust, mud and dirt, carrying such weight as I had seen piled on their heads, must show the scars of this labor in swollen joints, malformed toes, broken nails, skins cracked and filled with grime. From that afternoon at Sesimbra I never again looked away from the bare feet of Portuguese women, and I never saw dirt or deformities. One of my unanswered questions is, how do they keep their feet so clean, so smooth and so unscratched? The abundance of rivers and streams does not explain it for me. Women do not travel exclusively along river beds, nor even along the coastline are they constantly in the ocean. They travel on land and on foot, and their feet are beautiful.

In the distance on the water, we saw fishing boats heading for shore. Sophy, the sailor among us, computed they would not land for at least an hour. We could not wait for them, since this was the night we were to dine at Mrs. Scoville's.

Leaving the town, Sophy volunteered to drive up to the castle in order to see the view from there. I protested.

"Oh, please. No more climbing today. It's bound to be a comedown for the rest of you after the Serra da Arrábida—that beautiful Corniche Coast," and I shuddered. "I'd be grateful for a letup from heights. Couldn't we just drive quietly, and on the level, if the road allows?"

They soothed me with murmurs of comfort, and assurance no one would ask me so much as to rise higher than my own tiptoes for the remainder of the day.

We were tired, we were relaxed, not talking, thinking over probably, as I was, the saturating beauty we had seen, the vivid contrast in scene, the warm sun—only the middle of the day had been hot. The shadows were lengthening, birds were flying low as they do fly toward evening, no cars passed us in either direction. I wondered lazily if I ought not to ask Sophy if she would like me to drive for a little while. Perhaps she was feeling drowsy.

An ear-rending splay of notes came from immediately behind me, and very nearly precipitated me by the leap I accomplished straight over the seat ahead and into Gina's lap. Brother Theodore's literature rained about us. I think my head collided with Gina's, both on their way to the roof. The car executed a bracket that would have brought credit to an ice skater. At its completion, Sophy brought the bus to a stop. We turned as one, to look at Alec. We knew the source of that sound.

Head back, the corners of his mouth wrinkled in a smirk of triumph, he was regarding, fondly and proudly, the object he held in his left hand. Feeling our concentrated attention, he diverted his gaze to us. His eyes widened at the expression on our faces.

"You told me to stop counting the money," he explained, addressing himself to Gina. "So I thought I'd have another go at that fisherman's horn I bought, and—" he patted fondly the instrument from Hell—"by Jove, I've mastered it."

NINE

Quinta da Bacalbõa is the oldest inhabited Portuguese manor house. I continue the description of it, to be found in *Blue Moon in Portugal* by William and Elizabeth Younger:

"Bacalbõa was built at the end of the Fifteenth Century. It belongs now to an American lady who found it in ruins, restored it with taste, and still lives in it. The gardens can be visited if one has permission." The Youngers, for various reasons, were not able to visit it, but they continue, "Friends have told us of its domed pavilion, its clipped box gardens, its Azulejos and great water tank. It is heartening to find in this age such a feat of skilled private restoration of a work of art, and tragic to think that the Della Robbia medallions set into its walls were lost, for they must have shown wonderfully among the gold and green of the orange trees."

This friend, not of the Youngers, but of Mrs. Scoville, can add little to their description or to the passage in *The Selective Traveler in Portugal* by Anne Bridge and Susan Loundes. They say:

The palace has been superbly restored under her [Mrs. Scoville's] loving care. The extraordinary pavilion crowned with grooved melon-like cupolas is one of the most original features. Renaissance windows and loggias give on to wonderful views over the olive-silvered countryside as far as Lisbon, thirty miles away. On one side are formal gardens of clipped box planted with orange and lemon trees, and a great water tank backed by an excellent pavilion with three pyramided towers, where there are many remarkable Azulejos, including the earliest-dated panel in Portugal, that of Susanna and the Elders, in 1565.

Seteais, that name given the hotel in Sintra, and meaning "seven 'ahs' of rapture," is a meager count for the "ahs" from my companions and me during the hours at Bacalbõa. I do not know a Portuguese word for Seteais multiplied seventy times seven, but certainly we were a chorus, and "ah" was our refrain.

A long drive leads to Mrs. Scoville's *quinta*, and opens into a broad courtyard. As we circled this, our hostess came through a doorway to the head of a flight of stairs, calling down a welcome. As we left the car and climbed to meet her, Alec and Brother T. in the rear muttered a prayer that I would not include in my apology for being late an explanation that the men had had to persuade the garage owner to open his establishment to permit a second shave of the day in honor of the party.

"But don't think," I muttered back at the laggards, "I won't tell her during the evening."

"I have a bribe to offer," was Brother T.'s answer.

I had time to quash that with, "Please, God, no more pamphlets," before we reached Mrs. Scoville.

She led us across a great hall, larger than my living room at home, though I have always considered its proportions generous. Beyond a salon, we came out on a loggia, and from its balustrade, looked down on the boxed gardens of orange and lemon trees to the exquisite pavilion at its far end, on our left. In front of this, parallel with the loggia, we could see the water tank we had read about. In the untrodden-by-royalty ways among which I have dwelt, a water tank is a round container set on stilts. I often see one from a train window. Sometimes the name of the town it supplies is printed on it. I know a fish tank, it is larger than a fish bowl, and it holds water; but I have never seen identified as a tank a body of water more than twice the size of the average swimming pool, framed by gardens and a high wall espaliered with fruit trees.

We were on the first round of our chorus of "ahs" when Mrs. Scoville, behind us, asked to introduce her two house guests, just coming into the loggia. I did not need an introduction to one of them. Turning from the balustrade, I found myself looking with astonished recognition at the godmother of my son-in-law and a friend of mine, Winifred Kaltenbach. I not only had not known she was a far older friend than I of Mrs. Scoville—had been at college with her—I had thought she was at home in Rhode Island. Under the spray of ejaculations of astonishment and explanation to the others, and mutual pleasure at our meeting, I heard Gina say in an undertone: "And here, Alecmou, is coming a friend of yours."

I did not need to look at the doorway Gina, with a tilt of the head, indicated behind me. I knew from Alec's convulsive start, and the flush of color his recent shave exposed. The new arrival was the owner of the *quinta* that *is* a private residence.

"Miss Sousa," Mrs. Scoville said, as they shook hands. "I think you have not met—Madame Bachauer . . ." She made the rounds.

By Portuguese rule of propriety we had not met Miss Sousa. Sitting on her gallery at one end of the patio in her own *quinta*, she had seen our arrival, watched us cross the patio at the far end and, conducted by the maids, find our rooms. Her dogs had run to meet us, but she had not. The way to social exchange had not been paved. She had spoken through the window to Gina, and reproved Alec. This communication had been in her role of proprietor. Now the social paving had been laid. We could travel on it with cordiality.

Alec was the first one of our group to whom, with charming friendliness, Miss Sousa talked. Other guests, early arrivals, had been walking in the garden. They joined us on the loggia. Two of them, a couple, moved to Miss Sousa talking with Alec. She introduced them: "My sister-in-law, Mrs. Sousa, and my brother, Dr. Sousa." Until that moment we had not known of their existence. We learned from Mrs. Scoville they were joint owners with Miss Sousa and residents of the *quinta*. They had, too, we learned, an apartment in Lisbon, and divided their time between the two establishments. We never saw them at their country residence.

That evening at Mrs. Scoville's we did not mention our mutual residence; it would have been highly unsuitable. I thought, once, of confiding there was a leaky tap that dripped in my bathroom at night, but was at the instant shocked that I could have entertained such a thought. Dr. Sousa sat between Winifred Kaltenbach and me. He did not feel completely at home in English, he apologized. Would we be so generous as to speak either French or German? I cannot speak German, Winifred Kaltenbach does not speak French. Dr. Sousa was at ease, interchangeably, with both. Mrs. Sousa and her sister-in-law, I discovered when the ladies had left the dining room and we talked together, spoke beautiful English. I had heard them speaking French during dinner. We talked at dinner of a great many things, but not politics. I was longing to ask Dr. Sousa his opinion of the government under Salazar, but I had a feeling this topic would be even more unsuitable than the bathroom tap.

While the men were still in the dining room, Mrs. Scoville took us on a tour of the house, through a succession of handsome rooms, stamped uniformly by a remarkable combination of bright color and austerity—no flowered English chintzes here, nor dimpled cupids sporting on the ceiling, neither was there a Manueline effulgence. This was of an earlier day, and more sober.

A charming circular room, off her bedroom, contained only a beautiful sunken tub, circular, too. We climbed a marble circular staircase, the narrowest I have ever seen. Mrs. Scoville looked down at the tub balefully.

"I'll never stick to 'period' again," she asserted, "with a tub. There's nothing so cold to sit on as marble. Hot water doesn't faze it."

Returning to the drawing room we looked at albums of photographs that recorded Mrs. Scoville's thirty years of painstaking, scholarly work. I called the attention of the others to one picture of her on the loggia surrounded by fragments of tile, beside her a large basket, filled to the brim with other pieces.

"Thirty years of jigsaw puzzles," I said, "not counting the other work." Mrs. Scoville laughed.

"I will never forget a man who came to dinner. I had known his parents for years, they have a place not far from here, but during

114

that time he had been out of Portugal. After dinner the son was looking at these albums. He stopped at the very picture you were pointing to. He looked at it for a long time, then he faced me, his face very red.

He said, "I can't go away, Mrs. Scoville, without making a confession to you. It's been weighing on my conscience ever since I went into the garden tonight. On my twelfth birthday, I think it was, my father gave me a rifle. All that summer, the favorite sport for my friends and me was to sneak into this place—you hadn't bought it, it was a ruin. There was a row along the garden wall of tiles in circles, if you know what I mean. It seemed to us they were made for target practice, and we used them."

"I knew very well what he meant." Mrs. Scoville shook her head sadly. "He meant the Della Robbia medallions." Then she added, with the greatest magnanimity I have heard expressed, "I don't blame the boys. Imagine finding such made-to-order targets in an old ruin."

"I do regret," she added, "the loss of the statues in the building by the water tank. They were irreparable, but I did find they were figures of the Virtues. Such a charming insinuation into a pleasure pavilion."

When the men joined us, we were still looking at the albums in the drawing room. Alec, coming to join me at a table under a lamp, said in surprise to his hostess he hadn't realized the house had electricity, since only candles had been used in the dining room.

"What a difference that would make, wouldn't it, to you and your brother," I suggested wickedly, "if we had electricity at the Quinta dos Torres?" I tasted power at that moment, and honesty prods me to admit I love the flavor of it.

The Sherman brothers looked at me with imploring eyes, like spaniels. With equal fervor they would have been happy, I knew, either to offer a handsome token or throttle me, to prevent my suggesting to our hostess they come to her house to shave. Such intimate exposure would plunge an Englishman to the lowest

115

depths of ignominy. I allowed my moment to pass—I had savored it.

"The men love to read in bed," I improvised to Mrs. Scoville, "but we women have made them promise not to. We're afraid of fire, if they dropped off to sleep and left their oil lamps burning."

"Fire is always on our minds here in the country," Mrs. Scoville conceded.

I saw the two men wilt with relief.

We included the Sousas in our general round of farewells at the conclusion of the party. Since all the guests left simultaneously, the Sousas must have been close behind, or in front of us on the short trip home. Nevertheless, we did not see them as we crossed the courtyard to our own wing. At our departure no reference was made to the fact that in a few minutes we would be once more under the same roof.

TEN

A voice from the gallery at the far end hailed me as I came from my room next morning. The day was warm not hot, sunny not windy—like the little bear's porridge, just right—and it was Sunday. No excursions had been planned by the indefatigable occupants of the front seat of the Microbus. My own plan was to stroll to the lawn by the pool, settle myself in one of the comfortable lounging chairs I had seen there, watch the swans, write some letters, perhaps read a little, but not from any of Reader Theodore's guidebooks or pamphlets. For the greater part of the morning, I would loll in the sun. Every prospect pleased me.

Miss Sousa's was the voice that had hailed me. She came hurrying across the patio.

"My dear," she called, "I am so glad to see you. I hated to disturb you if you were sleeping late, but Mrs. Scoville telephoned. She thinks she has tickets for all of you for the bullfight this afternoon, if you would like to go."

Mrs. Scoville, I had learned during the evening, is a bullfight enthusiast. She had revealed and explained her enthusiasm.

"I don't go in Spain," she had said, "but in Portugal they are quite different. It's against the law to kill a bull. You won't see anything in the country more colorful; the technique is fascinating to watch, and there is such humor; lovely, absurd clowning." I had been startled into enthusiasm. At the outset of the trip, I had stipulated the one sight I would detour widely was a bullfight. I would derive no aesthetic pleasure from watching an animal goaded, tortured and killed. Evidently, my aversion had been geographically misplaced. This would be a fascinating spectacle. My companions had shared my change of mind. Having accomplished this, Mrs. Scoville had ruefully admitted the impossibility of our going to the one on the following day, to which she was taking her house guests. This was going to be a sort of double-header because a fair would be held at the same time. Seats would be at such a premium she had bought hers long since.

"Now," Miss Sousa said, "Mrs. Scoville's granddaughter has just arrived. She has a job and an apartment in Lisbon. She has brought some young friends. They are all going on to the bullfight. She says she knows someone there she thinks can get tickets for you and your friends, if you would like. Do you think you *would* like?" she repeated.

I repeated my enthusiasm for such an opportunity, and turned to carry the news to my friends. Miss Sousa put her hand on my arm.

"I, too, have an invitation," she said, a little diffidently. "You must not feel any obligation because I asked you, but we have our own little chapel here. The priest comes from the village to say eleven o'clock mass. It does not matter if you are not Catholic; we would be happy to have you come."

I assured her I knew I could speak for my friends, we would consider it a privilege; that one of us, Madame Bachauer, was indeed a Catholic. My idyl of a morning in the sun had long since been tossed over my shoulder. I went to tell my friends this day, like all the others, was being organized.

Gina and Sophy were as pleased and surprised as I had been by the invitation both to the bullfight and to the private mass at the *quinta*. The first message of the morning that was not a surprise was Gina's information the men had gone to the garage in Setúbal. (We were learning to be familiar, like the Sousas and Mrs. Scoville, and call it "Stubel.")

We snatched up scarves for head coverings, and hurried across the courtyard to the main house, where we were directed to the chapel in one wing. Dr. and Mrs. Sousa had evidently gone back to

Lisbon. Miss Sousa was the only member of the family there. Besides ourselves, the congregation was made up of the house servants and outdoor workers on the place. The chapel itself was simple, but beautiful. I knew our being there meant we were, now, truly, guests of the Quinta dos Torres.

After the service, talking to Miss Sousa and the priest of the places we had seen, I mentioned the Cabo do Espichel we had visited the day before. I said how beautiful the meadow was, that we had come upon it behind the church, carpeted with wild flowers, orchids and varieties in white, blue and pink I did not know; the glorious panorama from the lip of the meadow, but in contrast to that the eerie sense of desolation we had felt from the buildings in spite of some signs of habitation. We had not been able—and I thought of Brother Theodore's research into his pamphlets that day—to find any identification or story of the place.

Miss Sousa and the priest spoke almost simultaneously, each assuring me indeed the place had a history and a story. Originally a shrine, it had been during the fifteenth century the objective of a very fashionable pilgrimage from Lisbon conducted by the King and Queen once a year. There had even been, at one time, a theater where, during the period of pilgrimage, plays were given. The two rows of low houses, or cells, had been built by Don José I. They were rest houses for the pilgrims, providing them sanctuary. Today, I was told, a Virgin from the church is brought out once a year, and in procession carried to twenty-five churches around Lisbon. I shall remember the beauty of its bright meadow, the wide stretch of sea, desolation and the cry of gulls overhead.

The men returning from their ritual at the garage were told the news of the bullfight and hustled to an early lunch.

Mrs. Scoville's granddaughter and friends were waiting in a car at the foot of their driveway. At the sight of our approach, with a wave of recognition, they started off, we followed. We should never have found our way unguided. We learned she had chosen back roads and short cuts to avoid what she knew would be a press of traffic moving toward the fair. Occasionally, even on our cir-

119

cuitous way, we came upon evidences of it. As Gina said, "Everything what you can imagine for carrying": bicycles, motorcycles, donkey carts, donkeys and horses holding on their backs family groups, and automobiles inching along, their frustration boiling up through the radiator caps.

I did not know how the town of Alcochete would absorb the people we had passed on the road. We found it already foaming with visitors.

The bottleneck was a tiny shop on one side of the village square. Without Mrs. Scoville's granddaughter (we never learned her name) we would have been "poor little sheep who had lost our way." She found a place among the donkey carts where Sophy could tuck in the Microbus. She told us to stay in it until she returned. We were fervently docile; a few feet away from the car and we would have been lost to sight of one another. We watched her with her young companions make a way through the eddies of people in the square to the bottleneck itself, and even inside it. From the elevation our bus provided we had a panoramic view. Gina, scaling the height to the front seat on our departure, had twisted her ankle. Now she was beginning to feel some discomfort from it, and asked if I would mind changing places with her, so that she might, on the second tier, put her foot along the seat. Teddy moved back to the third row with Alec and I hoisted myself, with Sophy's help, to the place Gina had quit. Gina, cut off from the wide expanse of windshield to which she had grown accustomed, asked if I would be so kind as to bow my head, "a leetle—like in your Protestant shurshes, where you do not kneel down." I gave her more than she asked. When I had bowed to the horizontal, so that my eye level was scarcely above the dashboard, she sighed contentedly. "Now," she declared, "we are prepurred for a wonderful spec*tacle.*"

It was a colorful "spec*tacle.*" Every woman wore a brilliantly colored shawl. Many of them were in bright-colored full skirts, the first color in dress I had seen. The skirts swayed like Canterbury bells on a stem. They looked and swayed like bells because under-

120

neath were seven petticoats, we learned later, each a different color. As women stooped or moved quickly we could see flecks of blue, orange, pink, yellow. We pointed out to one another the handsome features of a man, girl, woman, child discovered, agreeing it was impossible to classify a "Portuguese type." Each of us had been told at some time not to expect the Portuguese to be handsome people. We declared a unanimous denial of this. We saw many beautiful children, and handsome adults, but we could never say, "There is a typical Portuguese." Some were dark-skinned, some fair; they had dark hair or light, aquiline features or broad.

In the distance we heard a band playing, and shared anxiety that we might not be in the arena in time to see the procession; or, perhaps, not have tickets at all. Brother T. called out, like Sister Anne, that he did see our guide coming toward us across the square. When we waved to her, she waved back with a clutch of tickets in her hand. Unfortunately, she told us when she reached the car, she had been unable to buy seats together. She had three in one section, and two in another. Although we reiterated our gratitude, it did not require so long a time as for Banker Alec to unlock his basket and count out the sum required. He might, perhaps, have accomplished the transaction more quickly without our impatient heckling.

We were in our seats before the procession began. Sophy, to no one's surprise, elected to sit with the two men. We had walked slowly to the arena because of Gina's ankle, and she asked to have whichever of the two sets of tickets was for a lower row. I sat with her. The stands were filling rapidly when we arrived; vendors moved along the rows calling out the chocolate-coated ice cream on sticks they sold. Gina and I each bought one, found it delicious, and immediately we had finished, were overtaken by an acute thirst, but no fruit juices or soft drinks were sold.

We were distracted by a brass band that blew a vociferous measure and immediately sobered into a lugubrious march. The audience rose to its feet. Standing, Gina and I located the band at the far end of the field on our left. To the accompaniment of the dirge, a group of men entered a box not far from us. Evidently, they were local dignitaries. The audience applauded, the band came to a mournful conclusion, we all sat down.

A fanfare of trumpets sounded, and from an entrance directly facing us the corps of bullfighters marched onto the field. They wore spangled, dazzling costumes. They came first to the gentlemen in the center box, bowed low, sweeping off their tricorn hats. After this homage, they paraded the field, separating into two lines when they reached the entrance from which they had come. Two horsemen rode out on magnificent mounts, the riders in stunning costumes that included spangled capes over one shoulder. They came directly beneath the box that held the officials, bowed low and, facing them, gave a superb exhibition of *dressage*. At its conclusion, separating, they made a circuit of the arena, each holding his hat high in the air, in acknowledgment of the thundering applause. At their exit, the double line of bullfighters closed in and marched out behind them.

A man on foot was the next to make an entrance. He carried over one arm a large cape. Immediately behind him a horseman rode in on a magnificent stallion. When they had paid their respects to the occupants of the box and been acknowledged with applause from the arena, they took their places in the center of the field. From the side on which we were sitting, a bull came trotting slowly into the arena. The animal paused, looked around, then ambled on. He stopped in obvious bewilderment as the man with the cape advanced toward him, barring his way, waving the cape from one side to the other and then in convolutions over his head. The man stepped to one side; the bull had not moved. The horseman took the place of the cape-flinger, and executed remarkable and beautiful maneuvers. Back and forth, in front of and around the bull, wheeling, pivoting, the horse and rider moving with such fleet dexterity they were like a pair of ballet dancers, one sustaining the other. As they danced, the man called continuously one syllable, one note, echoed by the cape-wielding partner in the background. Now it was like a corps de ballet, executing an intricate, interwoven figure. Suddenly I saw the dexterity and agility had a purpose other than beauty of movement. The actual accomplishment was the planting of *banderillas* by the horseman into the bull. He, poor stupid creature, with no inclination to fight, in spite of the exhortations from the two men, would charge now and again in a fumbling, halfhearted lunge. The *banderillas* were being inserted with splendid accuracy. Against the sleek black of the hide, I saw streams of red flow down the sides, the chest and legs of the animal. My stomach conveyed a sickening realization of what I was seeing. My revulsion at such an exhibition of man's indecency, in both the performance and enjoyment of inflicting pain, was so acute I knew if I did not leave immediately I would be guilty of a personal exhibition, both conspicuous and uncomfortable.

"I'm going to wait in the car," I whispered to Gina, and started to pass her. My words were as the application of a stick of punk to a Roman candle. Gina shot out of her place, and ahead of me made for the nearest aisle. An elderly gentleman, leaning well forward, engrossed in the performance, blocked her way. Had he not in open-mouthed astonishment bent far back immediately, I think she would have vaulted him. As it was, she took in one stride up, and another down, a stone parapet that bordered the aisle and a stairway. I had to be assisted onto it by another spectator, who, in stupefaction at our departure and method of it, extended a hand to me. By the time I had got to the top of the stairs, Gina was at the bottom, expostulating with a group of attendants in uniform. When I raced down to join her, I realized the men were endeavoring to bar the way—not only to bar the way ahead, but divert us from the place in which we stood.

"They can't believe we want to leave their damned performance," I explained, out of breath.

"I *make* them understand." Gina, who faces concert or crisis with Olympian serenity, became an avenging fury. She waved her hands, their backs to the silly people in her way, as if she would shoo them contemptuously to either side. She roared in a basso profondo, "Out, out! Do you hear? We go *out!*"

I marveled at their temerity. The men stood their ground. They did not look happy, but they conceded only a step backward, pointing in unison, shaking their arms to emphasize their insistence we go somewhere to their left.

"Why we go by the exit they choose?" Gina demanded, putting into words my own exasperation. "We go by this one—it is the first." Threateningly she moved forward the step they had relinquished. They shouted at us. Gina shouted back. They closed ranks solidly in front of Gina. This gave me an opportunity to slip around the end man on my left. When they discovered one had eluded them, they would be bound to recognize the defeat of their silly officiousness, and relinquish Gina. Probably we were trying to go through the sacred door by which the dignitaries had entered. Just this once lesser folk would use it.

I saw my chance—the men were concentrated on Gina, shouting and pointing. I slipped around the end man. He and the others had concealed a rail fence. It enclosed a pen. I could see over the top of it. What I saw coming into it through a kind of chute was a galloping, very angry bull, stuck full of *banderillas* and bleeding.

The beneficent Providence who watches over the undeserving saved us. Our road blockers heard the sound of the bull approaching. No warning could have come from me. The sight had frozen me into a paralysis of motionless silence, a condition I think I have never before experienced. The man I had eluded pirouetted me, with one mighty thrust of his arm, around in front of him, released me and snatched from the ground a long staff. The other men took up the same equipment. These long staves had been at their feet; certainly we had not noticed them.

Gina and I were on our way toward the exit they had indicated when, from a considerable distance, I paused and looked back. The men had surrounded the pen, facing it. They stood some paces back, each extending his long staff between the bars. Had

124

we succeeded in diverting the attention of his guards, I have a knee-shaking conviction the bull would have been as confined by that fence as if it had been woven with strands of raffia.

As we left by the exit so beseechingly indicated, I remembered Gina's ankle. Her answer to my inquiry was, "What is there to do with an ankle, when there is a bull?"

I have never heard a bull recommended as therapy for a twisted ankle, neither have I seen such an instantaneous healing.

The surprise Gina and I expressed at the sight of Sophy just outside our point of departure was not mutual.

"I watched you leave," Sophy explained. "It was quite a sight! There must be something in telepathy," she continued. "I was 'willing' you to go. I knew I couldn't take another drip of blood." She shuddered. "The men are staying. They'll meet us at the car. Brother T. says he feels he must be able to report it to us."

"Don't tell him," I begged, "but this is one time I would have welcomed a pamphlet—preferably in Portuguese."

His report, when the men joined us, was the afternoon had ended in a fine piece of absurd clowning. After the first display of horsemanship, and cape-tossing when the animal was enraged—certainly not the poor creature we had seen—the men who in the beginning had formed the procession re-entered the field. They gathered around the bull to subdue him by force of numbers. Some jumped on his back, others clung to his tail; the animal thrashed about, tossing them onto the ground, probably bruising and jolting them badly. This was the best possible news to the three sissies who had decamped. Finally subdued, the animal was deployed and led back to his pen by a group of oxen. They must have said good-by to him at the entrance to the pen, where I met him. Brother T. assured us earnestly he had read a heavy fine, even arrest, was imposed on any bullfighter who actually killed a bull in Portugal. This was the great difference from bullfights in Spain.

"Oh, *vive la différence!*" was Gina's acid comment.

It was her suggestion we go home by way of Sesimbra since it was only now midafternoon. "So certainly," was her persuasion, "we will catch the boats coming in. Then we can put the taste of fish in our mouths, and take out the bull."

Gina, with a map open on her lap, exultantly directed Sophy the roads to follow. They were almost bare of traffic; it had evidently reached the bullfight and the fair.

We came to the beach at Sesimbra just ahead of the fishing fleet. The waterfront was crowded with people. The water's edge of the beach was marked like a row of hemstitching by a line of women, barefoot, full-skirted, brightly shawled, waiting to unload the cargo their men had brought. As the boats neared the shore, their high, painted bows rose over the heads of the women.

The fish were taken off in deep baskets; frequently a woman carried two, three or even more, piled on her head. Each boatload had a special area on the beach without any visible sign of partition. Within a few minutes of the unloading, the beach took on the appearance of a series of shop windows. The captain of each vessel was like a storekeeper, arranging his display. Under his direction the helpers (women not participating in this—they were only the carriers) laid out symmetrically in rows the contents of the baskets. Only one variety was exhibited. A separation from the over-all catch must have taken place on the boat before landing. I did not learn the name for these fish, and I have not seen them elsewhere. They are long—at least three feet—broad, bright gleaming silver in color and thin as a ribbon.

Once the rows were arranged, the owner, stepping back to look appraisingly at the over-all display, would move from one row to another transposing the fish, by some measure of his own, to their most advantageous position. While we watched them arranging, rearranging, brushing encroaching sand away from each, we heard a singsong chant. Alec pointed to the far end of the line.

"There's the fellow making that racket," he asserted, and it was of considerable volume to rise above the chattering on the beach. "Look at him, he's an auctioneer."

We might have been listening to the commercial on the old Lucky Strike radio program. A man, with four or five attendants,

Vasiliu

helpers probably, who noted down each transaction, moved from one display to the next. At each one he paused, and immediately, a larger group surrounded him, probably the fishermen involved in that particular catch, and merchants who were bidding. The auctioneer did not pause in his staccato recitative but somehow bids must have been interjected, because he would come to an abrupt end, move on to the next display. Behind him the crew whose catch it was would gather up the fish very carefully, load them back into the baskets. Women swung them onto their heads, and carried them up the beach to the road where a line of trucks waited.

We watched more fascinated and pleased than we had been by the earlier sights of the afternoon, until the last catch had been sold. By this time it was very late afternoon. Shadows were lengthening, the sun was spreading a soft light over the landscape. We stopped in the village of Azeitão so that Alec and I could photograph women doing the family wash at a large beautiful community tank, roofed over and handsomely decorated. They were laughing and talking to one another as they slapped the garments down on the stone side of the tank.

"This is a meeting of the Women's Club," I murmured to Alec, as we focused our cameras, "and this is their clubhouse. I doubt they would thank you for a washing machine."

Miss Sousa was on her gallery when we came into the courtyard, at the Quinta dos Torres. I went to her to tell her our plans for the next day. She watched me without speaking, until I had reached her. I had sensed her look was appraising.

"Did you enjoy the bullfight?" she asked, when we had faced each other.

"It was very colorful," was my answer.

She nodded. "No, you did not like it," she said. "I knew you would not. I do not go."

ELEVEN

The Portuguese believes one of two things about an automobile: either it has no material existence—it is an illusion of the mind and, if ignored, will vanish—or it is an ephemeral, winged thing capable of doing anything a hummingbird can do. Of course, as a passing stranger, tongue-tied in his country, I could not elicit by direct question and answer what he does think is approaching when he hears the sound of horn or engine. I can only judge by his response to it. This is the most unequivocal negation I have ever seen demonstrated.

Whatever a Portuguese man, woman or child is doing when a car is approaching, he continues to do. He does not indicate by so much as a turn of the head in the direction of the sound an annoyance. He is not annoyed because he is not disturbed. He is not disturbed because he does not believe, or at least acknowledge, a motor is bearing down upon him. I would I had his serenity, but as a motorist I carry the burden of anxiety he has never assumed. Someone has to carry it. When he, perhaps with his family, is taking a siesta in the middle of the highway at the terminus of a curve that is itself the culmination of a long steep hill, he and his dear ones sleep on, untroubled by the sound of approach. That is why I maintain he, with a father's right of authority, has taught his dependents either, "This thing you hear is nothing—pay no attention and it will go away," or "This sound is from one of those large hummingbirds. It will stop in the air when it sees us or skim over. So do not let your rest be disturbed." Therefore, children coming home from school break the journey, and sink into sweet slumber, heads pillowed on book satchels.

There must be a reason to choose the middle of the road for a siesta; the Portuguese are neither irrational nor suicide-prone. I am the dullard because I cannot conjecture the reason. Perhaps the surface is cooler than grass, certainly it is less ticklish and scratchy. Perhaps its surface dressing wards off and keeps it free of insects, although eating outdoors every day we never encountered a crawling or flying creature. But conceding the advantage of these possibilities, why the middle, and not the side, of the road? I do not know, and so I say to motorists, "Never mind the dogs—there are few of them in the country—but *cave* the pedestrians, afoot or asleep."

Alcácer do Sal is fifty kilometers, and that is thirty-one miles, from Setúbal. Except that we were becoming accustomed to abrupt changes in landscape, we might have thought we had crossed a border into another country. Not only the scene, but the architecture, the colors, the people themselves in their dress looked different from anything we had seen. Alcácer is on the river Sado, so is Setúbal, but in Alcácer the river is bordered by rice fields. Houses blinding-white stagger from the field up narrow, steep streets. Somewhere we had crossed an undefined boundary; now we were in the south of Portugal, and the south is Moorish. The Romans had been there before the Moors, but there is little or no trace of them, except of course at Évora.

From Alcácer do Sal on that Monday morning we drove to São Tiago do Cacém for lunch. Our road took us across a vast plain. We were so aware of the space around us, we said to one another even the Microbus seemed to have diminished in size. The road was bordered sometimes by rows of cork trees, or eucalyptus, sometimes olive. Beyond the road on either side, stretched the cork forests. When the cork has been peeled, the trunks of the trees are glistening black or warm, shiny red-brown. Now and again in the distance we could see a gleaming white mound. At first we thought it was the sun shining on a vast dome, but coming nearer the first of these mounds, we found we were in a village of white houses, so close together that until we were very close we had thought it a solid mass.

When the mass separated into individual dwellings, it revealed another individual characteristic. This is the chimney on the house in the south of Portugal. No matter how small or mean the dwelling itself, the chimney is dramatic evidence of a householder's pride. Every man's house is his castle, but to the native of the

Province of Alentejo, his castle is measured by his tower, his minaret, his turret. It is of such grandeur the house seems to be there only for its support. I never saw two of these exactly alike. Some look themselves like miniature castles, some like campaniles. There are openings along the sides, vertical, again horizontal, always of interesting design. Delicately or boldly patterned, these openings are frequently edged in a pattern of tiles. It is rare to

find a chimney that is all white; on almost all of them color has been lavishly used.

The chimneys are far more gaily dressed than the people. Men and women wear black. The only variant is the shepherd, who wears the skin of an animal over his head, as we had seen first at Évora. From a distance, he looks like a large sheep, walking on its hind legs. Every woman we saw wore a black scarf pulled tight over her head, wrapped around the throat, fastened in the back, and on top of this a man's brimmed hat, black of course. The first two or three I saw had been borrowed, I thought, from a husband. Eventually I realized there could not be so many husbands simultaneously hatless.

The impression of Moorish influence is accentuated by the clothes women wear when they work in the fields. The skirt is pulled tight, then brought to the front between the thighs, and pinned there. In ignorance I had pointed out a group I saw at some distance, deploring the evidence that "shorts" had come to Portugal. I hoped they would never replace the full skirts and layers of petticoats beneath. Brother T., after a long thoughtful scrutiny, pronounced them "breeches." Gina gave the final identification.

"They put on a dress," she declared, "then they make for themselves from it a diaper, just like for babies." Women walking along the road usually covered the lower part of the face, with one end of the scarf wound around the head, or a handkerchief held so that it concealed the mouth and the nose.

The manufacture of umbrellas, we agreed, must be one of the most profitable industries in Portugal. Nearly every adult we passed was carrying one, always black. Alec deplored their appearance.

"They are never properly rolled," he said.

These people must consider sun rays and death rays synonymous. Scarf and hat are not enough protection against being struck by them; an umbrella is also opened the instant the clouds have rolled by. In the country I never saw an umbrella opened in the rain. In inclement weather, closed, it is carried horizontally on

134

the owner's head, if she is a woman. The men hook the umbrella handle over the back of their coat collars. Field workers do not seek the shade of a tree for a midday siesta. They open their umbrellas, dig the stick into the ground, then lie on the ground, sliding head and shoulders carefully into its shadow.

We reached São Tiago do Cacém at one o'clock. We had taken the road at ten after a final visit to the garage at Sestúbal. On its outskirts we paused, at my request, to watch a young woman with a baby on one arm. There is a special technique for this used by Portuguese mothers. The ubiquitous shawl around the shoulders is extended to include the baby, then the ends are crossed in front. The end that wraps the baby is tucked into the waistband very tight, the other end let hang to allow Mama to use freely her unencumbered hand. The parent we stopped to observe executed a miraculous sleight of hand, because after an overcast morning the sun came out. She took from across the top of a basket on her head her umbrella, opened it, shifted the baby from one to the other arm, and tucked into her belt the end of the shawl that had hung loose; all this with only one hand free at a time, and without so much as a tilt of the load on her head.

Prodded by Gina, Reader Theodore had dug among and into his collection of pamphlets and guidebooks and excavated the information that at São Tiago do Cacém there was a *pousada*.

There are ten of these, perhaps twelve in all throughout the country. This would be the first we had visited, and we were eager to know what Portugal offered its tourists. The Quinta dos Torres is neither a *pousada*, government owned and operated, nor an *estalagem*, an inn under private ownership. It *is* a private residence. To be permitted admission one must claim acquaintance-ship with a previous guest when writing for reservations.

Guests at a *pousada* are welcomed and made comfortable, but they are sent resolutely on their way at the end of five days. I do not know that a longer stay is not permitted, but it is not en-couraged. The government owner thinks guests should move on

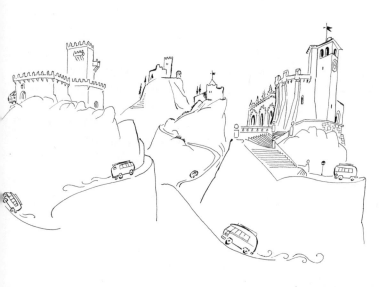

to see other parts of the country, and to allow other visitors to be made welcome.

The *pousada* at São Tiago is on a hillside. Leaving the Microbus in the courtyard we were directed through a charming lounge–dining room with a big fireplace at one end to a terrace beyond, and asked if we would like to eat there or have the meal served indoors. We chose the terrace. The sun was warm, there was a rose arbor overhead, and the view a delight. At the top of the ridge we counted six windmills. Reader Theodore told us at the top of the hill on the other side of the village we might see an old castle. I was beginning to be fractious about castles.

"Whose castle?" I asked with rude belligerence.

"Built by the Templars," Reader T. vouchsafed, and that flattened my challenge.

My irascibility about castles had been provoked during the morning, and the preceding day, and the day before that, by repetitive information gleaned by Reader T. from pamphlet and book that this village, that village, the town, had a castle at its summit. Come famine, drought or earthquake, whatever might have taken everything else away, or perhaps nothing else had ever been there, a castle was to be seen at the top of the highest point.

"Whose castle?" I had asked ingenuously, as Brother T. sighted the first one. "When was it built? Who was it built for?"

"This pamphlet, booklet, book—" whatever Reader T. was employing at the moment—"doesn't say more than that there is a castle. I'll look in the others." By the time we would have reached the next village, and Gina was demanding peremptorily about it, Reader T. would have exhausted his research material and begun a perusal of the index for the place Gina was marking with a forefinger on the map.

And again, "There is a castle on the hill."

And again, "Whose castle? When? Why?"

Always a castle, but never an owner or a history.

Now Reader T. was saying with no triumph in his voice, because he is a gentleman and a scholar, "The castle at São Tiago do Cacém was built by and for the Templars."

I do not consider it unreasonable to be interested in the ownership and history of a residence that must have boasted a hundred rooms and over. I would like, too, to know its given name, like "Windsor," or "Buckingham," or "Versailles."

"It's not as if," I expostulated as we sipped our *apéritif* of port on the terrace, "we were trying to find out about a bide-a-wee cottage. These are enormous, walled citadels. Each one must have been a community within itself, must have taken years, even generations to build, must have housed hundreds of people. 'Who?' That's all I ask, and 'Why?' in that particular place, in every place, for that matter, big and small, and 'When?' 'Where did they go?' In England or France you can trace the ownership of castles, châteaux, landed estates down through the history from its building to its present owners. But not here. 'Where has everybody gone?' For that matter, 'When did they come?' " I was as defeated

138

as the man in the De la Mare poem. "Nobody answered, nobody said."

Sines is a little nugget of beauty and charm. Like nuggets of gold, its discovery requires prospecting. Gina found it on the map. After a calculation that involved considerable finger-counting, she added the information it was thirty-four kilometers from Cacém. We would have to return to Cacém, she admitted, and on the same road, but on the map Sines looked so pretty we must see it. For Group Leader Sophy a journey to and from a destination by one road denotes lack of initiative, flabbiness of character. Gina had done her mapwork while we were drinking port. She never joined us in the before-lunch *apéritif*. She preferred to wait for her spoonful of wine in a glass of soda until the "shoebag hour." News of Sines and the waitress' announcement of lunch came simultaneously. As we moved from the sunny part of the balcony to the lunch table under the rose arbor, Sophy, smiling tolerantly at Gina, asked if she might have a look at the map.

"I'm pretty sure I can find another way back from Sines," she said modestly. "I daresay we won't have to return to Cacém."

We had finished the hors d'oeuvres when Sophy looked up from her studies.

"There is no other way. I think, just this once, I will eat a roll and butter."

Gina was radiant. "So you see," she said to the table, "that is the humble pie she is eating, but for me, I am walking in the air. What is success? At Carnegie Hall, at Albert Hall, everything what you like? Today I have the real triumph at the map over Sophy."

Lunch had a therapeutic effect on my irascibility about castles. In the car, thirty minutes later, when Brother T., with an apprehensive look at me, read diffidently from a guidebook, "There is a castle at Sines," I smiled magnanimously.

There is also a house where Vasco da Gama, that bold explorer, was born. It has been rebuilt, and is open to visitors. The town crier is more authentic than Da Gama's house, because there has been no break, down through the centuries, in his office. He patrols the streets, not as a custodian of the law, but as a news carrier. He reports births, deaths, boats coming into the harbor, includes editorial comment, and carries his own department of lost-and-found articles. I count this reward enough for thirty-four kilometers doubled, but an extra beneficence is the beauty of the little place.

Brother T., moving hastily from the news of the castle read, "It is so remote, and difficult to get to it is almost unknown to foreigners."

Even without that corroboration we foreigners admitted to one another we felt like discoverers. We came down a steep lane—I think it is the only one in the town a car could travel—to the beach. From there, looking back and up, we wondered the little white houses did not come "tumbling after." Alec supposed they clung together to keep from falling, and also because they were frightened of the rocks above them. They, or their inhabitants, might well have been. There were lobster pots so close to the shore we could see lobsters moving about in very large nets below the surface of the water. Reader T. informed us this tiny remote place is one of the principal sources of supply to the Lisbon lobster and crawfish market.

Beyond the village itself, we saw a lighthouse that marked the point of Cape Sines, but as far as the eye could stretch on either side, no other building. Deep cliffs, narrow beaches, bright blue water, in the center the nosegay of white houses, behind it green foliage and gray rock, and stillness all around; that is the panorama. It was siesta time. Two fishermen slept on the sand beside their nets. Two men sat at a table in the little café on the waterfront, their heads sunk on their breasts.

When we returned to the car from our walk along the beach Alec suddenly stopped Sophy as her hand was on the ignition key.

"Listen," he said.

We heard it then, a voice far off, as if it were calling. We looked at one another with a wild surmise. We were right, we

140

were in luck. From the far end of the village along the waterfront, we saw and heard the town crier bring to his fellow citizens the three o'clock news.

From São Tiago do Cacém, on our second round, the first retracing Sophy has done I estimate in twenty years, we turned south.

"We are coming to a place called Odemira," Gina reported. "Reader, tell us what it is that is there." A few minutes later Reader looked up from his literature. "Must I?"

"Read," said Gina.

"This is what Baedeker says." Reader paused to extend to me a glance of mute apology. " 'Odemira: population 2500. A small town on the right bank of the Mira, with an old castle.' "

"Quickly, quickly," Gina interposed, "I find another place." To Reader reproachfully: "Why you read that part. You know castles are not good for Emily."

"It's the only part there is," Reader protested. "That's all it says. No, here's another book—'On the long road up from Sagres through Odemira—' "

Gina broke in. "How is Aljezur?" She spelled it. "Read how it is." To me: "You will see, darling, not a single—I do not say the name."

Reader had found it. Squaring his shoulders, he recited, "Aljezur at the foot of a steep hill on which stands the tower of a former Moorish castle."

I spoke. "I had a German nurse named Alma when my twins were little. When a situation was almost past enduring, she would face it with the pronouncement, 'I don't say a vord.' Right now, after twenty years, I feel very close to Alma. 'I don't say a *vord!*' "

Further silence.

"Listen," Alec called from the back seat. He was always the first to hear an unaccustomed sound. "What is that, Gina, that thin—not a tune, not a creak, something between? Why does it make me think of Greece?"

We heard it then, a sad sound in a rhythm one could beat.

141

"Windmills," Gina called excitedly, "like in Greece on Chios and Mykonos. They are singing."

All of us had heard the singing windmills on Chios and on Mykonos; we remembered them, hearing their echo here. Sophy took her hand from the wheel and pointed to the left. "There they are," she said.

Three of them stood not far from the road, moving with stately rhythm to a doleful, creaking tune. We had exclaimed simultaneously at first sight of the windmills in Portugal. They were like the Greek ones, with their spokes and sails furled or unfurled, but we found it strange they should carry the same song.

"And, what is more," said Gina, "in the same key."

"That is what I was going to tell you from the guidebook," Reader T. interposed to Gina, "but you were afraid I was going to say Emily's unmentionable." He read again. " 'The long road up from Sagres through Odemira is accompanied by an intermittent song; self-absorbed, like a child humming to itself. It comes from the singing windmills. They sit there with white barrel-like bodies and their grey canvas sails play a squeaky music.' " (*Blue Moon in Portugal* by William and Elizabeth Younger.)

Lagos is a market town. Fairs are held there, Reader T. informed us, in August and September. That makes for me another reason to return to Portugal. For the first visit I was glad not to have so colorful a distraction, yet it could not have dwarfed the magnificent bay where Henry the Navigator made a base for his fleet, equipping and repairing them. As we stood looking at its bright water, one of the group of interested bystanders we invariably attracted drew on the road with a sharp stone the outline of a ship, and beside it wrote the numbers "150." He then spread his arms wide to indicate the expanse of the harbor. It was not difficult to translate this. One hundred and fifty large ships, warships, I suppose, could be anchored there.

The fair is probably held in the very place where slaves were once auctioned, the only slave market in Portugal. They were brought back from Africa on those ships of the Navigator's that had been outfitted in the bay. Around the square are handsome buildings, the most striking the customhouse. The architecture is almost entirely late eighteenth-century, understandably, since most of the town was destroyed by an earthquake in the early eighteenth century. An aqueduct, however, that still provides a water supply to the town was built in the late fifteenth and early sixteenth centuries.

We should have driven on out to Sagres, if only to stand on that lonely promontory and know more vividly where that remarkable, dedicated, fanatic Henry the Navigator, born in 1394, planned his expeditions that would bring the treasures of the world back to his own land. Not for his own enrichment, he was an ascetic—every account includes the phrase, "He died a virgin" —but for his country, and because he himself was greedy for knowledge. His reiterated orders to captains returning from long voyages was, "Go back, go further. Find out more."

We would have liked to stand on that lonely promontory where his observatory once stood, but the day had been long, we were tired. We pushed on.

It was after Lagos the climate of tempers within the Microbus took a sharp drop. Read on a barometer it would have indicated "Hurricane." It began with Alec's mild request to look at one of the maps with which Reader T. had flooded Gina. Gina magnanimously handed back two. The one she seldom relinquished from her hand had not the pristine freshness of a newly acquired treasure. It had been given Sophy and me in New York by friends, Katy and Herbert Greef, at the end of an evening when they had shown us their pictures taken on a trip to Portugal. They are thorough and appreciative travelers. They had kept a meticulous log of the places they had been. During the evening, Sophy and I had taken copious notes. As we left they had pressed the map on us, assuring us it was the best they had found, and the only one of its kind they had come upon during their trip. Therefore, it was travel-worn. The cracks that threatened to separate it had been re-enforced by Scotch tape.

143

Gina, seeing it, had at once taken possession of it. Brother T. had offered to find another. Gina, by now, had at least a dozen maps. None of them suited her; therefore she magnanimously gave Alec two of them.

At the moment of request he had finished, he said, his accounts for the day.

"Complicated," he added reproachfully, "by unexpected and scattered purchases of both cards and stamps by members of the party from the General Bank." Therefore, for two hours, he had been out three escudos.

No protest from Sophy and me, that the purpose of a general pot was to avoid such meticulous accounting, could dissuade him from the dogged completion of his self-appointed task.

Some minutes after his perusal of the maps extended to him, he reported he had found, he thought, a shorter way than the one Gina was indicating, to our destination for the night, Praia da Rocha. That was the moment the barometer fell. With awful slowness, she turned to face him.

"Alecmou," she asked, "you are telling *me* about roads? In five minutes from looking at a map, you know this, when from two hours of counting, you are three escudos in the rear?"

Alec waved this aside. "I know what I see," he repeated doggedly. "I see a road that is definitely shorter than the one we are taking, and this one is in none too good condition. In fact," he amplified, "I call it bloody awful."

"It is not," said Gina, "it is dressed."

"What do you mean 'dressed'?" said Alec.

"What I mean is, on the map, my map, the only good map, it is the Mobil Oil, it is saying, this road is dressed, that road is dressed. So other roads are undressed. You want we should travel on naked roads?"

"I don't know what an undressed or a naked road is, but I doubt if it would be worse than this one."

"There you are wrong, Alecmou. This map I have that is so

144

good it gets broken. We must paste it again with stinky paper."

"Sticky," from Alec, "and, anyway, it's called Scotch tape."

"No matter," Gina answered. "When you are getting all these maps for me, I didn't said I didn't want a garage map, I said only, 'Do you want to buy a map for me, or you don't?' All those you bring me I look just over quickly. I see there are roads in them that stop completely. Only the Mobil Oil, they go on. So these other maps must be burned, and you must write to the people who make them. They must make their roads go on."

Brother Theodore, sensing an approaching storm, quickly sorted from his mass of literature a copy of the London *Express* he had brought with him from home. He opened it and either read or used it as a screen. It was suddenly pushed violently into his face. Alec was scrambling from the back seat to the middle section. Leaning forward between us, he thrust his head next to Gina's, shaking his map at her.

"I tell you, Gina, dressed or undressed, here is a road that looks shorter."

"Give back that map tomorrow. It is no good. Only roads and roads, with no signs of dressing and undressing, and they stop."

By this time Alec's head was close to Gina's. Each was waving a map at the other. Sophy's head was out the side window, the rest of her wedged against the door by most of the rest of Alec.

"I tell you, Gina—" Alec rattled his map—"you have only to look here. My God, I can read a map."

"I do not believe you can read anything," was Gina's bland rejoinder.

"That's an insult," Alec told her.

"I know it is. That is why I say it."

In the end, over Gina's thundering protests, we took Alec's road. It was undressed, down to the bone. Workmen were in the process of clothing it with sand, gravel and rock. After some three miles on it, our way was blocked by steam rollers and other equipment. We turned around. Twice in one day, after twenty years, Sophy had to retrace a route. Gina crowed; Alec, in retreat

TWELVE

The two places in Portugal most frequently mentioned by some travelers with whom I have talked are Estoril and Praia da Rocha. Now that I have been in both these places, I think I know the kind of trips those travelers make. They are members of a flock of skimmers. Their leader could be a woman who, one late afternoon two years ago, stood next to my stepmother and me at the desk of a hotel in Rome. When she had attracted the attention of the clerk, she asked urgently if she could keep her room for that night.

"I know I only reserved it for twenty-four hours," she explained, "but now that I'm here, I find there is more to see in Rome than I thought. I figure I ought to give it half a day more."

The only two places in Portugal I would skip on a return visit —and if wishes could make that possible I would be in Portugal this very minute—are Estoril and Praia da Rocha. They are both resorts, and for me, a resort is a resort is a resort, and that's all it is. They have beaches, but so has Praia do Portinho, where we ate the lobster. Portugal is awash with beaches. The one at Portinho is not spied on by a row of summer hotels, boardinghouses and cottages. There are beaches at Sines, that tiny village "almost unknown to foreigners." The only building near them is the lighthouse. I doubt it provides Saturday-night dances and music every afternoon at cocktails. Praia da Rocha has these much-advertised attractions. They do not attract me. That is my own idiosyncrasy. Sydney Clark, in his excellent book, *All the Best in Spain and Portugal,* says, "Praia da Rocha is *the* unchallenged tourists' paradise of the Algarve shore." For me, its only distinction comes from the rock formations that give the name, Praia da Rocha, "beach of the rock." They rise from the water, and the beach itself, in tall masses. The sea and the wind have shaped them into beautiful architectural patterns, with spires, lacework wings as thin as filigree, hollows and caves at their base. These must be the delight of the spade-and-sand-pail set.

At the far end of our hotel, on what would be the boardwalk, but in Portugal is just a road, there is a dramatic mass of stone. This was once an old fortress. The walls are there, and inside them, a simple restaurant. The structure is dramatic because at this point the sea is far below. The thick-walled, heavy stonework hangs so far over the lip of the cliff its equilibrium looks impossible to maintain. We walked there after dinner and the view was magnificent. The day had been overcast, we had even gone through some rain, but by the time we had finished dinner, the clouds had scattered and the moon was brushing them to either side as she swam across the sky.

"The way your mother used to do the breast stroke," I said to Sophy. "Such dignity."

When we returned to the hotel, Brother T. excused himself diffidently. He thought he would explore a little further, and perhaps find some night life.

"There can't be any places open now where you can get pamphlets," I urged. He assured me he was not in search of them.

"But I like to sit in a café, and listen to the people around me. I hear there is rather a picturesque one, and I hear there is a casino, too. I don't play, of course," he added hastily, "but I do enjoy watching."

"How you hear such things?" Gina demanded. "We come in at the same time. We go to our room, we meet for the 'shoebag hour,' we come down to dinner together, but you know about cafés and casinos."

Brother T. apologized. "I showered quickly. I had time for a little walk before the 'shoebag.'"

148

"We couldn't have known that," I told Gina. "He brought back no literature."

We sat for a little while, Gina, Alec, Sophy and I, in a dreary lounge. We were too tired to explore with Brother T., too tired to make, at the moment, the added exertion of going up the stairs to bed. We had driven three hundred kilometers over roads in various stages of undress, and in rain. Gina is always concerned about the welfare of those around her, and they form a circumference that is very nearly the world. When she is in London, she is looking after, getting help for, concerning herself in the affairs of people dear to her in Greece, America, Egypt. The list includes any country in which she has spent a little time. When she is in New York she ministers by telephone, but she does not turn her back on London. She only increases her correspondence. The circumference of her generosity is not a hairbreadth less than that of her concern and her love. Time, certainly money, whatever she has, is lavishly spent. She enrolls others, who perhaps can provide a specific assistance, singing lessons, concert clothes for a young artist whose career is just beginning and must be properly dressed for the stage, a place to live. Once I found myself listening, because Gina asked me, to a whole afternoon of a play, half dance, half opera, performed for me by the composer, all in Greek. The composer, a beautiful pianist, could not sing, nor command enough English even to outline the libretto. But the dance-play will be seen and heard in New York next winter. Gina found a way.

That night at Praia da Rocha, her concern was primarily for Sophy, who had done all the driving. She would like to give her a massage. "My hands are strong," she said, as if that were news to anyone who has heard her play. "I can find every muscle that is tight, every nerve that is twanging. I find them and I make them give up." I thought I saw Sophy flinch a little. I heard her assure Gina she was not so very tired; she would only like to talk a little, and then go to bed. Gina, who is as perceptive as she is protective, did not push her offer.

"So," she said, "good. We talk. Only I do the talking. You will not make so much effort. I tell you a story. I am thinking about it ever since Brother T. say he is going to the casino. You would like that I tell you about how once I go to a casino here in this very country in Estoril? And what happened? Oh, my God, what happened!"

Alec had been lighting a cigar. He waved it in the air. "It's a wonderful story, Gina—fantastic! I had almost forgotten it. Now, then." He brought his cigar down to a level, pointing at her. He was the conductor. He had given her the down beat. She began.

"It is all long ago I am in Lisbon for a concert, the only other time I am ever in this country. On this night, after my concert, the Greek Ambassador here in Lisbon, who is an old friend, said, 'Gina, how do you like to go out to the casino at Estoril and make a little gamble?' How I like? How do I know if I like? I have never in my life been in a casino. So I say, 'Of course, I would like very much. The concert is over, my job is done, I am pitched up.'"

"Keyed up," Alec murmured.

"I am in a high pitch," Gina reiterated. "Always after a concert I do not sleep for hours. One must unroll slowly, slowly."

"Unwind," from Alec.

"I am unwinding this story, Alecmou. You must let me say it how I feel. So we all go to the casino, very gay, the Greek Ambassador and his wife, Alec, one couple, perhaps two more, I do not remember. In any rate we are a little group, very happy, so we come into the casino, and right away, Alec is excited. He loves to make the gamble."

"I do love to have an occasional fling at it," Alec admitted ruefully.

"And the others, too," Gina smiled at him kindly. "Only me, I say, 'I do not play, I have never been in a casino in the whole world. I do not know what one must do.' I am not prepurred, so I say I will watch.

"We go to the big table, everyone has sheeps, red ones, white ones, everything what you can imagine. There is a man at the head of the table. He is the croupier, I know. I have read of such people, and therefore, too, I know, they are playing roulette, because I see the round thing in the middle. Then it begins to speen around and around, and the croupier say, '*Faites vos jeux,*' and everyone at the table is putting on the sheeps, and sometimes they are winning, and sometimes it all goes into the pit."

"Pot," from Alec.

"Then something begins to happen in my brain. 'Tick, tick, tick, tick,' I can only explain it like this, that I think because we were very late in the evening the same croupier is working too long, perhaps he is tired, and he is falling into a rhythm, because that is what I am hearing in my head—a rhythm. And when I know that, I begin to count, and presently slowly, slowly, I know I am counting five over three, seven over four, I do not remember, but do you know what I mean? You know everything in the music is written in the beat—two-four time, six-eight, what you will—"

"Yes, Gina," Sophy and I agreed. We really did know that much.

"Forgive me, darlings," Gina said, contritely. "It is only I am trying to make it so clear so that you know what is happening. In a beat, like the music, you understand, the rhythm does not change. That croupier, with one hand starting the wheel, and after the number of beats each time it is the same, he is stopping, and with the other hand he is raking in the sheeps. So, now I find, if I join with him in the rhythm, and I count to myself, and I see on what he starts his little wheel, so many beats it will stop, and so many times around it will be at this number. It is so simple, it is to music. So, slowly, slowly, I move from where I am standing, I go behind my friends, I go where they can hear me, and I watch the croupier and when he starts, I start the beat. He does not change his tempo, so I say quickly this time, 'On seven.' So certainly seven is winning, because I am counting. And then I wait, and I count the beats, and I say, quickly, quickly, 'This time on eight,' or whatever that it is."

151

"And every time," Alec broke in, "we fairly scooped it in."

"But, of course," said Gina, "how could you not? It is to music, but do you know what is happening? By and by when my friends are winning everything that there is, the bus—"

"Boss," from Alec.

"—he is coming behind the croupier and he makes the announcement, 'This table is *fermé* for the evening. No more.' Of course he is finding out what is happening. He does not know why it is so, but he does not want it to be so any more. So he closes the table, and certainly we go home, because certainly I cannot go to another table and find the rhythm again. I think it was only this time because the poor man was so tired. Anyway, I do not try it again. I do not go to a casino since."

I had heard of mathematicians working out intricate numerical systems for breaking the bank, but I had never before heard of its being done by a musician who, watching a croupier beat time, conducted her orchestra of players to an evening's triumph of music over money.

In the morning sun the rocks at Praia da Rocha were a deep rose color and beautiful. We walked along the beach, stopping to watch two children absorbed in a game of checkers. Their board was a flat rock they had marked in proper squares. The men they moved on the board were large pebbles, red like their parent massive rocks, and white gathered elsewhere.

Portimão is just around the corner from Praia da Rocha. Guidebooks say next to Setúbal it is the largest center in Portugal of the sardine canning industry, and include the information that the place smells strongly of fish. I cannot believe all five of us are insensitive to smells. Surely, at least one would have sniffed unfavorably. The wind that morning must have been in our favor. We wandered happily about the town, delighting in the view from every part of the wide harbor that is on the estuary of the Arade. Fishing boats at anchor were nudging one another; the sun made their bright colors gleam. When we looked away from the water we saw the houses, or many of them, were painted a deep or very bright blue, or rose, the shade of the rocks we had just left, sometimes as dark and purple in cast as what we call "American Beauty." Gina called our attention to a stripe of Madonna blue that outlined the doorway of many of these houses.

"This takes me backwards to Greece, too," she said, "like the windmills. Always there is the strap of blue."

"Stripe," said Alec.

"Strip of blue," Gina continued, "around the door. It is for protection from evil. It is the blue of Heaven."

Within a few minutes of leaving the car, we had scattered. This had come to be the recognized pattern, recognized particularly by its Group Leader, who at the moment of seeing a wandering eye, and a tapping foot, would look at her watch, like the starter and timekeeper of a race. She did not set the distance to be covered but she allotted the time.

"I suggest back at the car in——minutes," according to the day's run. It was not a suggestion. It was a limitation, and we kept within it. We knew the places we wanted to see; she knew the mileage to be encompassed.

On the opposite side of the square from our parking place, I had seen swaying from a hanger outside a shop what looked from a distance like a bulky sweater. In every village in which we had so much as paused I had made graphic inquiries for a heavy sweater, the kind knitted by women for their fishermen. This was what Sophy's daughter had asked me to find, one for herself, one for each of her two girls. Someone she knew had brought such sweaters back from Portugal, and they were wonderful for skiing, she said, and had, in addition, great style. Everyone I had asked in the villages knew what I meant, and this accomplishment alone tended to make me giddy with success. However, I felt it not quite enough to take back to Charlton.

Success was mine that morning in Portimão. A fisherman's sweater was what I had seen swaying in front of a shop. It was heavy, it was coarse, it was in natural color. It had a slight variation in pattern, indicating either indifference or lively imagination

153

on the part of the knitter. I had not seen one before; I agreed with Charlton's judgment, it had style. But there was only one. The shopkeeper conveyed to me his difficulty in coming by any to sell. Women, he made me understand, made them for their men. They had no incentive, except money, to make additional ones; evidently, that was not enough. Once in a while a few were brought in and quickly sold. I was lucky to find one. Gina came into the shop while my package was being wrapped. She was drawn immediately to a pile of bright scarves.

"These are beautiful," she reiterated, "quite the nicest I see anywhere. I go outside now and wave one to Sophy. She must come. She will want to buy them for souvenirs to take home."

Her signaling brought Sophy on the run. It attracted a number of other people, too, who crowded in at the same time. Sophy was out of breath.

"What's the matter?" she asked anxiously as she came through the door. "Why are you waving that red flag at me?"

"Darling," Gina said soothingly, "it is not a red flag. You think I am treating you like a bool? It is a beautiful scarf. There are many I think you will want to buy."

Among us we purchased more than two dozen. They were in bright, clear colors and charming designs. They cost a little less than seventy-five cents a piece. The citizens who had followed Sophy participated in our selection, waving in front of us the ones that took their fancy, frequently breaking off into side discussions over differences of taste. I have shopped more easily and simply, but never accompanied by such vivid interest in my purchases.

Even with this handicap, we clocked in ahead of the two men. They reached the car at a sprint, out of breath, and a little irascible. They had gone to the bank, Alec explained, to cash checks, and in the accomplishment of this simple transaction, had been asked questions the equivalent of an examination for applicants entering the Civil Service.

In the telling, Alec's customary equanimity was restored, because since the questions were in Portuguese, and his knowledge of the language dim, almost to the point of total obscurity, his answers may have brought a considerable surprise to the examining board of bankers.

Brother T.'s regret was he had been left no time to visit a bookshop. I offered a silent prayer of thanksgiving, but Brother T. is perceptive.

"I was hoping to find some London newspapers," he said, directly to me.

Silves was our next stopping point of interest. On the way Reader T. obliged.

"Silves is the ancient capital of Algés. It is situated amid extensive woods of cork trees. It has a high-lying, impressive unmentionable." He paused for my benefit. "And a Gothic cathedral."

Sophy spoke hastily, "Are you noticing how beautiful these roadsides are?"

We were happily diverted, and not for the first time, by the charm of the borders on every road we had traveled. It is not only they are cut back so that a broad green ribbon edges the highway, but they are planted as well. These are not heterogeneous wildflowers growing in undisciplined profusion. There are hedges of flowers. There are well-pruned rows, predominantly of roses, but many others we could not identify. Once we stopped to allow me to leave the car and bring back a particularly delicate bloom of which we had passed a great number. None of us had ever seen so living a blossom as this became in my hand. While we watched, its petals curled, shriveled, and it died in the palm of my hand, as if I had torn it from its blood supply. I could not, of course, restore it, but it made me a little sick to see what I had done. A little farther along the road Gina told Sophy to stop, so that we might see more closely another bloom. Again I left the car, went over to look closely.

"I think I dare pick this one," I called back. "It's unmistakably a rose." Returning, I presented it as evidence. "I am no gardener," I testified, "let alone a horticulturist, but I've looked at enough flowers to know that never in my life have I seen a deep purple rose." Sophy corroborated this, and she is a gardener.

We passed, at wide intervals, little groups of men working on the road. This, too, had become a common sight. Even so it invariably brought speculation among us. "How could these little groups, never more than five or six in all, maintain the roads of a country?" They worked entirely with their hands, we never saw a machine of any kind, theirs was painstaking, minute labor, and yet the over-all condition of the roads is surprisingly good. Asserting this, Sophy added one qualification.

"It's impossible to gauge the amount of time needed for any specific mileage, because not only do the roads vary in condition, but you can't foresee that they may be winding, hilly, narrow or flat straightaway. I think if I were telling other people about motoring here, I would say, 'Count on a quarter of the time again, over what you have estimated, to allow for variation.' "

The castle at Silves—instigated by Reader T., this structure was now always called "the unmentionable"—was not destroyed by an earthquake in the eighteenth century that reduced to rubble the rest of the town. The cathedral also survived. The town itself has been rebuilt since the eighteenth century. Originally, its inhabitants were Arabs. These are gone, but the houses with their flat tops, each a terrace, have a Moorish flavor. The Gothic cathedral is surprising both outside and in. The exterior is of deep rose, pointed in white. The interior is overwhelmingly Rococo. "A very rich banquet," Gina called it. "A little heavy on the stomach."

Between Silves and Caldas de Monchique the exquisitely blooming roadsides swelled into an avenue of golden glory. We drove between solid, impenetrable banks of mimosa. Not one of us had ever seen anything like this abundance. Sophy stopped the car. We marveled. We walked along one side and then the other. We felt, we said, drenched by a shower of gold.

"But do not touch it," Gina warned. "Smell it, but keep your hands behind your backs; in Greece we say it brings the very worst of luck so never must you bring mimosa into the house.

156

And do you know," she continued, "I found exactly the same thing when I was in Calcutta."

We lunched at the Café Central in Caldas de Monchique. Caldas de Monchique is a watering place, but this was not its season. Nevertheless, the little Café Central gave us a delicious lunch. Its proprietor had no possible anticipation of our coming. At first view, we thought the restaurant closed. There was no sign of activity outside, no cars parked. When we had pushed open the door, half-expecting it to be locked, we saw no one inside. Almost immediately, however, a friendly, hospitable young woman appeared, assuring us on our inquiry that certainly we could have lunch. This was accomplished by eager pantomime from Gina and me, interspersed by more specific communication from Sophy.

At the sound of her first word, Alec launched into his version of Portuguese. To hear Sophy venture a phrase was an irresistible temptation to him. He must sound out his grasp of the language, and this is exactly what Alec's Portuguese was—a succession of sounds that, according to Sophy, bore no resemblance to words she had learned. Nevertheless, to her aggravated discomfiture Alec invariably made himself understood. His was the accuracy of a musician's ear, so he gave back perfect inflections in syllables of gibberish, a word he had picked up thrown in here and there. I have known in my life only one other person, the great actor, Mr. Otis Skinner, who attacked a language in this fashion. When his daughter, Cornelia, and I, earnest students of the language, were in Paris with Mr. and Mrs. Skinner, Cornelia and I wrung our hands, first in anxiety, and then in something approaching fury, when Mr. Skinner in our presence spoke French. With serene disregard for tenses, genders or even words themselves, Mr. Skinner would sail into a conversation in an accent so meticulously reproduced, his listeners invariably identified him as a Frenchman. Their only qualification was he came from a province with whose particular dialect they were unfamiliar.

The Portuguese received Alec's efforts with the same kinship. They did not catch the words, but certainly, he was speaking their language. At the Café Central he requested an *apéritif* of a delicate port, and then, allowing us a few moments for its enjoyment, and the cooks time to prepare a meal, we would lunch on whatever the house offered. This is what he told us he said, and this is what we received, though, Sophy expostulated, not any of the syllables he uttered made words, except those that formed "port," "please" and "thank you."

We ate a delicious soup followed by a delicate fish; with the fish the largest lemons any of us had ever seen. We thought them oranges, and had conjectured this was a novel flavoring, until we sliced and squeezed the juice. The waitress assured us, by pointing, they were grown in the neighborhood. The fish was followed by delicious thin *filet* of pork, potatoes and a large bowl of radishes as vegetable. Our dessert was a sweet quince jelly, not to be spread, but to be eaten with a spoon. Though I am not what my grandmother used to say, "partial" to sweets, I found this delicious. At the conclusion of the meal, Alec told us he had specifically ordered each dish.

The hotels and baths at Caldas de Monchique might have been in any spa, but the views of the forest and from the hills the countryside are beautifully indigenous. We drove to Monchique, a village beyond the spa, and at a considerable elevation. From there we could look across a wide plain to the sea. We agreed it was one of the most beautiful vistas we had seen during the trip, though an ensuing argument over what had been *the* most beautiful of all quickly died away, since the only point on which we could agree was that we had seen so many beautiful views the selection would have to be *"Chacun à son goût"*—wildflowers and bright water, forests, wide stretch of landscape from a height, or high, proud, brightly colored fishing boats in the setting sun.

In spite of the beauty of surroundings, the village of Monchique itself gave us the only unpleasant impression we had in the country; and yet this was so intangible as perhaps to be our own imagining. However, it was curious we should have had a unanimity of discomfort before anyone said it aloud. This was the first place in which people had not come toward us with frank, pleasant, hospitable curiosity. In this village people were walking about the square, men were sitting at tables in front of outdoor cafés. They stopped talking when we left the car. They watched us, but there was no friendliness in the look. Passers-by moved on and then turned back to stare. We felt a silence and arrested movement, but it was not friendly. Without a word of this to one another, after we had gone only a few steps we simultaneously returned to the car.

Sophy said only, "Shall we move on?"

We were a mile or so beyond the spa when Brother T. said, "Those people did not look like any we have seen before. They were sullen, and they were dirty. We've seen poverty, but this was misery."

Sophy added, "I saw more deformities in those few minutes than I've seen in the whole of our traveling here."

We spent a second night in Praia da Rocha. Brother T. visited the cafés again, but could not persuade us to join him. He reported next morning he had found neither the lights nor the night life very bright, but he added, brightening, and producing from behind his back his surprise for me, "I did have the luck in a little café, of all places, to find this booklet about Praia da Rocha."

THIRTEEN

Before I went to Portugal, I was told repeatedly I must be prepared for garlic in everything, including the soup. I had read a book about the country entitled *No Garlic in the Soup*. The warning and the book's title brought such anxiety I seriously contemplated taking enough packages from home of dried soup to carry me through the month. Garlic and onions are the only edibles I cannot stomach. That organ rejects them promptly, and violently. I can eat a dish of such exquisitely blended flavors I find it impossible to separate, or even identify the ingredients; but if garlic or onion has been included in the blending, a belated, but positive identification is provided for me. Therefore, the Portuguese cooking did not fool me, because that is impossible. Then where did other travelers eat? I visited, with my friends, a goodly number of restaurants, hotels, inns cited and recommended in guidebooks, and in not one was I given garlic or onions. In the beginning I would ask, with yearning emphasis, please not to include garlic—Sophy knew the word for it. I eventually stopped mentioning it; I was embarrassed too many times by a soothing answer, with overtones, that my supposition of garlic was so preposterous as to border on the hysterical. I learned there is one predominantly garlic dish, and that *is* garlic soup. When I had discovered this was the only dish to avoid, I followed the injunction my sister-in-law once gave me, when in a moment of confused excitement she urged me to "throw abandon to the winds." I have found this an excellent maxim.

Garlic soup is not the only soup that is a *spécialité* of the country. Mint soup, served cold or hot, perhaps is found elsewhere, but none of our group had eaten it, and we all declared it delicious. We women also wondered to one another, with a little annoyance, why we had not thought of it, and served it at home; it was so simple to obtain and to prepare. After all, we said, there is nothing exotic about fresh mint. Sometimes in Portugal bits of the leaves are sprinkled, like chopped parsley, over the top. The flavor itself is from a broth made by pouring boiling water over the mint. This broth is then added, according to taste, to any basic stock. It could just as tastily be added to a cream base. Well chilled, it is a delicious hot weather food.

The only ingredient not to my taste in Portuguese cooking is the olive oil. Somewhere I read, probably in one of Brother T.'s pamphlets, the difference between the Portuguese and the Italian or Greek olive oil is that in Portugal the olives are left deliberately on the ground for something like twenty-four hours, whereas in the other countries they are gathered quickly and the oil made immediately. The Portuguese like the rancid taste that comes from permitting the fruit to spoil a little. I tasted this rancid flavor only a few times; it is discernible when too much oil is used. I did not recognize the taste immediately. I thought, on my first experience, the fish I was eating was bad. When the same taste appeared in the French fried potatoes, I realized it has nothing to do with freshness. The taste is more likely to be in the food of a small provincial restaurant than in the sophisticated eating places of a city. This does not mean, however, that all provincial cooking includes too much olive oil. One of the smallest, and least pretentious, is the Restaurant Verde, at Olhão. We had stopped first at Faro on our way from Praia da Rocha. Faro is a port. It is the capital of Algarve and a busy town. We walked along its harbor front, bordered on one side by warehouses from which, we learned, fruit, wine, cork and anchovies are exported. We peeked in the Renaissance cathedral, and the Largo da Francisco, which has panels of *azulejos*. Though the history of the town goes to before the thirteenth century, there is very little evidence of the

161

early period. We were not tempted to stay long, and we were hungry. We drove on to Olhão. Wildflowers along the way carpeted some of the fields in color, wall-to-wall. One meadow was salted with white blooms. White villages we saw in the distance looked as if they had been strewn down the hillsides from an open hand.

White is the color in Olhão. Its houses are blindingly unrelieved by so much as a smudge. Their shape is uniformly a solid square. The roofs are flat with growing things in pots along the parapets. Evidently these roofs are terrace gardens. We saw several of them occupied by the householders.

We found the restaurant by the simple and practical method of driving slowly along the streets until we saw the identifying sign of an eating place. This one, with bright green façade, to corroborate its name, I suppose, looked clean and it was immaculate. We were the only patrons during the time we lunched, but we were watched from a courteous distance by four little boys who stood just inside the door. They had not come in to beg. When we spontaneously offered some of our meal to them, they refused with scandalized politeness. They were simply interested. The restaurant had one piece of equipment we later found repeated in other places of equal simplicity, but this was the first time we had encountered it. At the far end of the room a washstand was placed behind a pair of curtains, though the curtains were not drawn. We did not see it used at the Verde, but later, in other cafés, we not only grew accustomed to the sight of a patron going immediately to the basin to wash his hands before being shown to a table; we followed. On the tables, too, in this kind of eating place, we found a piece of equipment that baffled us in the beginning. It is made of cardboard, sometimes in the shape of a house, sometimes a design of no particular identity. The outside is covered by advertisements of the café in which it is placed. It is not flat; it can be square, oblong, cylindrical. It did not occur to us it was a receptacle until, picking up one to examine it more closely, I released a rain of toothpicks from a small hole in the bottom. The delicacy with which these implements are concealed is in startling

162

contrast to the conspicuous gusto with which they are employed.

Our lunch at the Verde included a soup, fish, meat cutlets, potatoes, all delicious. Slices of lemon are always served with meat, as well as with fish. I have adopted this, as well as the mint soup, for my own household. Salad is served with the fish as well as potatoes, and potatoes again with the rice or meat. The green vegetables are delicious, but they are not served unless one asks for them. The rapidity of service itself prevails as extensively in the simplest restaurant as in the Tivoli in Lisbon. Unless Sophy, with Alec's particular and peculiar assistance, made it clear we wished an *apéritif* of port before eating, soup would be placed before us immediately by a waiter or waitress on the gallop.

When we finished lunch, we took to the car again, and that was a mistake, since Sophy could find no place to park, and we wanted to explore on foot. Each time we approached the center of the town pedestrians courteously indicated we must not stop there. Finding at last a place that attracted no displeasure by our stopping, we left the car, and walked back toward the center, from which previously we had been waved off. Each of us must have been dull of wit not to have realized the whole section we were endeavoring to enter is barred to cars, marked so by stunning black and white mosaic pavement.

As usual we scattered immediately, investigating the shops of our particular interest. I saw Brother T. disappear through a doorway. I did not need to see for myself by its window display he had found a bookstore. This is not difficult to come upon, however small the community. The prevalence of bookshops in Portugal should make an American ashamed of the prevailing drought in his own town. To visit these shops is also to make one wince at our provincialism. Portuguese stock includes books in French, Italian and English, as well as Portuguese. The English selection, I admit, is narrow, and not quite up to the latest best-sellers. *Ivanhoe* is an over-all favorite. Nevertheless, I doubt if I could find the Portuguese equivalent of *Ivanhoe* in a bookshop of a small town at home—if I could find a bookshop.

The discovery I made in Olhão was a store that sold sweaters, and in that store, two fishermen's models. My "To Do" list could now carry full checks of accomplishment.

The purchase begun as a quiet transaction over the counter ended as a public celebration that substituted for fireworks a pyrotechnical display of oratory. The quiet opening was my request to see some sweaters. The proprietor eagerly displayed a few. Using one as an example, I pantomimed I wanted a heavy, coarse, hand-knit model made for fishermen. My pantomime of knitting and fishing increased the modest audience that had followed me into the shop. Word evidently got around there was a performance going on that would be a pity to miss. As the crowd increased I think the shopkeeper, seeing it, wanted to prolong the show; I do not like to believe my illustration lacked clarity.

Whatever his motives, the proprietor-director increased his cast. Selecting from the audience a little boy about ten, he gave instructions that took the child out of the shop, the spectators making an aisle for him, and across the arcade. The director indicated we would pause for an intermission. I took from my bag a cigarette. Six people offered lights. When I had exchanged a first bow of acknowledgment and thanks to this circle around me, and was on the second round, we were all distracted, though we had not been silent, by a high-pitched voice outside calling loud. The boy runner had turned herald; he was announcing his return, and the success of his expedition.

My attendants moved to get a good view, allowing me to see, approaching the shop, a new crowd headed by a middle-aged man wearing an open shirt, somewhat rumpled gray trousers, and flapping slippers over bare feet. He had the tousled look and dress of someone roused from a nap. The little boy, shouting, walked beside him. At least ten people, perhaps more, followed, men, women and children. The open space of the shop by now resembled the aisle of a subway train at five in the afternoon, but somehow, passage was made for the two leaders. At the moment we confronted one another, the chattering crowd stopped talking in mid-syllable. The gentleman so recently jerked from his siesta spoke. "I live in Miami. Is a fine place. You know it? But expensive." He extended his chest and thumped it proudly. "My old lady stay here, so I come to see her. I help you buy something? What you want?"

I explained; he explained to the proprietor. The proprietor had four sweaters of the kind I sought. I selected two. My interpreter benevolently took the purse from my hand, extracted the proper amount, delivered it and returned the purse to me with a bow. I expressed my gratitude, and my regrets that I had never visited Miami. We shook hands; I shook hands with the proprietor, and then with some fifteen or twenty people. Outside, the crowd scattered, after expressing its surprise and its approval that I rewarded the young herald. The interpreter, after urging me to come to see him in Miami, returned, I hope, to his interrupted siesta. I returned to the car, mission accomplished.

Brother T. had a pretty stack of literature; Gina was vociferously rueful. Alec had dissuaded her from buying a set of pendant earrings and ring in pearl at, she insisted, a fantastically low price. She interpolated her regrets with dark threats of the alternate profession she would embrace if Alec persisted in withholding her rightful funds. Infrequently we could hear Alec's obbligato disclaiming parsimony and protesting it was a matter of principle— one should not simply buy pearls out of a shop window. This should be a more serious undertaking, properly handled. The decision was made by Gina—she was not sure she wanted them, anyway. That was really why she had not bought them. I was the only one who heard Sophy mutter, "Had I known that, I would have taken them. I was dying to get them for Charlton."

We made no more stops that afternoon, other than to loiter in the car at Tavira. Its appearance had even stronger Moorish features than Olhão. In both places we saw with interest women shrouded in black, covering the lower half of the face with a scarf, or in curious contrast, with a bright-colored handkerchief. The chimneys on the houses were magnificent, and there were flowers everywhere, trailing from baskets hung on the outer walls of houses, in pots on the roof terraces, covering every garden wall and, outside the town, splashing the roadside.

São Braz de Alportel is a delightful *pousada,* beautifully situated as they all are. I think of imagination as a quality in an individual; I do not expect to find it exercised by a government. The government-built and administered *pousadas* show evidence in their location alone of delightful imagination. Instead of an obvious site in the center of a town, each *pousada* has been placed outside a community, and on whatever spot affords the best view. The São Braz de Alportel is evidently a favorite. When we had telephoned a few days before, asking for rooms, we were told the only accommodations available consisted of two: one room sleeping three, the other two. We had agreed at the outset of the trip we would rather risk inferior or no accommodations at the place of our first choice than limit ourselves to an inflexible itinerary. Unlike the lady in Rome, we wanted freedom to give more than a day and a half to a locale we might find especially provocative. Therefore, we did not demur at the rooms provided at the São Braz, though the sight of them surprised us. We had thought the room for three would be of extra size; we found it a small chamber furnished with a bureau, a chair and a pair of double-decker beds. The narrow aisle between these was itself divided by a sky-blue cotton curtain that could be pushed against the wall or extended the length of the room on a wire suspended above the height of the upper bunk. This was the privacy afforded two couples, I suppose, who might occupy that room.

Gina, Sophy and I occupied it, the obvious and only possible arrangement. We gathered in the men, nevertheless, for the "shoe-bag hour"—cramped as the space was; two people sat on each of the lower bunks, Brother T. with drink—and book—on *the* chair.

After a very good dinner we were tempted by a blazing log fire in the lounge to have a liqueur in front of it—Gina abstaining. The evenings were invariably chilly, and *pousadas* provide an open fire. We went, almost immediately after, to bed. I volunteered to occupy an upper bunk, insisting with honesty I like it. Gina and Sophy gave way; we gave way to one another over the process of undressing. While one prepared for bed the other two sat in the lower berths. We speculated, unsuccessfully, on how two couples would manage.

Finally installed in my upper quarter I noticed for the first time a wide gap between my bed and the wall, not wide enough to slip through, but enough to catch and wedge an unwary leg or arm flung out in sleep. Since Gina and Sophy were not yet settled in their places for the night, I asked if they would mind pushing my section against the wall. I thought Sophy below me would also find it more comfortable to be attached by one side. They applied themselves immediately and agreeably, confirming my proposal that if I had something solid on one side, I could arrange myself there and stay away from the drop on the other. They pushed, they applied themselves like battering rams; each unsuccessful attack made them more determined to succeed. I offered to remove my weight and add my strength. Sophy said that was nonsense. It couldn't be so heavy even with me in it.

It was at a moment when spent, they were pausing for breath, I discovered between bed and wall a fixture that froze my attention. When I knew I must share my discovery, my friends were at the heave-ho again, Sophy counting, "One, two, *push*."

I leaned down over their heads.

"Dears," I urged, "*please* don't bother any more. It really doesn't matter, I promise you."

"I will *not* give up," was Sophy's panting answer.

"*Please*," I repeated, "I *beg* you to stop."

"No, we do not," from Gina.

Nothing but confession would bring an end to it.

"Darlings," I told them, "you'll *have* to stop. There's a wedge up here between the bed and wall to keep them apart. I don't know for what purpose. I'm so sorry I didn't see it before. I hope you're not done in."

Each of my companions simultaneously dropped her length on a lower bunk, breathing hard. Gina spoke.

"It is not so much that our hearts and lungs are finished. Shild-bearing apart of anything else, out of question now. But it is that *sans doute* we have spoiled our keedneys."

Sophy was the first to turn off her light. Gina asked, apologetically, if we would like her to draw the blue curtain. She wished to read a little more. She had received mail forwarded from the Tourist Office in Lisbon. She had had no opportunity to read it. Sophy and I convinced her it would make not the slightest difference to either of us. A few minutes later when I had turned off my light and was just drifting off to sleep, I smelled a dreadful infusion into the room. I sat up, my hand clamped over my mouth and nose; my stomach was heaving. I entreated, muffled, but in anguish, "My God, what do I smell in this room?"

Gina called up to me happily. "It is from a letter I am just reading. It is from my darling friend Katy Kapsoyannis. She encloses them for me to sew in the hem of my new concert dresses to bring me luck and ward off the evil eye." She sighed with pleasure at such thoughtfulness.

"Two garlic buds."

FOURTEEN

São Braz was, I think, the first place at which we breakfasted together, and in the dining room. Usually, in the European pattern, breakfast had been brought to our individual rooms. If we had shared that meal elsewhere, I have no recollection of it; I shall not forget the one at São Braz.

The hour had been determined the night before. What with the limitation of the women's sleeping quarters, and by Sophy's and Gina's calculations, the mileage and sight-seeing to be encompassed during the day, a tryst at eight o'clock had been appointed.

We were punctual, but not communicative. No one seemed illtempered, only subdued and in a contemplative mood, awaiting the arrival of coffee. We exchanged "Good mornings," agreed we had slept well, and fell silent.

Without preliminary, not looking at any of us, Alec called out into the room a single word. Apart from the unexpectedness of such a loud break in the silence, the word itself was a shocking surprise.

I have not led, I think, a particularly sheltered life, but I had never heard that word actually spoken. I have seen it written on fences and the walls of buildings; it has only four letters.

I know I jumped; I think I saw Sophy and Brother T. rise a little. Astonishment, bewilderment, whatever may have tied our tongues, did not strike Gina dumb. It generated an explosion.

"Alec," she thundered, and there was no "mou" attached, "how you say such a thing!"

Alec answered briefly, still looking off into space. "I don't know how I came to think of it."

169

"Never think of it again," was Gina's rejoinder. "Not so long as you live."

Interested curiosity restored my powers of speech. "Gina," I asked, "how do you happen to know that word?"

Still glaring at Alec, she tossed her answer to me. "That kind of word someone always tells you when you are learning a new language."

"It must be all of twenty years since I learned it," Alec vouchsafed from his abstraction. "Remarkable."

I thought to myself he must then have been of age when he learned it; I counted that remarkable.

"I only ask you," Gina said, "put it away from your memory. I never hear you use such talk. I want I should never hear you again."

A waitress from across the room came to Alec and laid a knife beside his place. Alec looked at us for the first time. Waving it triumphantly before our eyes, the smile of a cherub on his face, "You see," he told us, exultantly, "I was right, *'faca.'* I learned it when I was here twenty years ago. I have not thought of it since. I may not have had exactly the right pronunciation, but I got what I asked for—by Jove."

We were subdued for the remainder of the meal, even after we had had our coffee.

The road between São Braz and Beja twists around and over hills; I would call them mountains, and did, until I experienced the ones we traveled during the afternoon. For once, however, I did not find it necessary to ride with a hand arranged like a Venetian blind before my face. By this method I find I can shut off the sight of a drop that would make my head reel; at other times, anticipating a hasty blotting out, I view the landscape through hand-made slits.

This time, however, without giddiness or trepidation, I joined the chorus of wonder at the panorama around us because the road was set far back from the rim, with planting between. Paradoxically, Sophy the Intrepid was the only one who felt anxiety, and,

bless her heart, she did not confide this to me until the end of the day. There was such a high wind blowing, she said it had required full strength to keep our bus, top-heavy as it was, from describing an erratic zigzag.

During the morning, we made only one stop. Brother T. instigated this. He had been reading about Castro Verde. We never questioned his suggestions, but I am particularly happy we did not demur at this one.

Castro Verde is a charmingly picturesque village of deep, winding, narrow ways. At its top, or very nearly, is a church one guidebook, so Reader told us, called "the parish church, dedicated to N. S. da Conceição." Baedeker calls it "the church of Nossa Senhora." All chroniclers agree its interior is remarkable. To me it is an enchanting sight. When we had finally wound our way to a summit and left the car in the cobblestoned square before the church, we discovered to our dismay its doors were closed. We were turning away disconsolate, unwilling to give up when we had come this far, but debating among ourselves where to go for help, when a voice called to us.

A young woman came from a cottage across the way, the cottage itself so small she stooped to come through its doorway; even the windows were scarcely a foot above the ground. Eagerly pointing to herself she indicated with a turn of her wrist, as of unlocking a door, she would have the church opened. Behind her in the cottage we could hear a child crying. With a gesture to wait, she ran back to her house and reappeared almost immediately, rocking a very young baby, soothed now, in her arms. She held a child by the hand; two others clung to her skirts. By the time we had recrossed the square to the steps of the church, we had annexed some six or eight other children from houses down the square. Indicating she would return, she went with her covey toward the back of the church. Gina occupied the time by distributing "Karamelles." The inevitable happened. Whenever Gina scattered "Karamelles" the original recipients multiplied by five or more, though none of us observing ever saw a member leave the original group in order to spread the news of falling manna.

The door was opened from the inside by the sexton. The young woman standing beside him saw the populace we had accumulated. Violently waving her arms, including the one that held the baby, she dispersed our audience and shooed her own children ahead of her to the steps. Bowing, she indicated we must not be disturbed on our visit. We must have the church to ourselves.

How we stared, smiling, even laughing a little, at the sheer delight of an interior solidly covered from floor to ceiling, not so much as a crack between, with *azulejos* in a shade a little paler than a delft blue on a white background. I have seen Rococo splendor, Gothic majesty, Norman austerity, but I have never before, nor since, seen the nave of a church so light, gay, joyous, mirth-provoking. Even tableaux of battles (the Battle of Ourique in 1713, Reader T. said) do not sober the temper of this place because beneath them birds, windmills, animals and flowers dance.

We came from the church to a scene that, for me, is as memorable as the nave we had just quitted. From the top step I looked down on the reassembled chorus of ragged, barefooted, but not poverty-thin children. They were watching for our appearance, all the large brown eyes turned our way. They stood silently in a circle; the center was the young mother. She was waiting, too. She stood facing us, still holding her baby, long since asleep, cradled in one arm. Her other hand was outstretched in our direction and, curled in the palm, a very little kitten. At the sight of us, she looked down at her hand, then holding it up a little higher, smiled and laughed gently. She had brought the kitten, perhaps, from her house, because she thought to look at it would give us pleasure. It gave me great pleasure. I shall not forget the young mother, the baby, her children, nor the kitten in the palm of her hand. She did not want to sell or give us the little animal. She wanted us to enjoy it with her.

The older children as we left ran down the hill, behind us, and the younger ones came tumbling after. Gina tossed them "Kara-melles" until the last one gave up the chase.

Pique-Nique in Beja is an excellent restaurant. We lunched very well. Alec observed dourly Gina's and my enthusiasm for the food was flavored by our openly expressed appreciation of the handsome young waiter who served us. Sophy regretfully admitted she had been so hungry for once her attention had not been distracted by the proximity of a handsome male.

Brother T. had been reading. Beja, he told us before we set out to explore, still holds traces of the Roman occupation when it was the "Pax Julia," and traces of the Visigoths and the Moors.

"One of the outstanding and most conspicuous points of interest," he apologized, "is the 'unmentionable.' It has a superb tower built partly of white marble, and it dates from around 1300."

For once I was tolerant of its existence, because for once a castle emerged from anonymity. It was built by King Diniz.

What I associate with Beja I told my friends—and I think I interrupted Brother T. in my eagerness to display knowledge of at least one place—is the story of the Nun of Beja, and her unanswered correspondence. I had their attention. They did not know this story. They asked for more coffee, settled back and I told them.

Love Letters from a Portuguese Nun holds a secure and permanent place in the literature of the world. The first general knowledge of these letters came from their publication in France in 1669, two years after they were said to have been written. This edition carried a note that the letters were translated from Portuguese. It is not known how the letters came to the publisher, because the originals have never been seen except, presumably, by the writer and those involved in the publication. Therefore, the whole story may be apocryphal.

"But," I insisted to my friends, "what difference does that make —the story itself endures."

Sister Mariana Alcoforado at the age of sixteen entered the con-

174

vent of Conceição. When she was twenty-five she met a handsome French military officer. His name was Noel Bouton. He later inherited the title of "marquis." He was at the time in Portugal on a military mission giving aid to the reorganization of the Portuguese Army. How the young Sister and M. Bouton met is not disclosed in the letters. Nevertheless, wherever the first meeting took place, there were many that followed, secret trysts because they had fallen in love. They became lovers. When hints at such a scandal reached the companions and superior officers of M. Bouton, that dishonorable gentleman folded his tent and quietly slipped away, back to France.

There is no record of a letter from him to the love he abandoned, but somehow Sister Mariana knew where to reach him. She wrote him five love letters. There is not in them a word of anger or of reproach. The paragraphs hold out to him with overflowing tenderness only love, passion, self-revelation without self-pity, compassion, understanding, forgiveness, all said in such clarity, simplicity and beauty the words still reach the hearts of their readers. The only heart it did not reach was that of M. Bouton. He never answered them; that much is known from the letters themselves. He must have sensed some worth in them, since they found their way, I suppose with his direction, to the French publisher.

The convent, built in the fifteenth century, is now a museum of archaeology. The cloisters, brightly decorated with *azulejos,* is from the sixteenth century. These statistics were contributed by Reader T.

We did not find the cloister decorations appealing; they were indeed brightly colored *azulejos,* bright green and white in diamond shape; it might be bathroom tiling. But the chapter house next to the cloisters has an exquisite, over-all pattern in *azulejos,* like a medieval tapestry. In spite of my stubborn resistance to the ubiquitous castle, I had to concede this one, that dates from the early fourteenth century, has a stunning tower of gleaming white marble, and an added spectacular adornment of two tiers of battlements, one above the other.

175

The Church of Santa Maria is not far from the convent. Reader T. told us it had been rebuilt in the fifteenth century. It is not like any other church we saw in Portugal. I have seen its like only in Albuquerque, New Mexico, with an exterior of a kind of plaster-like adobe. The contrast between this and the interior with lavishly Rococo altars is startling.

As we came out of the church the rains that had threatened all morning dropped suddenly and heavily like a curtain of water before us. There was no overture of a light sprinkling. We had had the threat in the low dark clouds; now we were in the midst of the full performance. We ran to the car and were drenched when we reached it. Sogginess quenched our interest for further sight-seeing on foot. Sophy is a weather expert. I treat her prognostications with a respect not far removed from awe. She can stick her finger in her mouth, remove and hold it in the air, and then say which way the wind is blowing. I drench my finger in the same manner, hold it in the air, and the only knowledge I glean from this is that it dries. At Beja, however, she did not offer her predictions with customary assurance. The rain had undermined it, she admitted. By her calculation the high wind of the morning was going to blow away the storm clouds. We still had the wind and the contents of the clouds. Therefore, Group Leader proposed we make no further stops, but push on to Elvas, where we had reservations for the night. She had recovered enough assurance to prophesy categorically this was no passing shower to be sat out. Therefore, we did not sit in Beja; we pushed long and hard.

Beja, itself, is like an apple core surrounded by miles of a white plain specked, here and there, with rows of eucalyptus trees. Beyond this are green fields of wheat and corn, but when we had passed these we were in the mountains again. The wind was high, the rain a fierce downpour, the road not the best, the day seemed endless. The lights of Dover are no more welcome a sight to the Channel-tossed traveler than the lights of Elvas were to our busload.

The *pousada,* Santa Luzia, is at the far end of the town from the road by which we entered, and at the top of a steep, winding hill.

"Excelsior!" someone said, as we staggered out of the car in the dusk and rain.

Like all *pousadas,* this one was cheery, comfortable, inviting. A maid and porter hurried out at the sound of our car to welcome us and carry in our luggage. Through the open door we saw a bright fire burning. There is an over-all similarity among the *pousadas* that includes one aspect of administration we found odd. The manager is never in evidence. In an inn, smaller than a hotel, one would expect, we thought, to see the innkeeper, the host, in short, the boss. He would be visible somewhere supervising the admittance and registration of guests, the distribution of luggage, the seating in the dining room or, waiving all those things, the payment on departure. If there is a *pousada* head, we never saw him or her; there are more maids than menservants. One of these brings the bill at the end of a stay, collects payment, and takes it somewhere. A maid, not necessarily the same one, on the arrival of guests presents the book for registration, and collects the passports, subsequently returning them. There is not only no desk clerk—there is no desk.

How we welcomed the "shoebag hour" that night, the delicious dinner and, immediately after, bed.

We woke next morning to the sound of rain, but the wind had stopped. Our rendezvous was for nine o'clock at the car, and everyone was punctual except Alec. Gina, apologizing for him, said he was having banking trouble. At the moment of paying the bill for all of us, he had remembered his intention of gathering from us the night before fuel for the pot that needed replenishment. What with the rain and the fatigue, and the sleepiness after a good dinner, he had forgotten all about it.

"So," Gina explained, "the bill comes and he is opening his banking basket, and there is very low money. We are almost washed out, he says."

"Cleaned out," Brother T. substituted.

Gina acknowledged this with an impatient wave of the hand. "So," she continued, "because the maid is waiting there, and you are waiting out here, he becomes agitated. He pulls from his own pocket and his purse all what he has, and that includes my money, you understand. He dumps it into the basket and out of this bank that now is not washed away, he pays the maid for all of us. The maid is out the door and I am in the bathroom putting in the case my toiletries and I hear a howl like something that is in a zoo at night. I have never heard that sound in a jungle, you understand, because I have never visited a jungle, but I have been at the zoo. I drop my toilette case, I rush in, I think he is stabbed, maybe he is bleeding. He is running up and down, smocking his head with both hands."

"Smacking," from Teddy.

"No matter," Gina conceded equably. "Smacking, smocking, smoking. He is howling, and I am shouting on top of it. 'What is it that is happening to you? You are dying?' 'No,' he tells me, and stops the howling, but he is still walking up and down, up and down. 'Of course I'm not dying, but I am an idiot. My God! What an idiot! I paid that girl from the bank.' I tell him, 'Of course, that is what the banker must do.' Then he stops his walking. He stands in front of me. He shakes my arms. 'Don't you understand?' he says. 'I put my money in the basket with the pot. Now I don't know how much was pot and how much was my money.' '*Your* money? *My* money, too!' I tell him, and now *I* am howling."

Brother T. offered to go to Alec's help.

"Better you stay here," Gina advised darkly, "and when he comes I think it better we do not say, 'How is the bank?'"

We had not waited long when Alec joined us. His habitual ebullience was conspicuously lacking. The smile with which he wished us "Good morning" was instantly replaced by an expression of melancholy preoccupation. He took his customary place in the back tier, and immediately drew from his pocket a large and crumpled piece of brown wrapping paper and a pencil. I think this was the only writing equipment the *pousada* had been able to furnish. He opened his basket, spread out in front of him on the seat the money he took from it, counted, muttering to himself, wrote down figures on the brown paper. His withdrawal enveloped the bus. We drove away in silence.

This condition could not prevail, however, at least among the four of us. By the time we were at the foot of the hill, the silence was invaded by Sophy.

"I've been saving up my one bit of advance knowledge," she volunteered. "I hope it will impress you. Plums come from Elvas. In Philadelphia everyone bought candied plums at Christmastime. They were as much a part of my childhood as fireworks on the Fourth of July. They were very sticky and delicious. I still remember the rapture of licking my fingers after I had eaten one. They came from Elvas in Portugal." Reader T. corroborated this. He read from Baedeker's: "It is also noted for its dried plums."

"Then we will have some," was Gina's declaration, "and we will lick our stinky fingers."

"Sticky," came sadly from the back seat.

"Alecmou," was her answer, "continue your counting. Do not use your ears."

In the darkness and rain of the evening before, we had not paused in the town. This morning the rain was intermittent, and not drenching. We gave it only the concession of raincoats before we left the car.

The aqueduct of Elvas is a magnificent and astonishing sight. One row of high and broad arches is topped by another until there are five in all. The aqueduct, as Reader T. instructed us, was built on Roman foundations. From its beginning to its completion required 124 years. It brought water along a wide plain to the city. Its completion was marked by a charming fountain, built in 1622, of marble columns topped by a cupola, and on this an equestrian statue. If not Ossa on Pelion, it is still a respectable piling. Water from the aqueduct spills into it. The streets of the town are steep and narrow, so are the houses. Some of them are so narrow, Sophy insisted, a man over six feet tall could not lie at full length across a room. Nevertheless, each one has a magnificent chimney, and the rooftop is a terrace with flowers in pots on its wide lip.

After a few minutes' walk we realized we were encountering a considerable number of soldiers. We had seen them before only in Lisbon. Reader T., urged by Gina, released from under his arm several guidebooks, always attached to his person. With some difficulty from passers-by on the narrow way, and lack of place on which to lay his pile of books, he wrested the information that Elvas is one of the chief garrisons of Portugal. I suppose it is the presence of the garrison that makes the town seem so crowded. Many other towns have streets as narrow but I was not aware of congestion in any of them. Suddenly as I backed into a doorway to yield passage, I remembered a moment years ago when my brother, at the age of five taken to downtown Chicago for the first time, clung to Mother's hand. He had looked around him at the corner of State and Randolph streets and said excitedly, "What's happening?" Nothing in Chicago that day, and nothing in Elvas the day we saw it—just people.

The Church of São Domingo is of octagon shape. The only other one I saw was on the way to Óbidos. São Domingo was built in the middle sixteenth century. Its interior has floor-to-ceiling *azulejos,* but for me they lacked the gay, ephemeral quality I had seen at Castro Verde. This is partly due, I daresay, to the contrast in lighting. São Domingo has only two windows. A lantern suspended from the ceiling does not add sparkling illumination.

We did not go into the cathedral, but we did pause to enjoy the black and white mosaic pavement on the square it faces. We chose instead, in Sophy's apportionment of time allotted, to patronize a shop where we could purchase plums. It was not difficult to find. There are several. Gina bought more than several boxes; she emerged with both arms filled. She refused not only our offers to help; she forbade us to make purchases for ourselves. In the doorway to the shop she distributed two boxes for each of us, the Elvas equivalent of "Karamelles." Even after this largesse, she still had an armful. They were to be presents, she told us, for friends in England and Greece. I doubt she would have been so encumbered had Alec accompanied us. The prospect of extra weight and space in their luggage would have brought his hand heavily down on her expansiveness.

Alec had not been with us, however; he had stayed in the back row of the car with his basket, his money, his brown wrapping paper and his pencil. He looked up bravely when he heard the car door open. "I've almost got it," he told us triumphantly. "I think I know, within a few pounds, escudos, dollars or something, where we all stand, and just how much I am out of pocket." He stopped short, his eyes starting. He had seen Gina stacking boxes of plums on the front seat in order to have both hands free for her ascent. He asked fervently of the Deity what his wife had bought, and of her where she had got the money to pay for it.

"I borrowed it," she told him serenely, "from Brother T. So now you must add that to your counting."

A sound from Alec was interpreted by Gina. Surprised, she turned to us.

"That is the howling he is making this morning I am telling you about. Why he makes it now?"

FIFTEEN

As we were leaving Elvas, Sophy stopped the car for a last look at the great aqueduct. Nature at that instance did us a pretty service, beautifully timed. The rain had been petering out for some time. At the instant it stopped the sun emerged, looking a little wan, but of sufficient strength to give light and shadows; simultaneously a girl came into our focus. She was young, slim and the most beautiful, we agreed, we had seen in the country. She carried on her head, with regal serenity, a tall water jug. Alec, roused from his counting by our quick exclamations of pleasure, leaped from his seat, clutching his camera and scattering in all directions his carefully laid piles of money. His only egress was by the door opening on my tier. He had to wait for me to gather up my camera, but he called the girl. She turned, smiled, waved her hand in acknowledgment, the jar immobile, and waited for us. That photograph with the Roman arches of the aqueduct towering behind her is one of my favorite souvenirs of Portugal.

We had photographed other women carrying such jars as this one, but the carriers had not been so beautiful. The jars themselves are of uniform shape, size and color. We had seen truckloads filled with them, lumbering through city streets or along the road. By their prevalence they might be, at home, Coca-Cola bottles. The jars themselves are of clay in Pompeian red and Etruscan shape. This confusion of identification is commensurate with my bewilderment and lack of knowledge. I do not know why Etruscan vases in a Pompeian red should be a Portuguese common carrier in 1961. I can only assert we saw them everywhere. On the way to the water

182

supply women generally carry them crosswise on their heads; filled, they are, understandably, borne upright. Every woman "prepurrs" herself, as Gina would say, for carrying by placing on her head a circlet the size of a deck tennis ring, and equally hard. It is wrapped around with cloth, usually black. She sets this squarely on her crown and places on it the burden she is going to assume, unless it is of such bulk it must be put there for her by a helper. Once it is in place it seems to be as much a part of her as her own head. At no time does she resemble a circus performer, who constantly exercises neck muscles in order to maintain the equilibrium of whatever he is balancing on top. I have seen a Portuguese woman with a bundle on her head at least four feet wide, with

a baby cradled in one arm and securely fastened by one end of the mother's shawl tucked tight into her waistband, stoop, pick up with her free hand another package and stride on, her skirt swinging in the rhythm of her step. I have seen little girls walking with the same unconcern under a bundle looking to be twice their size.

The other carriers we saw were donkeys. Until we traveled north we did not encounter oxen on the roads or in the fields. In the north they supplanted the donkeys, but in this part of the country we saw them only on the beaches where the fishing boats land. There, in pairs, they draw the boats high up on the shore.

When Alec and I returned to the car, our photograph made, we found the others talking about the women of Portugal. Gina was comparing them to the Greek girls. Alec, retreating to his back seat, gathering up his money once more, took no part in the conversation.

Gina was saying, when I took my place, she thought the people in this country traveled more than the same class in Greece moved about. Sophy modified this. "I don't believe they travel far, and certainly not out of the country, but I agree they do move, at least from one village to another."

We had seen evidence of this. No matter how remote a mountain road appeared to us, we would inevitably come upon the sign I once thought was a town, "PARAGEM," meaning "BUS," and nearly always there was a group of people waiting. Their luggage frequently included vegetables and live fowl. I suppose the passengers with such luggage were going to, or returning from, a market. All this impedimenta would be hoisted by the conductor, with the assistance of the passengers, to the roof of the vehicle. It was a common sight. Once in a village, waiting behind a *paragem* while it unloaded passengers and freight, we saw a sewing machine brought down from the roof. The woman claiming it was greeted enthusiastically by a young girl who resembled her. Between them they carried it away, and we saw them enter the door of a house along the road. Our conjecture was Mother had come to visit her daughter and help with the spring sewing.

only a few years ago. My auntie's husband, *mon oncle,* was a man what builds bridges and things like that. He has a factory about it. On one of the islands there is a big, big thing, building, bridge, maybe, I do not know. Anyway, *mon oncle* is saying he must be there for a long time to watch how it goes. So he and my auntie take a little house there. She is not very happy, you can imagine—from Athens to such a place. But what can you do? So she find a maid, an island girl, a nice girl, she said, but she knows nothing, nothing, so my auntie teach her. Everything what you can imagine she has to teach her. One day *mon oncle* says a big, important man from the government, who is also a friend, is coming next day to see this thing *mon oncle* is making. He will come on a boat he has, he will look at everything, he will have lunch with us, and then he will go back to Athens. 'Are you crazy?' my aunt say. 'What I can do for him for lunch, this high-up man from Athens? We know how he lives. How can we?' Then she say, 'No matter. He will understand. I will do the best what we can.' So then she is running around like a mad mouse, and finally she decides she must give him fish, that is the only thing she is sure will be good and fresh. So she get a fish, and she prepurr it herself. She put it to cool. Next day she feex everything—salad, all the else she will give him. She prepurr the table, now everything is prepurred, except one little tiny thing. This must not be done until the final moment, so it will be crisp and fresh, and that is the parsley. She tell the girl carefully, carefully, slowly, slowly, how she must bring in salad, how she must carry in the fish, and at the last minute place the parsley so. Now *mon oncle* arrive with the guest, they have nice little glass of wine, they go into the table, everything is lovely, the salad bowl comes, the girl go back, there is long, long wait. My auntie thinks she will go mad. Then door opens and girl comes in carrying slowly, slowly the platter with the fish. My aunt looks at it, looks fine, only one thing is missing. And then she look up, because the girl is breathing so hard, like a horse that is snorting. My aunt look at her, and can you imagine, sticking out from each nose—"

186

"Nostril," from the back seat.

"—is a bunch of parsley. My aunt have say to the girl at the last minute put the fresh parsley in the nose—of the fish, of course. Always in Greece we serve the whole fish with the head, and we put the nice, fresh, crisp parsley in the nose. But that stupid girl from the island, well, she had it in the nose—hers."

We were approaching the town of Borba. Sophy, on the alert for signs that we were on the right road, pointed to one. "It looks like marble," she said. "Can that be possible?"

Reader T. corroborated this. "Borba is famous for its use of marble that is quarried locally." Reading further, he informed us, "It is also known for its excellent wine."

Sophy's response to this was a cheer, and a startling pressure applied to the accelerator.

Not only the roadsides around Borba are of marble; every building we saw down to the smallest cottage had doorsteps, window and door frames of marble. We saw, too, a great many outside stairways, in marble.

This was the place of no sight-seeing for us. Sophy, Alec and Brother T. are abashed they did not see churches or other cultural objectives. Gina and I gloat over this blank. "It is for us," she said, "the day of the Treasure Hunt." On the first street we entered, we saw antique shops on either side. We did not stray from that neighborhood. Alec did not dare leave, he said; no telling what his wife would buy. He begged assistance from Sophy and Brother T.

"Emily will bear watching, too," Sophy told the men. They patrolled the street.

Nevertheless, Gina managed to acquire a charming little lead figure, and one or two other gems. Sophy deterred me from a headboard for a brass bed, marvelously festooned with garlands held by cupids. "Transportation," she had insisted, "would be difficult. Give that a thought. The shop will not know how to ship it. Even if we could put it on top now, when we give up the bus are you going to carry it on your back?"

I yielded reluctantly, and instead, bought two pictures on glass and other small pieces. Alec later joined Sophy in vigorous protest that by the time the pictures were padded for safety and wrapped they could not be catalogued as small pieces. I offered to go back for the headboard to provide them with a standard of comparison. I heard no more after that from the complainers.

On our return to Lisbon at the end of the trip, I learned about and visited the Centro de Turismo e Artesanato, Number 61 Rua Castilho. This shop not only packs expertly and ships purchases made elsewhere and brought there, but has, itself, a comprehensive and well-selected assortment of native products from skirts, hats, aprons, shirts to chairs and tables. It even has an excellent collection of Fado records. I doubt, however, it could encompass sending to Borba for my headboard. Perhaps it could; I did not ask. We bought some wine with no intention of having it shipped. We drank it that night at dinner, and gave Borba an appreciative endorsement of its reputation.

Although we were recalcitrant about the churches, we stayed a long time in the car near the fountain, known as the Fonte das Bibas, of white marble. We were not looking at the fountain, however. We watched women coming to draw water there. Swathed in black with a rust-red urn on each head, they moved in a dramatic file of silhouettes against the white marble of the fountain. They stopped, of course, to join others in an exchange of gossip. When the individual silhouettes melted into a seated group and folds of their shawls and dresses dropped over the white fountain, we saw pictures follow one another like a roll of film. Alec and I did not want to intrude with our cameras. We wanted these pictures imprinted in our memory.

Group Leader finally persuaded us to leave by putting the car in motion.

Gina bent over her map; Brother T. fanned out some of the literature between us.

"Now," Gina said, "we prepurr ourselves for a next place, when I tell you what it will be. Estremôz," she announced, after brief consultation with her chart. Sophy urged Reader T. to delay a little.

"We're not coming to Estremôz for some time, so do look at this countryside."

On either side of us olive trees flanked the road and stretched back row upon row, giving way to cultivated fields in the distance. Between the ranks of olive trees and the road ran solid banks of wildflowers. We talked as we looked about the mystery of the cultivated fields. Very occasionally we had seen people working them. In the late afternoons we would meet and pass some traffic on the road, donkeys and the women carrying heavy loads, frequently of small fagots. These for the most part are of a kind of heather or furze that grows in the open, uncultivated plains and beneath the pine woods. They are dried, tied up in small bundles. It is the kindling for the country; many times no other firewood is used. In our little fireplaces at the Quinta dos Torres only this dried heather was supplied. It burns quickly and fiercely, but it does not last long.

Children, too, would be on the roads with the men and women; we had seen them laboring in the fields. Frequently small boys were included in a group of road workers. There is no perceptible concession made to their years. I have seen them pounding stone with heavy sledges. Nevertheless, we said to one another, the extent of cultivation—fields, roadsides, vineyards, cork forests, olive groves—was out of all proportion to the number of laborers. Another discrepancy that bewildered us was the distance between the areas of cultivation and habitation. Our respective native pictures, that is, of the United States and England, are of a farmhouse surrounded by tilled acres. In Portugal, we pointed out, we were driving miles between the villages with no visible habitations, but unbroken evidence of labor in the fields. "Who does it?" We queried one another. "Where do they come from? Where do they go?"

"Elves," was Alec's assertion. "They live underground and work at night."

"Then that is settled," Gina declared, "and now we hear about Estremôz."

Reader T. gave an apologetic cough, and I knew what was coming. He read: "The 'unmentionable' stands boldly on a hill, above the flattish, surrounding plain. The town is surrounded by seventeenth-century fortifications." He brightened suddenly. "Emily," he said, "now I have news for you. You will be reconciled. I can even mention the 'unmentionable' because for once I can identify and give you a history of—" he paused for emphasis—"*the castle*. It was built in 1281 by D. Diniz." Sophy broke in with a complaint this had not shed a beacon light as far as she was concerned, since she did not know who D. Diniz was. Reader T. added, "His widow, Saint Elizabeth of Portugal, died in 1336." Sophy rudely snorted. "If you think that clears everything up?" she queried.

I endeavored not to be smug. "I just happen to know," I said, offensively, the others told me. "Diniz is in English 'Dennis.' He was the King of Portugal and a very good one, except for a little flair-up of filial impiety when he led a rebellion against his father. After this impertinent talking back to his parent, he devoted his attentions to the development of agriculture so successfully he's come down in history as 'The Farmer or Laborer King.' Nevertheless, he evidently had time left over for light wines, dancing and other amusements that provoked his wife to leave his board and, certainly, his bed. She was Isabel of Aragon, also called Elizabeth— I don't know why. She left the court, of which she disapproved, and when Diniz died, entered a convent at Coimbra she'd founded. She was eventually made a saint, and called 'The Peacemaker.' Where she made peace, I don't know; she never did with her husband. A legendary meeting with him is celebrated to this day in the city of Tomar. It's called 'The Feast of the Tábuléiros.' On this special saint's day to Isabel or Elizabeth, a procession is held, so elaborate the community can't afford it every year. It takes place in October. Young girls in the procession wear on their heads high towers of freshly baked loaves of bread garlanded with roses. The basic structure of this tower is a long stick which runs through the loaves of bread, and at the back is fastened to some sort of cap that fits on the head of the young girl. She's always accompanied by her favorite swain. He walks beside and a little behind her, ready to steady the edifice if it threatens to topple. The loaves of bread and the roses are the symbols of the legend or miracle of Saint Elizabeth. On her way one day to visit the poor and bring them loaves of bread, she was accosted by her husband. He rudely demanded to be shown what she concealed in the skirt of her gown, since it was obvious from the way she was holding up the hem she was carrying something secret. Frightened, she let her hands fall and from the skirt spilled to the ground an armload of roses."

"Very interesting," Reader T. commented. "That is also the legend of Elizabeth of Hungary."

The town of Estremôz is within a rim of ramparts, packed earth on one side and faced with brick. There are beautiful gateways that permit entrance. One of the first things we saw was a display of the "Etruscan" water jars. The town is evidently one of the chief places of their manufacture. Along these narrow streets, too, we saw cottages, blinding white, without windows, but with spectacular chimneys. The chimney and door provide the only light and ventilation. Evidently the climate ranges from piercing cold in winter to stifling heat in summer. The absence of windows is a protection against both. We saw, too, many objects made of cork. I had not known cork has the quality of a Thermos bottle. Shepherds and men and women working in the fields carry either a hot lunch in a cork pail with a tight lid, or cool water in a cork flask. The shop I entered to look at some of the articles made of cork was owned by a man who spoke a little English. He told me not only of this quality of cork to retain heat or cold, but something of the cork industry. It is one of the major products of Portugal. Half of the world's supply is provided here. I knew the cork itself came from the trunks of the tree. We had seen forests of them, stripped, partially stripped and untouched. We had asked one another the reason for these degrees. This heaven-sent instructor told me the bark is stripped only once every nine years, and that the trees are planted far apart because they will not thrive without plenty of sun. When we had thought some of the forests we had seen were abandoned because the ground beneath looked uncared for, we were deeply mistaken. What we had seen were crops growing to utilize every foot of space, since the trees themselves must be at such a distance from one another. The crops are gathered before the acorns fall. When these drop to the ground the farmers turn loose their pigs to fatten on them.

When I came from the shop with my information about cork, and a few souvenirs of that product, I found I had completed the time allotted by Group Leader. I met the others on their way to the car. They told me they had seen the town hall, the Misericordia Church and the hospital, all built around the square in the center of the city. They talked about the beautiful staircase in the town hall and had seen *azulejos* paneled there and in the church. They told me the cloisters of the church and the hospital were two-storied, and lovely. We did not go up to the "unmentionable." Our journey that day had to be a long one in order to reach the inn in which we had reservations.

At Montemor-o-Novo we lunched on bread, local cheese and a glass of port at a little bistro. It was clean and very pleasant; the proprietor, evidently astonished at our choice of his place for a meal, gave us solicitous attention. He explained his was not a café, not a restaurant; it provided primarily drinks. We would not have known this from its appearance because it had front windows. We had learned after much questioning an open doorway leading to an interior of impenetrable blackness—no windows—was the local bar. There is no swinging sign outside; somewhere in the interior there must be people and lights. They are not visible through the always open door from the street.

The patrons of the bar in Montemor-o-Novo we saw were workmen, clean and politely curious about us. Through an open door in the back we could see the family of the proprietor at its noonday meal. When we told him we would appreciate very much anything he might have on hand, and suggested bread and cheese, he brought us a freshly baked loaf, a mound of butter and locally made cheese. When we had finished our meal, he escorted us to the bus. Discovering on the threshold the sun was very bright, he excused himself, ran back and, in an instant, reappeared with his umbrella. Opening this over his head, he took us to the bus, boosted the ladies in and waved us out of sight.

As we drove through a narrow street toward the outskirts of the village Sophy asked if we wanted to delay for a little sight-seeing.

"Reader T. will tell us what we must do," Gina decided. "Read." Brother T. read: "Picturesquely situated above the valley of the Canha and overlooked by the ruins of a large 'unmentionable.' Beyond the town the road forks."

"We fork," Gina said decidedly.

We drove on.

It was a long push, over not very good road. At Santarém over a high lattice bridge we crossed the Tagus again. We had not been on this side of it since we had left Lisbon for the Quinta dos Torres. We had taken a large scoop out of the south and now compass, bus and camera were pointed north. We did not pause at Santarém; this would be a separate excursion. In Alcobaça, however, though we did not get out of the car, we stopped for a considerable time by the railway station that seemed also to be a bus terminal. Buses came toward us and enveloped us—twenty-five, fifty, a hundred, perhaps even more came toward us in a caterpillar train. Each bus was filled to capacity with passengers of all ages; its roof was stacked with food hampers and blankets. The passengers hung out the windows on either side, laughing, waving at bystanders who, gathered to watch, lined the square. The front of each bus was banked with green boughs as if it had been camouflaged. Suddenly we knew, as my brother had said years ago, "What was going on." This was a pilgrimage to the Shrine of Fatima. Now we knew, too, the meaning of boughs we had seen over the doorway of cottages in every area we had traveled. Some of the boughs were green-leafed, others were brown, leafless. They marked a house from which someone, or perhaps the whole family had made recently, or long before, if the branch was withered, a pilgrimage to the Shrine of Fatima. On our first visit to the Church of the Jerónimos at Belém, Sophy and I had seen the altar at the statue of "Nossa Senhora de Fatima" or the "Virgem do Rosario," as she is sometimes called, ablaze with candles and gathered around her niche a group of little girls who were being made ready, we were told, for this pilgrimage. Remembering these things, the statue, the children, the boughs over the doorways whose meaning had puzzled us, and now the buses carrying them, I put it all together.

I told the others this was what we were seeing. Reader T. consulted his literature and immediately confirmed this. "From May to October," he said, "the days of pilgrimage are on the twelfth and thirteenth of each month. The road is extremely busy on these days."

While we watched and waited, Alec reminded us of the railway crossings at which our car had stood. There had not been many of them, but each one had meant a long pause in the day's occupation. Alec had clocked one wait of twenty minutes. During that time we had been implacably restrained by a woman guardian of the gates. She would permit no reckless dashing across the tracks, in the very face of a steam monster bearing down on us. When the monster finally came in sight it did not flash across our view. Invariably it looked to us like a toy train moving slowly. Long before we saw it, we would hear from its engine shrill cries of apprehension. Whenever I hear that high note from a European locomotive I have instantly a visual image of a woman looking at a mouse. It would be impossible to cross a railroad track in Portugal unaware of the sound of an approaching train; nevertheless Cerberus, guardian at the gates of Hell, might have been the tutor of Portuguese railway guards, almost always women.

"So, now," Gina said, "we will wait even longer without a guard. Brother T. will read to us about Fatima. I do not remember the details." While Reader selected from his literature the account he preferred, Sophy reminded me that on the plane coming from New

194

York she had discovered the woman sitting on her right in our row of three was on her way from Wichita, Kansas, to be a volunteer worker in a shop of sacred relics at the Shrine of Fatima.

Brother T. read from Baedeker:

On May 13th in 1917, and thereafter on the 13th of each month until October, the "Virgem do Rosario" appeared to three shepherds' children. Since this, Fatima has been visited by countless pilgrims, and has grown accordingly. Impressive candlelight processions take place at night. On the edge of a huge square stands the small Chapel of the Apparition with a statue of the Virgin. The imposing Cathedral which terminates the square in the background was begun on the 13th of May in 1928. It is surrounded by extensive monastic and hospital buildings, as well as many stalls for the sale of many devotional objects.

Here is another account from a travel folder:

In a grazing field, two miles from Fatima on the 13th of May, 1917, three little children, a brother and sister named Francisco and Jacinta, and their cousin Lucia were leading a flock of sheep to pasture. Having seen a flash of lightning, and foreseeing a thunder storm, they made up their minds to gather the sheep and return to their village. They had taken but a few steps when they were surrounded by a shining light, and suddenly saw the figure of a very beautiful young woman above a little holm-oak tree. During the summer, from May to October, on the 13th day of each month, with the exception of August, the figure appeared again, and always at the same hour of noon. The children were asked to say the rosary, to do penance, to make sacrifices, and to procure the conversion of sinners. The Vision promised that the war would soon come to an end, requested the building of a church there, recommended the devotion to the Immaculate Heart of Mary be

195

spread to the whole world, and especially Russia, and said if these requests were not fulfilled, another war would be inevitable. She promised those that received Holy Communion, said the Rosary, and meditated fifteen minutes on the mysteries of the Rosary on the first Saturday of the following month, would go to Heaven. Though arrested, persecuted and threatened, the three little children did not deny their statement. The news spread like fire. During the last apparition in October, about 70,000 people were at Fatima. An extraordinary phenomenon took place, namely, the so-called Miracle of the Sun, which had been announced several months before by Lucia. Among the on-lookers there were freethinkers, who had gone to Fatima for the sole purpose of criticism. Even these had to admit the strange phenomenon. The color, the movement, the brightness and the dancing of the sun, all these might be natural facts, but one miraculous circumstance remained, the fact was that these happenings had been foretold with the greatest exactitude. Today Lucia is a Carmelite nun. The brother and sister, her cousins, are dead, but their lives had been transformed in such a way after the apparition, and due to a vision of Hell, that their beatification and canonization are being considered. . . . This is the story of the most unusual religious event which has taken place on the earth in this century, and the origin of the most celebrated Catholic shrine of our time, Fatima, a small village located less than 100 miles north of Lisbon in the friendly land of Portugal.

Sydney Clark, in his *All the Best in Spain and Portugal,* says:

I will only add that Lucia, the Carmelite nun, has two sisters living in Aljustrel, and also her aged parents still live there. I went to see the eldest sister, a humble weaver, and asked her, through a translator, to describe the miracle of October 13th, 1917. She eagerly did so, explaining among other things, that "The sun went in circles, so close, and then it came down so close we could almost reach up and touch it." Numerous newspaper reporters of large and respected journals have given substantially the same report.

I went to the home of Lucia's parents—her father is a wood-cutter—and though they were not in, I had a good look at the place. Its poverty was the most evident thing about it. The racket-complex has certainly not vitiated the character of those at the core of the Fatima phenomena.

Reader T. added one bit of information: "The great pilgrimage, sometimes attended by hundreds of thousands of people from all over the world, is on May 13th. Charabancs are chartered. The roof of each bus is piled with hampers of food for three or four days. Fatima has few hotels and restaurants. The pilgrims eat and sleep out on the open hillside."

The day we waited in Alcobaça for the procession of buses to pass was the thirteenth of May.

SIXTEEN

The Estalagem do Cruzeiro at Aljubarrota is on the main road between Alcobaça and Batalha. Miss Sousa, because she was a friend of the owners' family, had telephoned from the Quinta dos Torres and accomplished reservations for us on the night of the thirteenth. She had recommended it, adding it was usually filled, because it was excellent, but she would be glad to intercede on our behalf. This was the reason we had not dallied along the way, lest by not claiming them we would lose our reservations. Thanks to Miss Sousa's guarantee of our dependability, rooms had been kept for us, though we were several hours later than the time we had set for our arrival.

Our rooms were adjacent to one another, each opening on a balcony. The balcony extended over one side of the building; the section allotted to each room set off by low railings—easy, we discovered, to step over. The view was charming. Immediately below us lawn and gardens yielded to meadows, vineyards and olive groves in a valley, merging into hills and mountains beyond. In the far distance between two summits, we could see a V-shaped slice of sea, bright, sparkling blue.

Within a short time after our arrival, we had lifted chairs and two small tables over the railing barriers to make a community room for the "shoebag hour." Gina, established with her thimbleful of wine in a glass of soda, assured us the pleasant balcony, her fatigue and the wine would certainly intoxicate her; she must be very careful.

The large, attractive dining room was staffed by young waitresses, eager, quick, and without a word of English in their vocabulary. The dinner and the service were excellent.

At the end of the meal Alec, having selected an orange, discovered he had no knife. He would ask for one, he said, from the waitress. Like a volcanic eruption all of us, except Alec, simultaneously half-rising from our seats, protested. Gina's dictum was the loudest and most emphatic of all.

"You will not ask that word again," she pronounced with finality.

To reconcile Alec, I offered to peel his orange, since I had a knife at my place. I assured him I could do it as well as the Portuguese. We had watched in other places their way of eating fruit. It is done very delicately. First, a fork is inserted in an orange by which it is held. Then with a knife the top and the bottom are cut off. The orange is placed upright, sliced down all around, then across, making small quarters. Each of these is removed by a fork, like a slice of melon, and is eaten from the fork. I have seen a banana slit down its length, still with the skin on, then cut out in small pieces with a knife, and eaten with a fork. Our method of peeling and eating the fruit while holding it in the hand must seem to them barbaric.

This time, I told Alec, I was not going to adopt the Portuguese method for his orange; I would need practice. I would "prepurr" it for him as my father used to peel an orange to my delight and fascination as a child. I had never tried it, but certainly I could do it, and Alec, not to mention the others, would be fascinated. I would remove the skin all in one curling sinuous peel. The trick, I explained, was never to allow it to break off. Therefore, you had to cut deeper under the skin than you would do if you were peeling it by hand. Explaining this, I had a spellbound audience as I began my feat. No one spoke as I worked; I was nervous, but I cut steadily, round and round. I came to the end, delicately, slowly, made the last circle, and held triumphantly a spiral of unbroken peel.

"There, you see," I said, dropping it on Alec's plate. "I can do the trick—isn't it pretty?"

199

"Very pretty," Alec acknowledged. "Where is the orange?"

Startled, I looked back at my plate. In the center of it was a yellow nugget about the size of a walnut. The rest of the orange was on the inside of the peeling. I transferred the walnut to Alec's plate.

"I told you," I said, "you have to cut a little deep to make sure of getting the skin off in one piece."

"Next time," Alec said, "I shall ask for a knife."

Alcobaça is only six kilometers from Aljubarrota. We drove back to it at about noon on the day following our arrival. We had been lazy during the morning, breakfasting on the balcony and writing letters in the sun. We were relaxed, indolent. We had reached a stopping place of several days, no need to push our sight-seeing. We would look at the cathedral in Alcobaça and then after lunch somewhere in the town, drive perhaps to Nazaré.

You do not look at the cathedral in Alcobaça, that is, the Monastery of Santa Maria. You stop in your tracks at first sight. You stare up and up and up, beyond its flight of stairs wide as the façade of our *estalagem*, up the great carved doorways—by now the back of your head is between your shoulder blades—and on and on to the peak.

I was not surprised when Reader T. told us it is the largest in the country, and that the entire church is of uniform height. When he told us, further, that according to one writer, it has the largest and "one of the most insipid façades in Portugal" I was both surprised and displeased. He quickly and thoughtfully diverted me by telling me the plan of the abbey is an enormous square; it contains, in addition to the church, a Hall of the Kings, a library, a kitchen, a hospital and five cloisters.

When we had finally accepted the size of the façade and rubbed our aching neck muscles, we moved inside, and stopped again, necks snapping against our shoulders. Ahead of us stretched parallel lines of white columns that rose up out of sight until our heads were well back again. The columns stretch into the distance until they seem the very definition of parallel lines that never meet, even

200

in infinity. If there is color in the nave, I have no recollection of it. My vivid image is of an avenue of clustered pillars, white, reaching up into Gothic arches, a vast emptiness of austere majesty.

As we moved down the aisles, Brother T. whispered, "The monastery was originally founded in 1152 as an offering of thanksgiving for the recapture of Santarém from the Mussulmans, though there is a discrepancy of a few years among those who have written about it."

Brother T. loves figures. He also whispered to us the kitchen measures 102 feet.

We were not moving aimlessly. We, like the girl in the song, knew where we were going. We had directions from our Researcher, Reader T., where to find the tombs of Don Pedro I and his mistress, Inés de Castro. They would be in the chapel, to the right of the high altar.

We knew the strange, savage story of this very ill-starred love. Brother T. had reread it the night before during the "shoebag hour."

Don Pedro was the grandson of Diniz, or Dennis, whose castle we had seen at Estremôz. He was married to Dona Constanza. She came, as a bride, from Castile, bringing to Portugal among her ladies-in-waiting a beautiful young woman whose name was Inés Pires de Castro. She was known as "Heron Neck" or "Colo de Gãrc," evidently describing the set of her lovely head. Pedro, the husband, fell in love with "Heron Neck." His wife, endeavoring to block an attachment, chose her to be their son's godmother. When Inés refused, or was unable to permit this honor to stifle her love, she was exiled. Four years later, the wife Constanza died. Inés returned immediately to Portugal. Near Coimbra she lived with Pedro openly and happily for ten years, bearing him three children.

Into this placid domesticity came renewed threats of war with Castile. Inés was a Castilian. She might influence her husband to make an alliance that would absorb his country. Pedro's father was begged by his court to put Inés out of the way. The story is that he agreed, and went with the court to Coimbra. Once there, he could not bring himself to murder, and rode away. Leaders of the party that had almost persuaded him, and were themselves determined she should be removed, finally secured from him an order for her execution. These murderers, with Alfonso's consent, rode back to Coimbra. Self-appointed executioners, they cut her throat.

Pedro, in savage fury, waged civil war upon his father, and was victorious. Five years later, when he as the heir had become King, he sent for those executioners who had retreated for safety to Castile. When they came to him at Santarém, he had their hearts taken from their bodies. One version of the story says Don Pedro, himself, ate these hearts. He had only begun his siege of vengeance. He had Inés exhumed, ordered her skeleton to be dressed in the robes of a queen. When this was done, she was placed in an open coffin, with a crown on her skull. Then the King ordered all the nobles of Portugal with their wives to come to the church at Coimbra. When they had assembled, they were locked in, any means of escape cut off. They were then compelled by the King to move forward, one by one, kneel before the skeleton of Inés and pay her the homage due a queen. This completed, the church was unlocked.

The coffin was brought out in state and the nobles ordered to follow it in procession from Coimbra to Alcobaça. The roadside was flanked by peasants placed there with lighted torches. The end of this macabre procession and the final resting place for Inés was in this Monastery of Alcobaça, in a magnificent tomb Pedro had made ready for her. On his death, by his own orders, he was laid in a tomb in the position to lie close to his love, but feet to feet. He had said when Judgment Day came the two lovers would sit up simultaneously and the first sight for each would be the face of the beloved.

The tombs themselves are magnificent, but they are also exquisite in the delicacy of their carving. They are in white, and they rest on crouching animals. On the side of Inés' tomb are carved monstrous figures of evil, supposedly effigies of her murderers.

The kitchen of the cloisters looks to be every foot of the 102-foot square Brother T. had reported. An early writer called it "the most distinguished temple of gluttony in all Europe." It is tiled in pale blue from floor to high roof. A swift little stream runs through the center of the room along a stone course, emptying into a large pool that contained the fish for Friday. Along one wall are other large stone tanks under taps for washing the meat before it was cooked. The space for roasting will hold an ox.

We lunched very well at a little restaurant across the street, and afterward drove on to Nazaré.

Nazaré is thirteen kilometers from Alcobaça by road, and hundreds of miles by imagination. To have stood reduced to midget size in the awesome nave of the monastery, conjuring up the life and the people of its heyday, and then, within a few minutes, be transported by our rolling bus to a scene of vividly colored animation, is quite an exercise in elasticity and adaptability. Leaning against the sea wall, looking down on the beach below me, I had a curious experience that lasted only an instant, but was a real suspension in time. The people below me, the boats coming in, by their shape and color were of the period I had just been restoring in the church.

We might have come on a day when a tourist excursion invaded Nazaré. Then the sight of buses in the square would have put me firmly in the contemporary scene. By happy circumstance, we were the only invaders, and since our own bus always seemed to me to be a preposterous caravan, I could dismiss its presence as only a slight incongruity in the landscape. The people I watched below me were the first I had seen in Portugal of uniformity of type. They have black hair, a long thin nose, scarcely indented at the forehead. The Nazaré's is a classic Greek profile; almost every one of them near enough for me to see closely had gray eyes.

When Reader T. told me they are thought to be of Phoenician stock, I was not in the least surprised. What would make any newcomer blink his eyes, and shake his head in a moment's disbelief, is the impact of the splashing waves of colors. After the sight for days of women swathed shapelessly in black, the men in black, and almost as shapeless, the sight of yellow, green, blue, red, pink, orange—as Gina would say, "everything what you can imagine"—makes for a little joyful giddiness.

If Portuguese water jugs are Etruscan, the noses of Nazaré citizens Phoenician, I suppose Scottish plaid trousers for Nazaré fishermen are consistently outlandish. I doubt the plaid itself would be recognized by the chief of a Scottish clan, though the legend is they are derived from the kilts of Scottish soldiers Wellington brought to Portugal. The plaids of Nazaré are large squares, but they are in red, pink, green, yellow, orange, blue. The shirt worn with these can be of any color, so long as it is sufficiently startling in contrast. The women wear seven petticoats, each a different color, over these a pleated skirt that is stretched tight over the hips. Women in other parts of Portugal wear a bright shawl over a black dress. The women of Nazaré wear a black fringed shawl over a brilliant-colored dress. In Nazaré, too, the shawl is not drawn flat over the head. It is shaped, and I do not know what sustains it, to a sort of pyramid above the forehead. Universally they wear gold earrings, circles, half-moons or round medallions that carry the embossed image of a saint.

The fishing boats are as brightly colored as the clothes. Which was the inspiration I do not know. The boats were like the ones Sophy and I had seen on the Tagus coming into the harbor at Lisbon—long, narrow, with high-pointed, sloping prows, painted in over-all patterns and colors, usually including a pair of eyes, by tradition, to assist the boat in locating fish.

For an appreciable period of time, and understandably, I think, I did not notice pairs of oxen lying on the beach. Large as the beasts are, they were, after all, not painted in bright plaid. They ruminate among women, children, babies and fishermen. When the boats come in, a man or a boy rouses them, leads them to the water's edge, backs them close to a prow, fastens them as they would be yoked to a cart. They drag a boat well above the water's edge.

The social life of the town centers around the beach. I watched a number of sewing circles. Their members knitted, embroidered or mended, laughing, exchanging gossip, minding their own and one another's children, as on their outskirts men were repairing nets. For untangling fishing lines, the men engaged the services of a small boy, probably a son learning the rudiments of his father's means of livelihood, which he would one day follow.

For the only time I can remember on any trip, I did not at first sight of a new scene reach for my camera. I had hung it around my neck when I had left the car, and there it stayed. I think I was stunned by the colors and the shifting kaleidoscopic patterns they made. I stood by the sea wall, and looked, and looked again. I do not know how long I had been there when the others joined me, nor had I been aware of their scattering. I only knew they had gone away because of their return with firecracker-poppings of information, and delight of discovery. I must come quickly, they urged, to see a dear bride and groom they had watched emerge from the church, and set out on a promenade around the village. The young man, they said, was in full evening clothes, the bride in conventional white, including shoes. They were evidently the first she had worn, because she frequently had to stop, and leaning on the arm of her understanding husband, remove them for a brief interlude of comfort. I must come and see old women sitting in doorways, minding toddling children, and shops where the trousers and shirts of the fishermen could be bought, along with many other articles of homecraft.

Alec was astounded I had not, as yet, taken any pictures. He had already used three films. I might, I thought, have been playing the game I knew as a child called "Still Pond No More Moving." Now I was released and eager to move about. I saw the bridal couple. My friends had not told me they were accompanied. The mother of the bride walked beside her, on the outside; the groom's mother on the far end of the quartet held her son's arm. I photographed them, and then hurried along the beach, taking picture after picture, each group, beyond the one I was snapping, demanding by its charm another shot. No one paid much attention. Sometimes

young women would look up from their sewing and laugh spontaneously, not as a pose.

When I came back to the sea wall that divided the beach from the road, I found Alec taking pictures of a group of four little children. They had stopped playing, and were standing still at his request. The youngest member, a little boy of about four, was responding with particular generosity. Each time Alec, by demonstration, requested a smile, he complied wholeheartedly, simultaneously lifting his shift to disclose, and point to, with a chubby finger, his navel. Alec has eight or ten likenesses of that anatomic area. He told me where I would find Gina and the others. He was going to have a few more "goes" at the child, in the hope of catching the youngest with his shirt down.

He found us a few minutes later. We had bought lovely baskets the size of an ordinary knitting bag with a straw framework, but both sides of solid, heavy wool embroidery—in bright colors of course. Sophy and I each had a mound of small objects for purchase, but Gina had moved into a larger field. She would buy, she said, a skirt, such as these women wore, and a blouse like theirs, colored skirt, white blouse, with full sleeves and low neck. This would be a costume she would find wearable and attractive when she would be on summer holiday in Greece. With Sophy's help, she had learned she could have these made to order and to her measurements. They would be finished in two days. She could return for them, or they would be shipped. Alec, coming in at the end of this transaction, made no protest. He was enchanted with the models Gina showed him, pleased they would not be burdensome in weight, and could even be shipped. He gave a benign smile of approval that changed with startling rapidity to an expression more of astonishment than displeasure, when the shop owner took Gina's measurements. The method was simple and direct, with no nonsense about a tape measure. The gentleman simply clasped his arms around Gina's bust, then moved them rapidly down to encircle her hips. Gina, in his embrace, looked over his shoulder at Alec with a mirrored reflection of his surprise.

Before either of them could comment on the procedure, the measurer released his hold, stepped back, nodded several times with a happy smile, conveying he now had the exact girths and would proceed with his work.

While we were making purchases, Brother T. had slipped off on one of his customary sorties of exploration. He came toward us as we left the shop.

"I've been reading about a sanctuary called 'The house of Our Lady of Nazareth.' It has a pretty story." He told it. In 1182 a hunter in pursuit of his quarry was pushing his horse at a hard gallop, when suddenly he was nearly thrown by the abrupt stop of the animal. An early morning fog was so heavy the rider was unable to see beyond the horse's head, but out of the mist emerged a Vision of Mary. She held up a gently deterring hand, and then melted into the fog. Dismounting in bewilderment, the huntsman inched his way forward a little, and discovered he and his horse had been stopped at the very brink of a precipice. On that spot the sanctuary was built.

Brother T. seemed troubled by my insistence we visit it. During his telling of the story, we had walked the length of the street, where cottages and shops obstruct a far view. Coming into the open square at its end, Brother T. pointed.

"There it is," he addressed me. "A funicular will take you, or you can climb it by car on a back, circling road."

I took one look at the funicular that was crawling up the face of the cliff like a bug. I urged my friends, "You go, not me. I'm returning to the beach." They too chose the beach.

"The views," Gina said, "are everywhere. Nazaré is only here."

Once more we strolled the shore front. Women passed us, their skirts swinging, their heads high, and on top large trays of silver fish. We leaned over the wall and watched the oxen drawing up the boats. Now the fleet was in. The activity, the swirl of color we had first seen was multiplied far beyond my capacity in arithmetic. Women ran to the boat belonging to their men, soon reappearing up the beach, trays of fish on their heads. Pairs of men carried between them great containers of fish to a place on the beach where they would be sorted. Other men hauled off the boats and spread on the sand nets to be mended. Oxen pulled, and were shouted at. Men called from boat to boat the news of their catch.

I had turned my back on the scene for a moment to retie a scarf around my head. A light breeze had stiffened, my hair was blowing. Across the street from me I saw a little boy of perhaps six slap a little girl, who could not have been over four. He slapped her repeatedly. Gina was standing beside me, her back to the wall. I went across the street, with speed and purpose. I yield to Gina the chronicling of the next few minutes; it was contained in a letter she wrote to my daughter, who, in turn, shared it with me. This is what Gina wrote:

I imagine you have heard all about our expedition in Portugal. I am sure that Emily told you how I have almost found myself on top of the bull at the Bullfight and what a dilapidated sight Emily and I were when we were pushed out from one of the exits. I expect you have also heard about the fights Alec and I had with our map reading, but *certainly* she has never told you about her *pièce de résistance* when we were in Nazaré.

As you know, the official interpreter of our party was Sophy: she has done very well and we were all very proud of her. Of course Emily was so confident with Sophy's Portuguese that she also thought she could speak the language!

So one day in Nazaré, a little fisher village near Lisbon, we were walking very happy near the sea looking at the wonderful costumes of the women and the marvellous brown faces of the fishermen. Emily was busy, busy taking photos one after the other, when suddenly on the corner of a road she saw a little girl crying because a little boy was beating her head. Emily's motherly feelings became so strong at this moment that she rushed up to the little boy and, forgetting completely that she did not speak one word of Portuguese, began to shout at him, shaking her finger in front of his nose, in a terrifying voice, and this is what came out: : "FFFOU MMMUHHMMM TSCHOU UNNNGGHHTTRRR UHNGGUGGGUUGGU BAD! BAD!!"

The little boy stopped beating the little girl and became completely frozen with his hand in the air: his eyes became bigger and bigger and then suddenly he run for his life up a little street. Emily was so pleased with her success that she turned with a big smile to the little girl and gave her a candy from her bag, saying in a lovely soft and kind voice "BOOLOOBOU?" "SHUSHUMUMU?" "NANANA *ANY MORE.*" The little girl stopped crying, but looked now even more frightened than when she was being beaten. Now Emily was really proud of herself: Two big conversations. So now she turned to three fisherwomen that were sitting on the ground watching the scene and began to explain to them the whole story—"BRDRAT FFFRRRNNN SHHRRR FFRAF-FRAAFROU, *THE BAD BOY!!*" The three women looked at Emily with open mouths and did not move an eyelash. This Emily took as a sign of admiration and returned to us with great dignity.

I said to Emily, "What were you saying?"

"Why," she said, "I had to give the little boy a lesson and then I explained to the women how naughty he was and that they must not let him do such a thing again."

"Oh, I see," I said, "and in which language you spoke to them?"

"In Portuguese, of course!" answered Emily.

So you see that it is not always me that is the cause of our aventures, but Emily plays also a big role in these happenings; of course she will not mention this in her book, but I insist that her family *au moins* knows what happens!

211

SEVENTEEN

Only within the last few years have I realized my most vivid memories are stamped by sound, not sight. Thinking of a rhythmic squeak and hearing in that inmost ear of memory its pitch of tone, I can be a child again, rocking in the swing that hung suspended by chains from the ceiling of my grandfather's front porch in Muncie, Indiana. Then I can see the green wicker of the other porch furniture, and smell the syringa from the bushes that hedged the porch. The sound comes first. A child's laughter takes me into one of the most beautiful courtyards I ever saw. Its cobblestoned floor was dappled in sunlight, its far end held a broad, curving staircase. Over the banister flowed a golden waterfall of mimosa. A little girl stood on one of the steps, leaning so far over, the mimosa closed around all but her laughing face. Her hair was very black, her skin a pale tan, with red just beneath in her cheeks. She laughed because she was trying to throw into the open mouth of a little boy standing on the cobblestones below small pieces she tore from an orange she was eating. I hear the free, chortling laughter; then I remember the courtyard and those children were on the Island of Rhodes.

The village of Aljubarrota is sharp, clear and permanent in my memory, because of the sounds I heard there.

Alec, as usual, was the first to hear. He wakened me, calling softly from his adjoining balcony, sometime between midnight and dawn. He was saying over and over, "Wake up, Emily, a nightingale."

Then I heard notes tumbling over one another like a brook in

213

spring when the snow has melted. I had never heard it before, but sitting up in bed I thought, with my eyes smarting, my throat tight, Alec need not have said, "a nightingale." I would have known. This drowning sweetness, not like other birds' piping, but layer upon layer of sound, could only come from the throat of that bird, and they lied who said any human being sang like a nightingale.

Alec, bless his unselfishness, roused the others. I sat in my bed. I could have moved, I suppose, but it did not occur to me to go out to the balcony. Even if it had been possible to see the bird in the night, the sound was all I wanted. I might have been a dry cistern opened to a sudden rain, and like a summer rain, the nightingale stopped in full song. There was no tapering off to a drizzle of notes. I do not know how many minutes the sweet drenching lasted, but suddenly it had stopped. I lay back, surprised by an enveloping lassitude. I would wait for the song to come again. I slept instead, and was wakened again some hours later. Now it was early morning; light came through the open door from my balcony. Birds were chattering, but one clear note from a distance rose above their shrill talk. I rose, too, with a leap. This time I was the harbinger. I ran to the balcony, and called to either side, not loud, but insistently, "Wake up. Cuckoo."

My friends stumbled out, pulling on dressing gowns. I retreated briefly and hastily to fling on the covering I had forgotten. We listened to that blithe spirit, that wandering voice call clear and sweet, "Thirty-one o'clock," returned to our rooms. I slept again.

This time we all slept long and late. We did not assemble on the balcony for breakfast until perhaps half-past nine. The sun was bright and warm, dissolving the mist in the valley below us, slowly drawing it up to the mountaintops. We were talking about the nightingale's song when Alec held up his hand. "Listen," he said, "what is it?" Our duller ears caught it then—fresh, clear notes in tune.

"It is not a bird, it is a tune," Gina said. "Someone is whistling." And then, excitedly, "It is Fado music."

We left the table hurriedly to stand at the balcony railing, leaning over its rim, searching the wide, misty landscape. Sophy pointed her finger, arm outstretched, a little to our right. "Look," she said, "there. In that vineyard. See the man?"

We were not sure at first he was the whistler, but we could not find anyone else within our wide range. This figure was moving slowly, but not aimlessly; he was evidently occupied.

The air was not quite clear of mist, but as we debated and questioned what he was doing, the sun brightened, flicking away the last of the haze. We knew then this was our man, and what he was doing. A heavy tank was strapped to his back; he held in one hand the nozzle of a hose that came from the tank, in the other a handle of some sort. He was a farmer spraying his vineyard on that Sunday morning, and whistling Fado. With the handle he pumped spray from the tank, at the same time directing the hose. I would have thought such effort must interrupt his breathing. From the unbroken melody that came by way of his lungs, this man might have been dangling a yo-yo. Note upon note, measure upon measure, the tune floated over the valley and up to us.

"In perfect pitch, too," Gina commended.

He came to the end of a row of vines, and of his song. Over the balcony rail we applauded and cheered. He jumped visibly, looked around, then up, found us, laughed aloud, bowed so that the tank threatened to slide over the top of his head, straightened, moved to the next row, and with head thrown back, sang, loud, strong and clear, another song.

"I think he does not breathe at all," was Gina's decision.

We returned to our table, and to our breakfast, but the songs came up to us, one after another until, I suppose, the spraying was done. When we realized there would be no more music, we went to the railing again, giving him another round of applause, and a chorus of "Bravos!" He had been looking for us, standing still. He bowed again to his happy audience, waving the hose above his head in the salute an artist makes to the top gallery of the opera house. He walked away, down and beyond a row of his vines.

To name the place and the *estalagem,* I must refer to my diary, but for all my life, I shall remember the look of it, because of a nightingale that sang, a cuckoo that called, and a man who, spraying his vineyards, whistled and sang Fado.

We were at the Great Church at Batalha in time for the eleven o'clock mass. Batalha is only fifteen or twenty minutes north of Aljubarrota, following the road our *estalagem* faced. History has brought the two places even closer together than their actual mileage, because the Monastery of Our Lady of Victory which includes the Great Church was established and the buildings begun by King John I in 1388. It commemorates his great triumph over the Castilians, at the Battle of Aljubarrota when Portugal finally won its independence from Spain.

The Betsy Ross of that revolution was the wife of a baker whose shop was somewhere along the road between the two towns. This baker's wife, according to legend, was an active and fierce combatant. She is said to have run from her shop as the Spaniards were passing and killed twelve of them with a long-handled shovel that on more quiet baking days was used to carry the loaves in and out of the oven.

Batalha's monastery is counted Portugal's finest national shrine, and the culmination of exuberant Manueline decoration. The magnificent front is of stone, incredibly refined in intricate carving to the texture of lace. The carvings twine and overlap one another, rising higher and higher so that their delicacy is absorbed into a vast splendor.

Sophy, suggesting we try to see one church peopled, had timed our arrival for eleven o'clock, when we knew there would be a service. Marveling at the glory of the exterior, we realized members of the congregation were coming up behind, women and little girls pausing at the threshold to put a scarf over their heads— always of exquisite lace, white or black. Alec suggested he and I go inside. Perhaps we could take some pictures before the church filled. The others followed us. Sophy told us later, with some

216

bitterness, she and her companions had very nearly somersaulted by the suddenness with which Alec and I stopped in the doorway. We stopped because we were struck motionless. I do not know their comparative measurements, but the nave at Batalha looked nearly as long as the astonishing one at Alcobaça. The floor of this one was occupied in length and total breadth by people. I am glad I did not see both these great monuments either empty or filled. The contrast made each the more vivid. As at Alcobaça, there was no furnishing in all this vast interior. The congregation stood or knelt on the stone floor. Before kneeling, however, each man took from his pocket a handkerchief and spread it on the stone floor very precisely where it would protect his knees. Watching from the door this wave of people swelling to their feet and subsiding again to their knees, I saw how clean they were, how soberly and reverently all of them, even the very little children, followed the service, and how shabby and worn the soles of their shoes, turned toward us in the doorway, row upon row, as the congregation knelt.

We tiptoed away from the service in order to see the Founder's Chapel that is on the right of the entrance. Beyond a magnificent doorway, the arresting sight in the center of the chapel is the sarcophagus of John I, Victor of Aljubarrota. His Queen, Philippa, daughter of old John of Gaunt, lies beside him, her hand in his. Each wears a crown, and they lie under a canopy of delicate tracery. Around them are the tombs of the Infantes, including the great Henry the Navigator. Each tomb bears the motto of its occupant. As we came outside again from the Founder's Chapel, Brother T. told us we must find the chapter house. He did not tell us what would be there; it would be an unexpected sight. It was both unexpected and moving. It is the tomb of the Unknown Soldier guarded by two sentinels.

The unfinished, or octagonal chapels, as they are sometimes called, are another unexpected and beautiful sight. Their unexpectedness is in their incompletion, because they are roofless. One writer about them, Reader told us, asserts the great Manuel, whose architects decorated the walls and the doors with this particular ebullience, became diverted to the great church he was building at Belém, and the work in these chapels was abandoned. It is for this reason the munificence of their extravagance and the glorious carving are exposed to rain and sun. Each pointed arch that bounds the cloister is interrupted by four slender pillars. They support an overpiece like an open fan of delicate carving. We were in the charming cloister garden, a miniature labyrinth—its zigzag paths outlined by low, clipped hedges—when Sophy reminded us the Greek Ambassador to Portugal and his wife were coming to lunch with us at the *estalagem*. If we were to be there when they arrived, we must leave. On the road back, I said I found it difficult to realize we were within two hours of Lisbon by car, though we had been driving nearly a week. Gina offered to show me on the map how it was possible. Sophy forestalled her.

"Don't bother. She won't understand it. One look at a map and she becomes an illiterate."

I changed the subject by pointing out a reminder of home that brought no surge of nostalgia. Local artisans make and display along the roadsides pottery articles for sale in the same lack of taste in color and design that affronts the eye of sight-seeing motorists in the United States.

My carping dissatisfaction with some aspects of "the folks at home" was aggravated by our delightful guests at lunch. Mrs. Lappas spoke English with the ease and fluency of an English or American woman. Gina whispered to me she spoke some four, perhaps more, other languages in the same manner. Her native tongue, of course, was Greek. The Ambassador spoke English only a little less easily. He could with equal facility, Gina told me, move into several other tongues. He had recently been Ambassador to one of the countries in South America. Their charming daughter in her early teens speaks English as her mother does, Spanish, French and Greek, as if the phenomenon had occurred that she had been born in each of these countries.

"Americans are yokels in language," I told Sophy after the guests

218

had gone. "What makes me simmer is, for the most part, we don't care. Like all ignorant provincials we like our provincialism. We say, 'Oh, you'll always find someone who speaks English.' Why should we, for heaven's sake? Why does everyone have to come to us in our language? It's so arrogant, as well as provincial. We ought to start American children in the first grade learning another language in addition to their own by ear and imitation, the way they've learned their own. I've no patience with people who say, 'I've no ear for language.' They must have, or they wouldn't be speaking at all. They didn't learn English from the written word. Why have I a Middle Western accent, and you a Philadelphia one? Because those are the places in which we were born. We speak as we heard it in our childhood."

Sophy assured me she was in no position to contradict or soothe, because she agreed.

Flattened a little by her inability to provide me with argument, I subsided. For the most part, I am a devoted American, and I think I know my country rather well. Born in the Middle West, educated in the East, I have traveled the length and breadth of it every winter over the last many years on speaking tours. I make this round of the Creamed Chicken circuit because of my love of the country, and the people in it. I cherish the opportunity it gives me to meet, talk to and make friends with every section, and heaven knows our country is sectionalized. I do not love the American who comes abroad with ignorance and arrogance.

I had made a speech; I saw Sophy furtively looking at the open page of the book she had been reading. I released her attention. I gathered up the day's contribution of literature from Brother T. and settled myself and my accumulation on the balcony. Within perhaps half a minute, I exclaimed aloud, evidently so forcefully it brought Sophy to the door with an irritated inquiry about my vehemence.

"A coincidence that's so preposterous you couldn't put it in a story," I told her. "I finished my outburst to you; I settled myself to read something that would distract me from my irritation.

219

Out of all the pile Brother T. has left, I pick up the London *Times*, I start turning the pages, and literally this is the first thing that catches my eye. It's a piece, unsigned. It just says, 'From a correspondent,' and it's titled 'Another Housewife in Portugal.' The subtitle is 'Pleasant Experience Over More Than Half a Century.' But this is the paragraph: 'In this country [Portugal] where courtesy is the rule, and where the right kind of approach instantly wins a generous response, the discourtesy of many foreigners fills those of us who live here permanently with mortification. We often wish that before people were allowed to come to Portugal, they were given lessons in how to behave in a land not their own, and even sufficient instruction in the language to teach them words for a little basic conversation and courtesy.' "

Monday was a market day in Alcobaça. We had intended to stop in the town only a few minutes in order to buy the travelers' trivia—stamps, postcards and, for Brother T., a tube of tooth paste. He had explained he was not really in need of one, but had been captivated by the piece of advertising literature that accompanied a sample tube provided by the inn. I doubt there are many tourists to Portugal who have read it. Brother T. read aloud the English translation. This piece of literature, handed on for my collection, measures about 3 x 2 inches.

This was what had pleased him. We found it pleasing, too. "Thanks to its quality efficiency and agreeable taste, it is appreciated, and it was studied in harmony with the Portuguese liking."

Alec accompanied Brother T. to the chemist's for the purpose of purchasing fluid for our cigarette lighters. Gina and I strolled along the street while Sophy went ahead in the car to have the gasoline tank replenished. When we had reconvened, Alec reported only 50 per cent success. Brother T. had his tooth paste, but the chemist had been unable to supply fluid. Sophy asked the garage attendant applying a hose to the tank if he could tell us where we might find the lighter fuel. Sophy translated to us the man's scorn of the purchase of such a commodity. If we would give him our lighters, he would be delighted to fill them. Diverting the hose from the car, he applied it to each of our receptacles with splashing generosity. Each was, of course, a blazing torch the first time it was subsequently lighted.

We could not move on from the town when there were market booths to visit. They were set up under trees at the side of the church. Sophy parked the car and we strolled among displays of fish, fruit, flowers, craft, small livestock. Alec remained close at Gina's heels to avert large purchases. At the end of our promenade, he made us wait while he wrote in his diary covering the page of May 16 in large letters: "Between 10:30 and 11 A.M. in the market at Alcobaça, Sophy, Emily and Gina did not make a single purchase."

Óbidos was the objective of our day's excursion. We knew it was a walled town, but on the way Gina asked Reader to give us more information. He demurred a little.

"We're having such a pleasant time," he protested. At Gina's insistence, the amenable man said, "Its old embattled walls and towers and the fifteenth-century aqueduct are dominated by an impressive—" he paused—"'unmentionable' which houses the Pousada do Castelo." His protest was the squeak of a mouse to my roar of protest.

"Do you mean to tell me," I demanded of no one and every one, "we are going to *eat* in an 'unmentionable'? Of course, it will be at the top, and of course, we will have to climb up to it."

Happily for me and my companions, they overrode my objections. Gina's solace was by way of a suggestion I keep my eyes closed, so I would not need to look down. To my bitter complaint that without practice I would experience some difficulty in eating without looking, Sophy tossed over her shoulder the proposal that I look only at my plate. I made no further protest.

Brother T. diverted me from the brooding melancholy into which I had slumped by calling attention to a church we were approaching. Sophy promptly stopped the car. The church had arrested us because it is hexagonal. A lantern of extraordinary size hangs above its entrance. We found the door locked and no building around it that might have housed a caretaker. Returning to the road and car, we urged Reader to tell us what he could find about it. He could not find it mentioned in the first few books he took from his library, but in *The Selective Traveler in Portugal* mention is made that it was built by the same architect as the Lisbon Museum, the date between 1740 and 1747, that it is the scene of a *"romaria,"* that is, the combination of fair and pilgrimage on the third of May. Our inability to enter was appeased by the added information that "the inside of the church is of little interest."

Now the "unmentionable" was in sight, towering high above the wide landscape over which we were traveling. Within a very few minutes, we discovered the breadth of the landscape dwindled to an entrance gate so narrow I declared joyfully at the sight of it our bus could not possibly go through. I should have known better. The only quality that surpasses Sophy's skill in driving is her determination not to be thwarted. Sydney Clark says in *All the Best in Spain and Portugal*: "Entrance through one of the gateways of the 12th Century walls is so narrow the Ford in which I entered could *barely* squeak through, and then, not without getting a scratch on one nether flank."

Sophy took our Microbus through without a scratch on either flank, but with a great deal of advice from Alec, Brother T. and Gina, who does not drive a car. Immediately inside, we were on a medieval narrow cobbled street, preposterously steep. It looked even more constricted than its actual width because it was bordered by solid rows of whitewashed cottages with tiled roofs of red. Their roofs betrayed their old age by an overlay of gray-green lichen. We had not gone far when, even with Sophy at the wheel, the street became impossible for a car to climb. We proceeded on foot. The way was made easy for me because cottages cut off the view below, and when we had left the street, a beautiful, winding stone stairway was enclosed in such high thick walls I could look over it, and even down with relative equanimity. Between the steps and

its guard wall, and along the entire length of the stairway, flower beds were in full bloom.

I can guarantee to kindred cravens this climb will not make the head reel and the stomach drop because of the height. Nevertheless, the head can swim a little, and certainly the breath come short, because the stairway is high and very long. Evidently this condition on arrival is prevalent, because the major-domo who welcomed us immediately indicated chairs, and courteously waited a moment before inquiring if we wished lunch, or only to look about. The lunch was delicious, the menu more elaborate than in other *pousadas* we had visited, and the service was given by waiters, overseen by a maître d'hôtel. This had the manner and sophistication of the best restaurant in a city; nevertheless, it has only five rooms, each one a double, but only one with its own bath, and it costs a little over three dollars a day, including meals.

After lunch the others walked around the parapet. Remaining inside I found a pamphlet that contained in English a brief history of Óbidos, that the *pousada* was part of a sixteenth-century palace, that the windows are Manueline and that an inscription over the doorway of the palace includes the date 1413. When the others returned from their silly walk and hailed me from outside I bestowed on Reader the pamphlet I had found. As he took it from me with profuse thanks, I happened to notice he was hurriedly stuffing something with the other hand into a side pocket of his jacket. When he released his hand, the object popped up. I saw it was a crumpled replica of the piece of literature I had just given him. He knew I saw it, and had the grace to blush.

"I'm so sorry," he told me. "I just happened to see them when we arrived." He might have added, "When the rest of you were lolling in your chairs, gasping for breath."

Down in the town again, we hunted and found the Parish Church of Santa Maria. It has a painted roof and elaborate *azulejos* from the floor up to a frieze of paintings. On the way from the church to the car, I lagged behind the others. I was peering through doorways into dark interiors of shops. Part of

224

their fascination for me, I knew, was their dimness. I conjured up prospective buyers groping about, and then taking out into the street the object they had put hands on to see what it was. I hailed the others unexpectedly. I had found contents of a shop easily discernible and enticing. I was examining them closely when my companions joined me. I called to them as they approached. "It's the prettiest furniture. I've never seen any like it, bamboo or straw or something, hand-made in wide plaits, chairs, tables, about two dollars apiece, if you could believe it. They would be divine for the porch at Watch Hill." Alec very nearly fainted on the cobble-stoned street.

Someday when I have found out how they can be shipped, I shall go back for them.

We returned to Aljubarrota by way of Nazaré, not the straight way, if one were traveling by map, but we traveled by inclination. We visited Caldas da Rainha, a spa with warm, sulphur springs, quite charming, we thought. Reader told us: "The bathing establishment was founded as a hospital in 1485 by Queen Leonora." But we did not visit it.

The place I should like to visit again—I think I could spend at least a month in the summer very happily there—is São Martinho do Pôrto. We were not looking for it; in fact, we did not know of its existence, but the road looking inviting. Reader could find no mention of it anywhere except in Baedeker, which says: "It is a small town situated on the slope of a sand hill at the northeast margin of a narrow bay, and is a popular bathing resort for children." It would be popular for me—lovely beach, salt water but quiet, and beyond it the ocean. It has not the obvious look of a resort. We put on it a unanimous stamp of approval. As we drove on to Nazaré, Reader found another endorsement. Sydney Clark mentions the Pousada de São Martinho and says of it, "Its location on high ground above the striking sea-side village of São Martinho do Pôrto is beautiful. The tariff is very moderate." Further grounds for approval.

We gasped at the sight of the Nazaré beach and the life on it,

225

as if we had not seen it before. I cannot imagine ever growing accustomed to that swirl of color and activity. When we had looked from the wall, and walked on the beach, we went to the shop where Gina had made her purchases on the chance her clothes might be ready. The blouse was finished, the skirt would reach her in Greece, the proprietor guaranteed. Encircling space with his two arms, and shaking his head dolefully, he indicated he, alas, had no need to take measurements again.

It was late afternoon when we took the road to our *estalagem*. We had been almost the only travelers in the morning, but now men, women, children and donkeys were on their way home from the fields and vineyards. All the women, the donkeys and many of the little girls were heavily burdened. Gina said it reminded her of Greece.

"Gypsies, too," she said, pointing.

At an unexpected sight, I interrupted her. "Everybody look. There's a man carrying a load on his head. This is the only time we've seen such a thing. Evidently there's one man in Portugal who doesn't let his women carry all the burdens."

Gina, turning to give a long scrutiny as he passed, made a clucking sound of commiseration.

"No, no, *ma chère*," she said, "you are quite wrong. *Sans doute,* the poor man is a homosexual."

EIGHTEEN

Standing on my balcony next morning, enjoying the view while I waited for breakfast to arrive, I heard extraordinary sounds from Alec's and Gina's room next door. I recognized Alec was saying something with insistent repetition, but I could not identify a rasping croak that occasionally interrupted him. Since obviously they were awake, I called a "Good morning," adding a "How are you?" and "How did you sleep?"

Alec stepped out on their balcony in pajamas and bathrobe. He looked harassed.

"Gina has a bad throat," he told me. "She's not feeling at all well."

The croak I had not identified called an urgent invitation to come in. Alec helped me over the railing. Gina was sitting up in bed, her cheeks a little flushed; determination I knew well in her eye.

"Darling," she whispered urgently, "as you see, and certainly you can hear it, too, I am suddenly undisposed."

"Indisposed," came automatically from Alec.

Gina shook her head impatiently. "Un, in, you with your pro-positions. Very well, I am over the weather."

"Under," Alec echoed wearily, "but never mind."

"So you see," Gina continued to me. "Alec wishes me to take honey for my throat, and certainly that is very good. But, darling, he says when the waitress comes, he will command it, and I am forbidding he try again those Portuguese words he remembers. You agree?" I assured her I did, indeed.

Alec was exasperated.

"I've told you I can make that girl understand, and if you insist on being so ridiculous, I will not speak Portuguese. I can show her what I want. You'll see."

A knock on the door silenced Gina. Alec, facing the door, squared his shoulders and assumed an expression of lowering mournfulness, something like that of an actor portraying simultaneously Napoleon and Hamlet.

"*Entre*," he said, and immediately repeated it in French. In Portuguese this is pronounced "ĕn-tray." The maid, young and pretty, came in, carrying the breakfast tray. She smiled, and said, "Good morning." Gina answered with a Portuguese phrase by now we had all learned: "*Bom dia*," pronounced "boh deéah." Alec bowed. Silently, he indicated that breakfast was not to be laid, as usual, on the balcony, but on the table to which he pointed in the room. When the maid had finished laying the table, Alec moved ahead of her to the door, stood with his back against it, his arms folded on the chest.

"Now, then," he said. "I will tell you what I want." The young girl, not understanding a word of this, and looking slightly bewildered that her exit was suddenly blocked, waited. Alec changed his position. Approaching her, smiling and waving his forefinger before her face in a tantalizing way, he inquired, in a syrupy voice: "Marmalade?" He pronounced it in what is perhaps the Portuguese fashion, "mar-me-*lah*-de," and with a hasty glance toward Gina, amended it. "Marmalade?" he repeated. We saw a startling change in the maid. Her mouth opened, she looked over her shoulder apprehensively at Gina, back at Alec, shrugged her shoulders, and seemed to say something, but Alec was too quick.

"Mar-me-*lah*-de?" he repeated, and shook his finger again, this time very decidedly. "No, no, no." Having made this point, he resumed the tantalizing weaving. "*Dolce*, I mean 'jam'?" He shook his finger again. "No, no, no." The girl's mouth remained open, but she did not jump again. She stood as if she were well into hypnosis. Gina and I, I daresay, looked in much the same condition.

228

"Now," Alec continued. "I am going to show you what I do want." With that he gave a little jump into the air. Extending his arms, flapping them up and down, he skimmed around her and me to the door of the balcony and back. As he embarked on this remarkable performance, he articulated loudly, "Bzzzzzzz." The maid turned all the way around to follow him in his flight of the bumblebee. When he had completed the circle and stood in front

of her again, enlightenment came into her face. She smiled, nodding her head several times.

"Oh, *sim, sim, sim*"—pronounced "see," Portuguese for "yes." "*Mel.* Bzzzz, Bzzzz, Bzzzzz. *Mel.*"

A peculiar sound from the bed distracted my spellbound concentration. The sound was Gina's laughter. The sound was a squeak. I think she intended it to be a derisive hoot. "Oh, ho, so we have all that showing, and it is '*melle.*'" She turned to me. "'*Melle*' is the Greek for 'honey.' That would be the one word I would not be nervous for Alec to say."

When Alec turned to protest he could not possibly have known this, but would like to call our attention to the fact that he had conveyed his meaning without speech, the young girl seized his momentary withdrawal and hurried from the room.

A letter from Alec some months later was an illuminating postscript. He wrote:

A rather extraordinary thing happened the other evening. We were dining with a young couple. He is a brilliant pianist; they are both Portuguese. Gina said during dinner she would like to tell them the story of how I tried to get honey for her in Portugal. She had no sooner reached the point when I said "Marme*lah*de" and then shook my finger, and said, "No, no, no," when the young people looked at each other, gasped, and began to laugh. Gina and I were both startled. Gina said, "No, no—that is not the end of the story. It's only the beginning." Still they continued to laugh. Finally the wife said to her husband she thought they ought to tell us why they were laughing. He told us. It seems "marme*lah*de" is the colloquial term a boy uses when he propositions a girl. He says it in exactly the way I said it to the girl. "Marmelahde?" meaning "Well, how would you like a little—marmalade with me?" So, evidently, I propositioned in front of my wife the young waitress, then immediately turned her down. I daresay that's why she looked bewildered. I thought at the time she was a little annoyed, I couldn't think why.

Later that morning Gina and Alec went back to Lisbon. Assembled in their room, we had all ruefully decided it was the best plan. By the original schedule we would have been together only two days more. Gina had concerts in England she had been unable to cancel. With a loss of voice, and an accompanying cold, she would be better off in bed in Lisbon with a doctor available. A telephone call to the Lappas' brought the offer of their car to bring Gina and Alec back, and a doctor who would see Gina as

230

soon as they arrived. With such friends as the Lappas close at hand there was no reason for Sophy, Brother T. and me to accompany them. It was a lugubrious parting. We had known the ending would have to come within the next few days, but not that it would be so dismal. Sophy, Brother T. and I agreed what a young niece of mine used to call the "solutionation" would be our own immediate departure. A new place would help us be less acutely aware of their absence.

Within an hour of their departure, we were on the road, and in Coimbra at noon. We had stopped at Batalha for one more look at the beautiful church. Today its nave was empty of people, a silent avenue of tall, white pillars.

We were glad to be in Coimbra for an early lunch, because the special event that had made us choose this day for our visit would begin in the early afternoon. The Astoria, where we lunched, is one of the best hotels in Portugal, and that places it among the best hotels in Europe. It has luxury of space, food and service. The high-ceilinged dining room has windows that look out on two streets, in the heart of the city. On the day we sat at the windows of the Astoria dining room, the streets were filled with people; so was the dining room, for that matter, even at such an early hour for lunching. This was one of the great days of the University. Families had come to see their sons. There were many of these groups around us, outside and at near-by tables; little boys and girls dressed in their best, watching, with respect, their older brother. The parents beamed with pride, endeavoring not to show it.

Coimbra is the city that holds one of the oldest universities in Europe. It was founded in 1290. We had come to see its traditional, annual ceremony called "Queima das Fitas," the "Burning of the Ribbon." Reader T., of course, had come by this information in his own burrowing fashion. Baedeker and other guidebooks make no mention of the particular festivity. It is a day that, something like our commencement, marks the progression of students to a higher academic echelon. Therefore the ribbon each one wears as his badge of attainment is burned, and is replaced by one that marks his advancement. The burning is only part of the celebration. There is, Reader told us, a parade of floats; there are concerts, dances and various sports events. The parade would begin early in the afternoon, and this is what we had come to see.

The site of the University was no surprise to me. When we had finished lunch, Sophy suggested we stay at the table a few minutes after it was cleared. She would spread out a map of the place to locate the position of the University in the town. I assured her this was an unnecessary delay. I would take any bet offered that whatever point in the city was the highest and steepest would hold the University.

"We have only to walk to the street and look up."

I was right. One guidebook phrases it: "The University crowns the hill on which Coimbra is built."

The city itself spreads on either side of the river Mondego. In that section the streets are level, and not wide. The prevalence of trolley lines makes motoring slow, and at the corners hazardous, when the tail of a trolley swings around. Labyrinths, scarcely broad enough to be counted as streets, rise and turn in V-shaped corners in an ascent I consider unfit for man, beast or car. The bus climbed it. So did I, inside the bus, temporarily leaving my stomach below.

We came out on a broad plaza, a vast quadrangle fringed by the University buildings. The ones here are modern. The square was filled with people and every minute becoming more crowded. We counted ourselves lucky to find a place just off the square where we could leave the car. People milled about aimlessly, waiting for the parade to start. We were jostled good-humoredly; we walked slowly by necessity. We did not mind; the difficulty of moving gave us greater opportunity to look at the people around us. Coimbra students are more easily identifiable than any undergraduates I have encountered because of their academic dress. It consists of black trousers; a coat that in its day was called, I think, a "Prince Albert," that comes to the knee, or very nearly; a white

232

shirt, black tie. Over this is a black cloth cape, not shaped, but wrapped around like a serape, or in the manner adopted by villains in old melodramas. The bottom of the cape is jagged, as if it had been inexpertly snipped with scissors. I learned from Brother T. the reason the cloak looks this way is because that is exactly how the effect is achieved. A student snips a piece from the bottom of this garment when he has a sweetheart. In my day at college a girl was respected in proportion to the number of "scalps" she could boast. However, her conquests were not visibly tallied. The snips in the cape of a Coimbra student are put there for counting.

We had almost reached the end of the quadrangle when a sudden shower surprised everyone. The day had been, sunny, this was only a passing raincloud that spilled, but it drove the leisurely ambling crowd into frantic activity to protect best clothes worn for the occasion. Immediately ahead of us was a roofed archway. We made for it along with a hundred or more other people. I was immediately separated from my two friends, and carried almost off my feet under the arch. For a minute or two I knew real panic. Somehow, one arm had got pushed back. I was so tightly wedged in, I could not bring it forward. I thought, wildly, it might be pulled from its socket. All this time I was being pushed ahead to the far side of the arch by the people coming up from behind, seeking the shelter of its roof.

The rain stopped, as unexpectedly as it had begun. Almost as quickly as that, the crowd spread and thinned. I found my friends on the far side of the arch, standing in the inner court. I told them I had very nearly lost an arm, but otherwise seemed intact, and suggested since we seemed to be very near its steps, we visit the great library.

It is not important to visit Coimbra on the day of a parade. A parade is much the same the world over, a Mardi Gras in New Orleans, a Mummers' New Year's Day in Philadelphia, Greek, Irish or Polish processions in New York on the Sundays of their national holidays, but there is no library in the world so beautiful,

233

I think, as the library in Coimbra. It was built during the years of 1717 to 1728. It holds only three rooms. They are large and high, separated by a tall and wide marble arch. Slender pillars along the side, patterned and embossed in gold, support stacks in a gallery above. At the far end of the last room, so that it is immediately visible from the doorway of the library, is a large and striking portrait of King John V, in whose reign this Baroque beauty was designed.

"It's like an enormous jewel," I whispered to Sophy as we stood literally transfixed in the doorway. I know now, much later, why at that moment I thought of a jewel. To have associated this interior with a bright flashing stone like a diamond is a preposterous incongruity. In my grandfather's house, a wrought-iron lantern hung over a sort of enclosed balcony, halfway up the stairs. The lantern was sheathed in a dreadful piece of stylish artwork, a glass shade studded with glass jewels; the light of the lantern made them glow a deep rich green, red and yellow. These were the jewels I was thinking of when I stood in the doorway at Coimbra. On my grandfather's balcony they were dreadful, but the green, gold and yellow-red of the Coimbra rooms glowed like them, and were beautiful. The gold is in the balustrades, the columns, the painted ceilings. The walls and the predominant color of the first chamber is green; the middle a contrasting and deeper shade; and the last a deep yellow-red. The furnishings are only tables, a few chairs around each one. Each table is of heroic size, inlaid in intricate patterns of a pale beige. At intervals along the wall are panels of *chinoiserie* overlaid in gold lacquer.

As we came from the building and stood on the steps a moment, Sophy said, "After what we've seen, the sun looks vulgar."

In the outer quadrangle the parade had begun. The crowd had concentrated there, but because the space was greater, there was not the congestion that had frightened me a little under the arch. I had not seen women students until our return to the square; perhaps they had been at a ceremony of their own. They were easy to identify. Their academic dress was distinctive, but not so

234

flamboyant as the capes and frock coats of the boys. The women wear a black tailored suit, a little like a man's tuxedo in cut, or perhaps the similarity comes from the white shirt and black bow tie that are the accessories. Every student wore an identifying ribbon—dark blue for the Department of Arts and Letters, light blue for Science, red for Law, yellow for Medicine, purple for Pharmacy. The ribbons are actually carried, not worn. It is a conspicuous and extra-long bookmark in a volume a student may be carrying, or extends well outside the edges of a brief case.

The only visible uniformity among the students is their dress. Their features and color of hair, eyes and skin are widely variable. A young man standing near me as we waited for the floats heard me pointing out to Sophy and Brother T. the striking variation among students. I think this young spectator was an alumnus of the University. He spoke English understandably and seemed to know the University intimately. He told us with pride their "republics," as he called them, corresponding to our "fraternities," are open to students of any race, color, religion or political creed, except Communism. The candidate must receive unanimous votes from all the members, but he is judged solely by his personal qualities. He told us, too, there are special courses given in the summer for foreign students. Many Americans come to these. I had not known before of their existence. He wrote down for me the name of the place to which application should be made for such courses. It is "Faculdade de Letras de Coimbra, Portugal."

The quadrangle began to be even more tightly packed with people than before, though I would have believed this impossible. Evidently the floats were coming. I would not have thought the square could become noisier, but it did. The most spirited contributors to the increased noise were the bands of students who came equipped with bottles of champagne, opened, that they shared with anyone in the vicinity who cared to partake of their hospitality. There were many takers. At last the floats began to come up over the brow of the hill, and turn off into a street away from the quadrangle. They were gaily and amusingly dec-

236

orated. Each one was a satiric representation of some aspect of the University, and cheered by the spectators. I do not know that we left at the peak of the celebration, but it was at a moment we felt unanimously and insistently a need for quiet.

As we walked toward the car, Brother T. said, ruminatingly, "Did you hear that young man telling me about undergraduate life? He said freshmen are very much restricted; they are not allowed to be on the streets after six o'clock. If one is seen by a senior, the senior has the privilege of shaving the freshman's head. I wonder how many shaved heads there will be tomorrow morning."

Because of the roistering around us, neither Sophy nor I had heard any of this conversation. Sophy and Brother T. had not heard the young man express his regrets to me that because of the crowd he could not take us back to the inner court to show the views from the balconies. He could have pointed out among other things, he said, the "Garden of Tears," called by that name since the time Inés de Castro was murdered there. I was fascinated, too, by his assertion that in a lily pond in the garden there are lilies of a shade of red not found elsewhere. The local legend is the color has come from the blood of Inés.

We found the peace and quiet we sought in the Augustinian Monastery of Santa Cruz, even though its location is in the very heart of the city, noisy trolleys passing. The only other church I had seen with a porch is the one at Évora. This one at Coimbra is very Baroque, and a little absurd. The interior, however, has no absurdity; it is long and narrow. The walls are brightened by *azulejos* in predominating Madonna blue. The cloister, too, and it is double, has beautiful *azulejos* in panels, multicolored. We were the only visitors to the church. There was no guide in evidence. Thankful for this, we strolled about, following our own inclination. We were momentarily disconcerted to find our inclinations had led us into an elegant office occupied by an elegant prelate. He was writing at a desk. In his absorption he did not see us as we entered, and we, in turn, were gaping at the painted ceiling and beautiful carvings on wall panels. Our mutual discovery took place simultaneously. We backed out with embarrassed and incoherent apologies, but he gave us a courtly bow of forgiveness.

During our stay in the church the sky had become overcast, and the temperature dropped perceptibly. Group Leader, without having to wet her forefinger, told us a storm was brewing. "We ought to move along. The Palace Hotel at Bussaco where we would spend the night is—" she stammered a little.

"Don't tell me," I broke in. "I know—on the top of a mountain, of course." Sophy nodded.

Brother T., at Group Leader's request, sat beside her on the front seat. He was to take Gina's place as map reader. Sophy had waved aside his courteous insistence I take that place. Brother T. yielded when she assured him, with a map in my hand, only God knew where I would lead them.

Brother T. led us to, and over, a road I doubt a dozen motorists have traveled since the invention of the automobile. Men, women and children came from their cottages at the sound of our engine. They had ample opportunity to watch us pass; the road was dirt, narrow and so deeply pock-marked it jolted us mercilessly and caused us to stutter when we tried to talk. We swept through villages and countryside at something around fifteen miles an hour. Brother T. and I, hanging onto whatever would keep us approximately in our seats, could observe the details in the passing scene, since its passage was almost imperceptible. Sophy, gripping the wheel, concentrated on the gullies ahead. In tones that vibrated, and syllables unintentionally stressed, I managed to direct Brother T.'s attention to the pinafores worn by both girls and boys. We had seen them everywhere we traveled in Portugal, but whereas the pinafores of school children in France are black, these are white, starched and spotless. Since the reason for a pinafore is the protection of the garment underneath, I could not, I said, understand why the protecting garment itself should be so vulnerable to dirt. Brother T.'s jiggled reply was he had found no reference to this in his literature, and could, therefore, give me no legend or historical events that would account for it. He did give me information, jerkily, about water wheels we had seen near Coimbra and in other parts of the country. Each time we had seen one we had speculated on its purpose and its mechanism. Our Researcher had, at last, found both a description and explanation of its *modus operandi*.

Sophy asked if he would mind just taking one more look at the map before he read about the water wheels. Was he sure this was the road? He looked long and earnestly.

"It is the only road on my map," he told her. "I am so sorry." To ease his embarrassment, Sophy apologized for her interruption, begged him not to take responsibility for the existence of only one road, and urged him to divert us from its perils by instruction about water wheels. They are picturesque and charming sights to come upon. The wheel covers the width of a stream. It is divided in sections by wooden crosspieces. These crosspieces breasting the current, Brother T. read, turn the wheel. At intervals of two or three, a squat, earthenware jar with a wide mouth is lashed to the slat at such a pitch that the jar fills with water, and empties when with the revolution of the wheel it has reached the top. It empties into a long, wooden chute, and from this the water goes along narrower opened chutes, made from tree trunks, and these, in turn, spill into the area to be watered. There is no fixed number of these earthenware containers on a wheel. It depends on how many the stream is strong enough to take.

Somewhere along the way, under Brother T.'s direction, we went through a town called Souzelas. We found no mention of it in any guidebook. Early along the way, Group Leader's weather prophecy was vindicated. It poured and grew very cold. The rain was hardest, I think, as we began the climb on a winding road, more like a circular staircase, to the summit and the Palace Hotel. The road wound through a forest that is the most famous in Portugal, and includes the cypresses of Bussaco known to botanists and tree experts all over the world, according to a guidebook.

They are not known to me. I cannot even say they are visible from the road because my eyes were closed. We had moved from dirt with bumps to stone that was wet and slippery. I reiterate to myself during such travail, "This, too, will pass," with no conviction that it will. This one did, however, as other ascents that have tried me have done.

We reached the top and drew up in front of one of the most monstrous edifices I have ever seen. When I opened my eyes, realizing we were on level ground, and had come to the end of the climb, I was looking at an assortment of stone excrescences, towers, pillars, fretwork that seemed impossible to have been conceived by only one architect. It is a three-tiered confectioner's dream, originally designed, I should think, for a wedding cake, but adapted to a summer residence for the royal family. Since it was completed only in 1905, the family had very little time to enjoy it. I wonder if their release from it might not have been one of the few compensations for the loss of the throne. The hotel, itself, is the epitome of luxury, in rooms, food and service. The views from it are magnificent. There are paths through the woods that are charming, we were told. In the downpour that accompanied our visit we could not explore them. Two miles away is the watering place of Luso. Guests from the hotel, we learned, make the baths there an objective of a daily walk, but the hotel itself has a large swimming pool.

The clerk at the desk, welcoming us, said how fortunate we were to have been coming only from Coimbra in such weather, since we had only to follow the wide main highway from the town directly here.

Sophy and I did not look at Brother T., but we heard him murmur, "I think I shall confine myself to guidebooks."

On the counter in front of me, I saw London newspapers for sale. I could think of no quicker solace for Reader T. He had not seen them. Choosing the two nearest I handed them to our disconsolate map reader.

"This is a present," I said, "with love." I opened my bag to

240

pay the clerk, and my billfold was gone. We emptied my large sack on the counter. There was no billfold. It had contained my driving license, various credit cards, including charge-a-plates at New York stores, and $150 in American currency. Providentially, my express checks and passports were in another case. Vividly, and almost immediately, I remembered the crush under the arch, and the way my left arm had been held inextricably behind me. That was the arm from which my handbag had dangled. At the moment of retrieving my arm, I had instinctively looked at my bag. The clasp was closed, so I had thought it untouched. During the day I had had no occasion to look in it for my billfold. Brother T., in addition to map-reading, had taken over from Alec the post of banker.

We dined well in a banquet hall occupied by ten people, including our group of three. Before separating for the night, we telephoned Gina and Alec, and had reassuring word from Gina herself. One of her favorite words in English is "dilapidated." She uses it quixotically. Joyfully, her voice restored, she called into the telephone, "I have made a complete dee-lah-pidated recovery."

Next morning, as our bags were being packed into the car, the clerk from the desk came up to us as we stood on the terrace. He waved a newspaper as he approached.

"I wish to say good-by," he told us, "and read you something. It will make you happy." The local Coimbra newspaper reported, as the clerk translated, a shocking number of pickpockets had invaded the scene of yesterday's celebration at the University. The police were swamped with complaints from visitors whose purses had been stolen. They were taking immediate action to forestall such a deplorable occurrence again.

Other announcements have made me happier than this one. I wondered how many visitors to Coimbra were in a position this morning to share my pleasure.

NINETEEN

Coimbra, we had read, is the third largest city in Portugal. In spite of trolleys and congestion of traffic, it did not feel like a city. I cannot define the quality that causes a visitor to say of a place, "This is a city," or "This is a town." I only know the quality is there, and is perceptible from the outskirts to the center square; and it has nothing to do with actual size. Oporto is the second largest city in Portugal, and it is a city, unmistakably, from its suburbs to the Infante de Sagres Hotel in its center. Some guidebooks call it "Porto," others, "Oporto." Whichever name is used, they agree it is a fascinating city. The three travelers in a Microbus corroborate this. It lies at the mouth of the Douro; the two-leveled bridge by which one crosses the river and enters the city is a magnificent structure, giving one immediately not only a superb view on either side, but the anticipation of a rich, handsome and vigorous metropolis. It carries its years well. It boasts its age, dating its birth as a little community in 2000 B.C. Indulgence must always be given to statements about affirmations of age; they are bound to err a little, one way or another.

The Infante de Sagres is a metropolitan hotel, of luxurious comfort in rooms, food and service. The people on the streets have the look of city-dwellers, that ranges from the sophisticated dress of fashionable residents to the shabbiness of the poor. For all their shabbiness, however, the poor do not beg in Portugal. We had been approached only two or three times in all our motoring, and those were halfhearted and tentative. Coincident with the absence of begging, there is an over-all courtesy. Though

"Cockburn's Lunch Port," "Partner's Port" and others. A sort of monument to the English colony is the "English Factory House" built in 1785. It is an extraordinary institution, not a club, and certainly not a factory. Whitehead, who was the Consul at the time, began its building then. The purpose was a meeting place for the British wine merchants. To visit it requires a letter of introduction from one of its body and, fortunately, we had one. A magnificent stairway leads to the banquet dining rooms and library. Lighted by large and exquisite crystal chandeliers, decorated with charming painted ceilings, and furnished happily in the period of its construction, its history is documented about the walls in the less formal rooms by photographers and other memorabilia. The street on which it stands was at one time known as "The Street of the English," but it is now called "Rua do Infante Henrique," since it is the street of the palace in which the English Philippa of Lancaster gave birth to the great Henry the Navigator.

The Factory, and it is a grave blunder to refer to it as a club, is an integral part of its immediate surroundings and, in fact, of the history of the growth of the city. Nevertheless, to move from its stately eighteenth-century British restraint in décor to the ebullient flamboyance of the Church of St. Francisco is not a jump, but a pole vault. Perhaps its location, too, next door to the Stock Exchange, made us think we would see a dignified austerity, not too remote in tone from the Factory. The Church of St. Francisco, begun in 1233, is said to be the epitome of Rococo in its gilt-wood decoration. Every pillar bursts into flowers, birds, fruit, encircling angels. An easier transition would have been to go first to the Ordem Terceira Church that is adjacent, and on the same level. The interior of this is in black, white and gold, and of quite a different beauty, the beauty of omission and restraint. We interrupted our sight-seeing to lunch at the Escondidinho Restaurant. The meaning of the name, we learned, is a "little hidden place"; its title is almost an understatement. We had been told this was the best restaurant in Oporto, but we passed its doorway three times. It is small, charming, intimate, its interior brightly decorated in blue tiles. Although the food was superb, the other customers were so interesting as to be almost a distraction. Perhaps we were interesting to them, too, but they did not show it. These were the fashionable residents of Oporto. I think we were the only foreigners in the restaurant that day. There were many luncheon parties. Every woman was in black. They greeted one another with formality, their voices and laughter were low, and yet, in curious paradox, there seemed to be an easy jocularity with the waiters. Several of the customers, men, shook hands with them, entering and at the conclusion of the meal, and with the maître d'hôtel. We had seen this same democracy in the very elegant dining room of the Avis Hotel in Lisbon, where Sophy and I had lunched one day. We had thought we were, for once, seeing two Portuguese women lunching together until the man who stood talking cozily with the head waiter rejoined them.

That afternoon we toured the city and its churches. There is a magnificent view from the Bishop's Palace and the Sé. A great bell tower, Tôrre dos Clérigos, which means "Tower of the Clergy," dominates the city skyline for miles around. The cathedral, itself, is a little reminiscent of the fortress-like church in Évora, but the interior contains a chapel that is the antithesis of a stark fortress. The Chapel of the Blessed Sacrament, and it is on the left of the high altar, is solidly made of silver. When I had recovered from my first astonishment at the sight, I wondered aloud, remembering my meager assortment of pieces at home, how it was polished. Reader T., I discovered, had already ascertained this. The whole furnishing is detachable in pieces, but the amount is so vast it can only be cleaned every few years.

We were moving from splendor to splendor. The Convent of Santa Clara is reached through a courtyard. Children were playing there when we arrived. We had heard their shrill squeals and laughter from the street. They were shabbily dressed, rather dirty and very polite. They stopped their play at sight of us; two or three came forward, indicating in pantomime they would make our entrance possible. One of them applied a heavy knocker to a plain wooden door, another pulled the rope of a bell alongside. I visualized from this plain exterior an interior to match—whitewashed walls, probably, and dark wood. Of all the churches we saw in Portugal, this was the most resplendent. Later reading *Portugal and Madeira* by Sacheverell Sitwell, I find he calls it "one of the major beauties of Baroque art." The chapel is completely encased in goldwork, the ceiling is studded with gold, and the chancel solid goldwork. Two black statues of saints stand out effectively against the gold. This church is small. Standing in the center of the nave, and literally dazed by the sunburst around and overhead, I found into my head had come involuntarily a song from *Porgy and Bess*—"Little David was small, but *oh, my!*" —and checked an unseemly desire to laugh aloud.

Simultaneously, next day we wanted neither churches nor city. We took to the road again. We paused at the river to watch boats like barges with sails, high slim prows and long curved tillers. In the stern we saw large casks, ebony-black. Brother T. knew at once they contained port, and these were the sailing barges, the conveyors of the wine; he had, of course, read about them. Oxen in this part of the country are the land conveyors of produce. Heretofore, we had seen them only on the beach at Nazaré; now they dotted the landscape, roads and fields. Their yokes were elaborately carved and painted. Houses we passed showed greater prosperity than we had seen before, and were, correspondingly, less picturesque. Nevertheless, their construction was evidently of such satisfaction to the owner he wished no mistake in the identity of the residence. In large script, across the front of a house, or on the gate, reads *"Vivenda———"* and the householder's name. Even minor inhabitants are frequently identified. In topiary, in front of one establishment, conspicuously unattractive in color and design, was cut a very-much-larger-than-life figure of a Scotch terrier.

The Misericordia Church and Hospital in Viana dos Castelo would have been reward enough for the excursion, had we not enjoyed all other aspects of it. This is not like any other building we saw. Its façade is three-storied, supported on caryatids; each tier

is lined with boxes of bright geraniums. The town hall is on the same square, built on arches, of beautiful design. We wandered the streets, and then, following a stream of people, came to a market along the river Lima. The booths stretched, I should think, a quarter of a mile, containing everything from vegetables and fish to dress materials and shoes. I left reluctantly.

We had not expected Braga to be so large a town with trolleys and considerable traffic. The streets themselves have a particular charm. Standards, at intervals along the streets, are topped with flowers. We lunched at the Hotel de Braga, and were surprised this time by the mediocrity of food and service in a large hotel in a town of this size.

"The outstanding feature of Braga," Brother T. began reading to us at lunch, "is its . . ." and his voice trailed away.

" 'Unmentionable,' " I said gloomily. "We haven't had one recently. I knew I wouldn't be spared for long."

"It's not an 'unmentionable,' " Brother T. amended apologetically, "but it is on the summit. It's a church that is famous for a pilgrimage, and a view," he added hastily. "At Whitsuntide, pilgrims make the ascent on their knees." At which I knew if the devout could climb on their knees, the impious and reluctant member of this party would be taken in a bus.

The view, like all vistas from a summit, is broad, but so are the steps on the grand staircase leading to the church, incongruously broad, and punctuated by statues. The cathedral and churches in the town were more to my liking. Braga is known to have been occupied in 585 by the Goths, and by the Moors in the early eighth century. From the early eleventh century, it has been one of the great ecclesiastical centers. The churches represent architecture over this long period of history from Romanesque to Gothic to Baroque. The Palace of the Biscainhas, entered by a covered courtyard, and including a staircase of deep blue *azulejos* in a pattern of landscape and figures, is of a charm to make one caper with delight. It is a complicated business to obtain permis-

248

sion to see much of the palace, but even if one were to see only
the gardens it is deeply satisfying.

We stopped in Guimarães on the way back to Oporto, but I
balked at the "unmentionable" at the summit. I balked so effectively I was even urged by Group Leader to leave the car, and
permit them to scale the heights. It was a lovely arrangement.
I explored the town, delighting in the square, enclosed by an
arcade that contains the palace and the town hall. The arches of
the arcade are large enough to drive through. The church of
Senhor da Pasas is more curious than pleasing. It is a sort of flat
Rococo of stone and blue and white tile, with an excrescence of
a balcony. I made a mutually satisfactory bargain with my companions when they picked me up. If they would not tell me about
the view and the "unmentionable," I would not go into detail
about what I had seen.

Back in Oporto, Sophy went to her room to write letters;
Brother T. and I took a walk. We dropped in, of course, at several
bookshops, from which Reader did not emerge empty-handed.
With mutual approbation, we saw a book fair in the process of
building. It would be ready for an opening within the next few
days. A series of open-air kiosks were the display booths; each was
the shape of an open volume, and, made of metal, could be closed
at night. The fair would last a week, I think. At least, this is
what I gathered from the clerks in the adjacent bookshops. We
did not find a clerk in any of the shops who spoke English.
Nevertheless, an outdoor book fair, open from early morning to
late at night for a week, is a sight I should like very much to see
at home.

The sight Brother T. and I caught up with less than a block
from our hotel will stand in my memory for all time, as a kind
of symbol of the paradox of Portugal. Certainly, it was, in its way,
a monument. I caught it first. Seizing Brother T.'s arm, and pointing, I said, "Thank goodness you're with me, to verify this. No one
would believe my telling it." Striding in magnificent unconcern

and freedom of movement along one of the busiest streets in one of the largest cities in Portugal, a woman, barefoot, carried on her head an office desk upside down; wedged securely among its legs a desk chair, also upside down; and in the center of this a strong box.

TWENTY

Leaving Oporto next day in the morning, we spent the night at the Pousada de Santo António at Sarem. In the morning before leaving we had done a little shopping, purchased some Fado records at a near-by music shop, some linen along the same street and, for me, a jewel. In appearance it may not have been a gem of purest ray serene, but for me it was beyond a price—a little plug that attached to the cord of my dictaphone, converting its idiosyncrasies to the requirement of European electricity. In Lisbon, and in Oporto, I had been able to revitalize my machine with the ordinary attachment, because their hotels made this electric concession to Americans. Nevertheless, I needed this mysterious liaison contrivance, and had asked for it at almost every town and village. There had been no liaison between me and the shop people I visited, but the man in Oporto understood at once my need, and with equal promptitude delivered the little beauty over the counter. From the moment the young men in Lisbon had taken their hands off the machine, it had worked to perfection. I had confined its use, however, to the solitude of my room, after one trial in the bus. The playback of my observations on the passing scenes, murmured low so as not to disturb the others, had been lost beneath the overlay of vociferous differences of opinion between Gina on the front seat, and Alec in the back, that he must stop his money counting and look, or quixotically, he must not interrupt her map-reading by conversation about the scenery; demands from Alec she extend to him some of the "Karamelles" from the store for children and, in turn, her specific and detailed

251

apprehensions about the state of his stomach that would ensue from candy; then interludes of reading from Brother T. and interjections from Group Leader having to do, usually, with eating. Therefore, I need not have carried the unwieldly object that was to permit easy use of the machine in the car, and also the need of recharging. I need not have paid the excess weight it involved. I had paid dear for an introduction to the lads of the Volkswagen garage in Lisbon. Nevertheless, in one way, if not another, the meeting had been charming, and now one of them had in his possession this costly souvenir from me. When we left I owned an object weighing a few ounces that took care of the whole mechanical problem.

Everyone who writes about Portugal talks of the dress of the fisherwomen in Aveiro. William and Elizabeth Younger in their *Blue Moon in Portugal* write: "The girls seem to have stepped out of an operetta. They wear flat, brimless 'pork-pie' hats, which are a jaunty attractive headgear. The men wear knitted stocking caps and checked shirts. Even the yokes of the oxen are different, for they are high and almost triangular, drilled with holes and painted."

For this reason, we followed the coast road with Aveiro as our objective. We saw no "pork-pie" hats, nor stocking caps, nor even oxen, let alone their painted yokes. I think we had come at the wrong season of the year. The fishing fleet, we understood, was in distant waters. The women were at home, I suppose, with their hats off. I have no information or guess about the oxen. Nevertheless, the place itself was not a disappointment. It is a strange little city, crisscrossed with canals, and approached by wide dark marshes, punctuated frequently with towering mounds of glistening white salt. There are buildings, too, in Aveiro, well deserving of visit, particularly the convent that is now a museum. Like Santa Clara in Oporto, the chapel is covered solidly, walls, ceiling and altars, with gilded wood. The Rococo interior of the whole convent is a delight.

We could have explored by motorboats for hire the lagoons

and canals interlaced through the town, but we considered this an opportunity we could miss with equanimity. We remained in our own vehicle, and continued our way.

The *pousada* at Sarem is one of the best; our rooms were large with a beautiful view and the food was excellent. We were a little chagrined, as well as pleased, to discover this. We had passed the sign on the way to Oporto and asked one another who would conceivably stay in such an out-of-the-way place? The inn itself is not visible from the road.

Next morning, Sunday, it was raining when we left about ten, and cold. We looked yearningly at the comfortable lounge and open fire but, by Group Leader's schedule, we must be in Tomar for lunch if we were to be in time for the opening of the great event that was the object of our journey from Oporto. Brother T., it is redundant to mention, had found in a pamphlet an announcement and description of one of the largest fairs in Portugal. It would be held in Santarém, starting on Sunday, the twenty-second of May, and running for a week. Sophy, poring over her own maps and literature, had drawn a ring around Tomar. This must be our base: it was the nearest place to Santarém with recommended lodging facilities at an *estalagem*. Because of the rain and not-too-good roads, we did not arrive at the Estalagem da Santa Iria until nearly two o'clock. This was the only *estalagem* or *pousada* on our trip in which the proprietor was identifiable, and visible. It was a man, calm, efficient, quiet, exercising authority over the staff. When we had been shown our rooms, and hastily freshened up for lunch, he met us at the door of the dining room, saw us to a table and was about to leave when Sophy detained him. We knew she was going to ask what time we should leave in order to be at Santarém for the grand opening of the fair. We had an idea something was awry, from the look of amazement on her face when the proprietor answered. Again, she seemed to ask much the same question. With a shrug of the shoulders, he gave much the same answer. She asked Brother T. if he happened to have with him literature about the fair. He produced several pamphlets; she extended one to the proprietor, her finger marking some part of it. The proprietor looked where she indicated, again shrugged his shoulders, and told her what she finally shared with us.

"He says the fair at Santarém will open *next* Sunday. He doesn't know whether the date in these pamphlets is the printer's error or the time of the fair was changed without anyone's bothering to notify the travel bureaus or whatever agency issues this literature. He says in either case it is not important because they were not anticipating visitors, anyway. So this is how Portugal woos the tourist trade," she concluded.

The proprietor, his information given, left us. He had been courteously unconcerned by our dismay. He obviously did not wish to intrude on our resolving of a quandary. We were in Tomar on Sunday, the twenty-second of May. We had planned to visit the Great Fair that afternoon and the following morning. We would then move north, following a full schedule of provocative countryside and places to see. From the northernmost point we would continue by car to Paris. Brother T. would fly home to London from there, Sophy and I would motor on to The Hague, where I would pay a visit to my daughter and her family. The Microbus would be received by the young man who had brought it to Lisbon. Sophy, after an intoxicating moment when she returned the car *intact,* would fly to London. It was a well-laid plan, and it had certainly gone agley.

By the end of a very good lunch our spirits were brighter, but our plans were still fogbound. The proprietor came to our table, and addressed himself to Sophy. She translated to Brother T. and me. A dance was to be held that afternoon at three o'clock; perhaps we would like to go. Instantly Brother T., who through the crisis had maintained a Jovian serenity, looked like a man on the brink of panic. His eyes widened, his brows lifted, his face paled visibly.

"I'm afraid I shouldn't be of much help," he stammered a little. "I've never learned how to dance."

Sophy reassured him. "I don't think it's that kind of a dance. It seems to be some kind of exhibition."

fringe of a grove of trees. Under these, tables and chairs were arranged on one side of a center aisle, and on the other, rows of seats. Beyond them was the stage where the dancers would perform. Somewhere in the trees loudspeakers were blaring recorded music. The record it was playing, the one we had heard faintly, the one I had called eerily familiar, was "When the Swallows Come Back to Capistrano," in Portuguese rhythm and harmony.

The audience began to assemble around four o'clock. The program began at five. In the meantime we had chosen seats at one of the tables. The choice was wide. We were the only ones of the early arrivals on that side of the aisle. The rows of seats, we learned, were less expensive. They were also hard, narrow chairs. By five o'clock both sides of the aisle were filled to capacity. We were thankful we had chosen a table under a tree, because at the moment the performance seemed on the verge of beginning, the sun came out. It might have been a violent thunderstorm from the agitation aroused in the audience. Umbrellas were immediately raised, causing a splatter of shrill protest from those whose view was blocked. The parasols were lowered again, under clamorous protest from their owners. Men and women not wearing hats hastily covered their heads with a scarf, a program, occasionally a woman's handbag. Mothers took from their bags handkerchiefs, knotted them at the four corners, and placed them on the heads of children. When all the forms of protection had been installed, a red-faced, heavy-set man of middle age entered the stage from one side, advanced to its edge and began a speech. He was evidently the impresario of this troupe. I do not know what he said, but the length of it made the three of us murmur to one another doubts the dancing would begin before dark. I kept in mind my customary solace, "This, too, will pass," and eventually it did. From that moment on, the afternoon, what was left of it, was unflawed delight. The dancers ranged from a group whose senior members were, I should judge, six years old, possibly eight, to adult ensembles. Their costumes were beautiful, and their technique excellent. Little by little we learned from the program, and Sophy's con-

versations with spectators at adjoining tables, this was an organized group that combined a school and a performing company. The long-winded gentleman was the director; he had recruited his dancers from all parts of the country. At this time of year they were on tour in buses; during the winter they attended school. They had become a national institution, well known throughout the country. Each folk dance they presented was authentic.

During the intermission, waiters appeared to take orders for ices and fruit drinks. The program itself did not end until about eight o'clock. Walking back to the hotel, Sophy admitted we had been so transported by the afternoon she was now delighted not to know what the next days might hold for us.

They held a leisurely exploration of Tomar. That is one of the most appealing towns, I think, in Portugal. Its narrow, twisting streets are punctuated here and there, unexpectedly, with a wide, handsome square. This is where the celebration occurs of the "Roses and Loaves of Bread" legend. Replicas of the maidens are everywhere with their towering headdresses of loaves of bread and roses. The most charming, to me, were small and in gold filigree, that is a special craft of that part of the country.

Our *estalagem* is one of the most delightful spots in the town. It faces a tree-lined park, and is itself on a little island reached by a bridge from the main street. In the actual grounds of the inn there is a pool where the turbulent river pauses. At almost any time of day we could watch women doing their washing there.

On the night of the dancing the troupe and many parents, I think, were given a dinner at long tables in the *estalagem* park. The balcony of my room overlooked it. I watched the festivity. There might have been well over two hundred guests. The last thing I heard, before sleep mercifully silenced it, was the voice of the dance director. He was making a speech.

We left Tomar on Tuesday, stopped at Santarém, found there was a possible hotel and made reservations for the following Sunday. By lunchtime, we were back at the Tivoli in Lisbon.

During the next few days, we alternated chores with sight-seeing.

Now it was agreed we would abandon the trip north, come immediately after the fair to Lisbon, leave the car, Sophy and I go by train to Paris for a few days, then I to Holland, Sophy to London. Brother T. would fly from Lisbon to London.

On Thursday, we drove to Mafra. It is only about an hour from Lisbon. The trip out provided for Brother T. a corroboration of what he had tentatively advanced as a "national characteristic." As a scientist, he must always put a Q.E.D. after his theorem. Sophy and I had immediately endorsed by positive opinion his suggestion that whenever in this country you thought you had seen an established pattern, you would inevitably find its contradiction.

The contradiction on this motor jaunt so satisfying to Brother T. was hair-raising to Sophy and me. At every railroad crossing on our trip, we had been stopped by a guardian of a gate when a train was within twenty minutes of her territory.

Driving the easy highway to Mafra, Sophy suddenly said, "This road suddenly looks and feel different. Where are we?"

Looking about me with more particular attention than I had been paying, I shouted, "We're on an airfield. We're about to cross a landing strip. There's a plane just coming down."

We were on a military post, totally unguarded. We crossed the strip as the wheels of a plane settled on its far end. There was no watcher of the skies, no guardian of the gates, there was no gate. The highway crosses the field, and strip. I had not the courage to look behind me, but if other motorists met the plane, we did not hear the crash. We were traveling faster than we had traveled at any time during the month.

Mafra was built in 1713, as a royal residence and, in part, a monastery. The reason for its construction was the fulfillment of a vow made by D. João V. If his wife would present him with an heir he would express his gratitude in this fashion. What a dwindling to the current tradition of a box of cigars! This building covers seven acres, none of them exhibiting any particular beauty or charm. The vast place is now a museum; therefore a guide is compulsory. He leads his charges through a mile or so—

it seemed longer—of corridors and dismal rooms. One of these is sufficiently arresting to provide background material for a nightmare. From floor to ceiling, including the furniture, it is covered with trophies of the chase. A number of chairs are made of interwoven antler horns, the backs and seats upholstered with the skin of the animal.

After the first fifteen rooms, Sophy explained we wanted to see only the library. Our Group Leader had met her peer. Smiling at her, our guide continued his program: he stopped at each room to give, in what he believed was English, a detailed account of it. I have not found a guide in any country who did not include the measurements of whatever he is showing. There is no aspect of a room I find less interesting.

"This, too, will pass," I was saying to myself, when we reached what we had come to see. Mafra is said to include a thousand rooms; I do not believe we had skipped many of them. After such a novitiate, I should have thought we were qualified at last, but the doors to the Mafra's paradise were closed and bolted. Our guide pulled a cord hanging at one side of the entrance. In the distance we heard a bell ring. Ten minutes later, the door was opened. Another guide was standing on the far side. He ushered out a preceding group, and at the same time permitted us to enter. We crossed the threshold of the library. Once inside I realized our detention was probably a necessary precaution, because in this vast beautiful room the books are on open shelves. It would not be difficult to extract a volume or two if one were unscrupulous and clever enough. I still do not know why the guide who takes one through the long journey must wait outside.

If it is possible, I think one should see the library at Mafra before visiting Coimbra because of the two Coimbra is far richer in color and overlay of decoration. The beauty of Mafra is primarily in its light—all white and gold, illuminated by a line of tall windows on either side. The gilding is in exquisite Rococo. It is a narrow room with a curved barrel ceiling. With all its dignity, this is a gay room without the somber lavishness of Coimbra. We

260

made the return passage on the double. Leaving the guide behind, we flashed past the antlered and all the other rooms, until finally we were out again into the vast courtyard.

The day was warm and sunny; we were on our way to Ericeira, a beach resort. It is a charming place, and the Hotel Ericeira is delightful. It is perched high above a long, curving, sandy beach, but it has its own pool. We swam in it before lunch, drank our port on the terrace in the sun and had a delicious meal. We came home by way of Sintra, and could not pass it without a little re-visiting; therefore, it was late afternoon when we "picked up" the highway to Lisbon, as the old motoring guides used to say. (My favorite expression in that literature was "pick up the car tracks.")

The day had been long and hot; at Mafra we had walked acreage that seemed mileage; we were headed for the stables; we wanted bath, "shoebag hour," dinner. In the back seat I was ruminating the way seemed longer than I had remembered it before, when Sophy said this aloud: "We should have turned off the highway into the city long before this, it seems to me."

Brother T. admitted he had been looking up a bit of information in his guidebooks, and hadn't noticed.

"We just miscalculated the distance, that's all," I told Sophy, "because we're tired. We certainly haven't reached Lisbon yet, or there would have been some indication. I haven't seen any signs except one, about a half-hour ago, called 'A. E.' "

The car made an erratic bracket on the highway. Sophy spoke.

"Like your children's nurse," she said, " 'I don't say a vord,' except that 'A. E.' marks the exit to Lisbon. Remember when we left Sintra I asked you to be on the lookout for—" and she gave me two words I do not even now remember, and only at that instant realized one began with an "A" and the other with an "E."

"It never occurred to me to look for abbreviations," I told her. "Next time you'd better tell me all the possibilities to look for."

"Next time," was Sophy's answer, "I'll do the looking."

The "shoebag hour," we agreed, had never been more welcome, soothing and appreciated than it was that night. We dined at the

Negresco, the restaurant Sophy and I had discovered before the arrival of the others. It is not only one of the best in Lisbon, but could take a high place on a list I might make of the best restaurants I have visited in Europe. The manager welcomed us in English. This irked Sophy a little until he told her he had remembered our first visit. He added it had made him think of America; he had been there. Brother T., who has extra-social perception, inquired how long the manager's stay had been; he himself had passed the preceding winter in New York, and enjoyed it very much. The Negresco manager's stay, he told us, had not been so extensive. The United Fruit Line's boat, for which he had once worked, had put in at Miami for one day; like Brother T., he had enjoyed his stay very much.

The assistant manager, during the course of the meal, engaged our attention apologetically. He said he had overheard us pronounce a food, and wished to know how to say it correctly. He brought from a pocket a small notebook. When I began to spell the word slowly for him to write down, he shook his head. He did not put it that way, he told us; he wrote it down as it sounded—that was how he could learn to pronounce. Diffidently he showed me his notebook, with page after page of extraordinarily ingenious phonetic spelling. I remember particularly "xad" for "shad," because "sh" is the Portuguese sound for "x."

When he had gone, I told my companions about the owner of the beauty shop at the Tivoli. I had found her surrounded by English grammar notebooks, and some novels. She was eager to try her English with me, and was quite good, amazingly good when I learned she had had no lessons, but had, like the man at the Negresco, written down phonetically the pronunciation she heard from her occasional American and English customers.

This determination to learn English, I said, was noticeable in towns of any size.

"I think they smell the tourist breeze that's just beginning to blow in this direction. They're preparing for it. They can't afford to go to schools; perhaps night classes of adult education aren't

262

available, I don't know; but their determination and application are remarkable."

"They've even begun it in the police force," Sophy contributed. "At the moment it needs considerable straightening out. Yesterday I asked a traffic officer directions for a wineshop I'd heard of—I wanted replenishments for the shoebag. This is what the officer told me: In Portuguese, he said, 'Straight ahead.' He followed this with '*Et puis, à droitsky.*' What's more, simultaneously, he pointed to the left."

Leaving the restaurant, we suggested to one another, because the night was so pleasant, we walk home. We had gone only a little distance when one of the absurd little trolleys ambled slowly by, rocking a little from side to side, reminiscent of the walk of a cowboy or a sailor. I proposed we take one to the Tivoli.

"I've been wanting to ride in them ever since the first day in Lisbon. Now we're leaving, and I haven't done it."

My friends happily acquiesced.

Although I had pointed out the trams went so slowly passengers boarded them anywhere, we went to the actual trolley stop. We felt not quite proficient enough to swing ourselves on as it went by. We boarded the trolley properly, found it was carrying very few other passengers; therefore, each of us could select an independent seat by a window, mine directly across the aisle from Brother T., Sophy immediately in front of him. Our windows were open, the breeze was delightful.

Brother T. sighed happily, saying, "I see what you mean. This little pet goes so slowly it gives one a chance to watch the passing scene in detail, and yet spares you the effort of walking."

We talked of this in happy agreement for a minute or two. By now we were approaching the Tivoli. Sophy suggested we move toward the front of the car and be at the door when it stopped.

We were on our feet and had just begun to move forward when a sudden spurt, so violent it was almost as if the trolley moved out from under us, knocked us back into our seats. Our little ambling pony had become an Arab steed. What had been a gentle

263

rocking from side to side had turned into a perilous heave-ho. Had we not been scarcely out of our seats, and still near enough to clutch them, we would have been lying in the aisle. We turned around simultaneously to look at the conductor behind us. I do not know what the others had in mind. My own vague prompting was to see if he were as astonished as we. Perhaps the motorist had gone suddenly mad. The conductor, like us, would be hanging for dear life to his pole on the back open platform, and frightened to death.

He was holding to the pole, swinging from side to side, his head thrown back; he was having the time of his life. I would not have been surprised to hear from him, "Hi-ho, Silver!" What I heard was Sophy, from whom Portuguese suddenly seemed to have decamped, begging, "No, no, no—*Tivoli*. For us the *Tivoli*. We must get out at the Tivoli."

The conductor answered. Swinging back and forth, his free arm waving like a pendulum, he called, "No, no, *no*, Tivoli," and laughed delightedly.

We flashed past the Tivoli—at our speed it was a blur of light— buckety-buckety; down a hill we went like a roller coaster, swooned around a corner and then we jiggled slowly down through the stages we had leaped over until we were in the original amble, eventually at a stop.

Shakily we descended from the car, the conductor waved a good night to us, and off into the darkness our little pony ambled jiggety, jiggety, jog. Perhaps this was the one night in his life when the motorist permitted himself something he had dreamed of for years. Perhaps under cover of darkness, and a pact with the conductor not to give him away, he always, at the ten o'clock run, takes this lap of the course on the gallop.

We were much too far from the hotel to be able to walk back. Eventually, we found a taxi.

Next day I was reminded of Brother T.'s assertion at the Negresco that the Portuguese were becoming astutely sensitive to the arrival of tourists from other countries. Mr. Rodriguez, of the Travel Bureau, had come to call on Sophy and me. He brought us our railway tickets, and confirmation of hotel reservations in our changed itinerary.

When he lingered after the business transactions had been completed, I realized he wished to make this occasion a social call. Previously, he had conducted his services by mail, by telephone or by messenger. I asked if he would like something to drink. Obviously pleased—he was very young—at joining the cocktail hour in the lounge of the Tivoli, he said he would like a little French vermouth over ice, and to make us all kin, added "We Portuguese, too, like ice." This led to a conversation about Portuguese taste in wine and food. Thinking it a good opportunity to learn about out-of-the-way restaurants that would be fun to try, I asked him what places he would choose, apart from the obvious ones. I was almost immediately sorry I had asked. The young caller acted the man-about-town, but it was not a convincing performance. He had obviously not been in Lisbon restaurants. A little later he said the Travel Bureau was comparatively new, and all its personnel young, but very interested and eager to make a success. I formed a theory about this gap in their knowledge. I think the personnel of the Portuguese Travel Bureau has had neither time nor money to investigate restaurants and hotels. They are not noncommittal as a matter of policy, but lack a firsthand experience. There is probably no expense account that would allow the staff people to patronize eating places and hotels. This service to customers would have to be added when the Bureau could afford it. Mr. Rodriguez, himself, young, eager, round-faced, ears a little prominent, hair in a short crew cut, looks like an Irish-American college undergraduate. He had given us efficient, thoughtful and considerate help in his area of knowledge. I learned from him, too, as he sipped his vermouth, Lisbon had been until recently only a stopping-off place for travelers—a day, not more, before leaving Europe or moving on into the rest of the continent. Of course, he had amended, during the war, Lisbon was filled with people from other countries, but they were certainly not tourists, and there was no traveling about. Only now, he said, tourists were

265

beginning to pause in order to see Portugal itself. They were trying, the Portuguese, in every way to make ready for this new company. In a few years, he said confidently, English would be spoken everywhere. Brother T. joined us.

Introducing them, I said to Mr. Rodriguez, "Dr. Sherman is not an American."

"I know," Mr. Rodriguez interrupted, bowing courteously. "He is English. I can tell from how he smells."

I thought I saw Teddy stiffen a little, but with grave politeness he inquired, "In what way?"

As Sophy afterward observed, people speaking in a language in which they are not at home invariably make a statement with more vehement authority than a native would use. Mr. Rodriguez replied, "Why, certainly, I can tell you. They all smell of soup."

This was disconcerting. No one vouchsafed an answer.

"Yes," Mr. Rodriguez repeated happily, "all Englishmen smell of soup, and when they come by boat, they smell also of the boat and the sea. When I am not sure and a customer comes into the Bureau just what he is, I smell hard, like this—" he sniffed noisily— "and then at once, if he is English, I catch the smell—soup, very clean, very fresh."

"Soap" had not occurred to any of us. We were happy when it did. We relaxed. I felt Brother T. had been isolated by this extraordinary distinction. Feeling he would be happier if restored to kinship, I inquired of Mr. Rodriguez how an American smelled.

"Americans do not smell at all—not of anything. There is no smell of an American, but all Englishmen, they smell very loud."

When Mr. Rodriguez departed, Brother T. suggested now he had learned his conspicuous effect on the senses of the Portuguese, perhaps it would be more considerate of him to dine alone in his room. Sophy and I overrode his unselfish considerateness. Sophy overdid it a little, I thought, by sniffing as enthusiastically as Mr. Rodriguez and protesting with a vehemence that attracted the notice of nearby patrons she considered he smelled lovely.

We dined at the Vera Cruz restaurant. The place was not easy to find because it is on the second floor of a building that houses on the street level the Volkswagen showroom. These were in the process of remodeling. Eventually, we found the door under some scaffolding, and with the help of a gentleman who evidently knew the restaurant well, and was also dining there, found a stairway at the end of a long corridor, strewn with shavings and odd bits of lumber. We considered the restaurant so delightful the other two affirmed they would be glad to climb a ladder to reach it. I would not go so far, but only because I do not care to be on a ladder. The address of the Vera Cruz is Number 12, Avenida da Liberdade, and it is especially popular for lunch. We were glad to find it not so crowded at dinnertime.

Saturday, we took the road again to Santarém, arriving at the hotel in time for lunch. From the moment we entered the outskirts of town, we knew this time there would be no mistake about the date. The folk from all parts of the country in every sort of costume and conveyance were filling the streets. The little foyer of the hotel was so filled it had overflowed the people onto the sidewalk. Working our way through to the desk, we communicated to one another an anxiety that our rooms had not been held. We were mistaken. The Portuguese are scrupulous about their agreements.

Sophy and I were to share a room; there were not enough singles to go around. She did not go upstairs with me. The proprietor sent a page with her and Brother T., to bring back from the car parked up the street our luggage. When she joined me, I showed her enthusiastically what I termed a charming and unusual feature. Though there were no windows in the sleeping portion of our accommodations, the room swelled into a kind of sun parlor with chairs and tables and windows on three sides. The bath was at the other end of the room, separated only by a drawn curtain. I had been unpacking, but on Sophy's arrival, paused to sit down with her in the little parlor. At the moment she was echoing my satisfaction in the arrangement, we heard through the open windows of our sun parlor a sound close by of a toilet being flushed. The next few seconds wafted into us the horrifying realization our sun parlor was not open to the sky. High above, in the top of the shaft on which it was located, was a glass roof. This provided the light. There was no air. The only other openings on the shaft were from the community toilet on each floor.

The manager was astounded at our protests that we must be given another room. It was the best in his establishment, the only one with its own bath and toilet. The very utterance of the word was a threat to my stomach's equilibrium. He was finally persuaded we would be happy in less luxurious surroundings. Each of us was thereupon provided with a pleasant, single room with windows on the street. He had not wanted to show them to us in the first place because we must share the community bath. He had thought it all right for the gentleman, but not for two ladies. We considered this manner of sharing infinitely preferable to the involuntary participation from the other room.

After the briefest unpacking, the three of us took to the street again. Every building, shop, house, restaurant had a balcony, and every balcony was festooned with flowers and banners. The streets themselves were filled with pedestrians, overflowing from the sidewalks. Cars made slow progress. The horn-blowing was incessant, to which no attention was paid. Even at Coimbra, we agreed, we had not seen so many handsome young men. They wore tight black trousers, black or white silk shirts, a black-brimmed hat, tipped jauntily over one eye. They walked with a grace of which they were aware. Sometimes they sat around tables at an outdoor café. They were the young horsemen, trainers and riders who would show their animals during the week. As we walked toward the edge of the town, the crowd thinned. We noticed two young girls, about fifteen or sixteen years old. They were obviously watching us, breaking off to talk to each other, and then to look again. As they caught our attention, one of them left her companion and came directly in our path.

"I ask pardon," she said, "but you would like to see the Tagus and the park?" We told her we would like that very much. She beckoned her companion. We moved on together. They were students at a boarding school in Santarém, they told us. The one who had spoken first was less shy than her friend, and more at home in English. When Brother T. complimented her on her knowledge of the language, she admitted, blushing, she was so eager to know the language well she had "taken the courage" to speak to us, hoping we would allow her, she said, to be friends, because this would give her the opportunity to practice. She did not say how she knew we were English—I did not press the point, lest she, too, would admit to a keen sense of smell.

We had a thoroughly delightful afternoon. We walked a great distance; she told us much about the town, how old it is, that its name came from Santa Iria. Brother T. whispered, "That is St. Irene, who was buried here in the seventh century." I thought the town, not betraying its actual age, had the over-all look of the seventeenth, perhaps the eighteenth century, and we walked most of its streets. By the time we had returned to the hotel, we had the occupational aching legs and feet that attack all tourists. We persuaded the girls to join us at one of the outside tables for an ice cream. Our interlocutor gave me her name and I wrote it down: Marie Lisette Boulosz. During our conversation over the ice cream, I made one grave social blunder. Artlessly I asked if she had the skill to carry a load on her head, such as I had seen on other young girls. Her eyes flashed for a moment, she laughed a little uncertainly, then gave me the benefit of ignorance. She explained girls like her and her friend would never dream of carrying anything on the head. I had overstepped a class barrier.

They left us immediately we had finished our refreshments. They had to report back at the school by six o'clock. We had an early dinner. Even then, the dining room was more than filled to capacity. Nevertheless, the food was good, the service under such difficulties remarkable. Before I went to bed that night I put a great many notes into the dictaphone. Since I now had the magic plug I had bought in Lisbon, I attached it, in order to recharge my machine. I had just finished pressing the right button, and setting it in action, when a maid came into the room to turn down my bed, and bring a pitcher of water. I pointed to the machine, and pantomimed, by putting my finger on it, and withdrawing it quickly, as one does to convey to a child a finger on a hot stove will be burned. I repeated, "Don't touch, do not touch," each time I jerked my finger back. The maid nodded, understandingly, and repeated in Portuguese, *"Não mexer"* and, laughingly, steered a wide circle around it on her way out the door.

We watched the parade on Sunday from the steps of the Tribunal. Our friends of the day before had told us our best view would be from that place. A great many other people thought so, too. The steps were broad. On their far side I caught sight, suddenly, of the two girls, evidently with their parents and younger

members of the families, come to town for the event. I pointed them out to my friends and the girls caught sight of us. We could not meet across the crowd, but we waved enthusiastically.

The procession was magnificent, led by bullfighters on foot in black and velvet and spangles. Coaches carrying the dignitaries followed, gilded and painted, some drawn by six, some by eight, white horses. Groups of riders came next, the young men we had seen on the streets; even larger groups of men on horseback, too, but wearing the uniform of the Portuguese cowboys, that is, the men who herd the bulls. They wear a sleeveless red jacket, a hat like the stocking caps we had seen on the fishermen in Nazaré, but these are red or green. They carry long staves, like the ones that had protected the bull from Gina and me. They rode mag-

Vasiliu

nificently, holding their staves high in the air with the sunlight on them like steel lances.

We followed the end of the procession into the arena and took the places we had purchased in the grandstand. By experience, we knew the moment to leave. The instant the cavalcade had paraded the bull ring, and the riders completed their superb exhibition of *dressage,* we were on our feet, past the spectators incredulous at our departure, down the conventional exitway, and out. In the entrance courtyard to the stadium we were engulfed immediately by an eddying crowd. I supposed they had not disbanded after the procession, but Brother T. surmised they were there in hope of securing tickets, which either they had been unable or could not afford to buy. Brother T., as usual, was right. We chose a young couple, shabby, unable, we knew, to buy tickets. I think I have never seen such stupefaction, incredulity, openmouthed delight as I saw on their faces when we gave them our places.

We went to the fair that evening. It was not an anticlimax to the week's delay and our complete change of plans. It was, as Gina would say, "everything what you can imagine." Magnificent animals, bulls, horses; booths of crafts (I bought some wooden toys and a beautiful straw basket). Sophy, who, during the entire trip, had permitted herself only small objects, and deplored Gina's and my impractical selections, went to pieces. She bought two large rugs, one white sheep's wool, the other interwoven in softly blended colors. They could be shipped from Lisbon, she told us loftily, now that she had found the Tourists' Service. She made no mention of the space they would occupy in the bus in transit.

When we were too tired to walk any further, we turned into a restaurant. Discovering windows looking out on a large, brilliantly lighted square, we chose places there and ordered beer.

Sophy had no sooner said, "I think there's going to be some kind of performance in that square," when an old friend strolled into the center and began to speak, amplified to the ears' torture by loudspeakers in the trees. It was the dance director we had heard

272

just exactly a week before in Tomar. As he had done in Tomar, he finished eventually. The dancers came on. The program was even more varied than the one we had seen superbly executed.

It was late when the performance ended, but we found the aisles between the booths as crowded as they had been earlier, the breach of time indicated by the number of babies asleep in their mothers' arms. Sophy engaged the services of two little boys to carry her purchases.

"You notice," Brother T. whispered to me, "how manly they are. They do not put the rugs on their heads."

On the way to my room in the hotel, I passed the chambermaid, still on duty. She smiled at sight of me, imitated my pantomime of the burned finger, and repeated, *"Não mexer."*

The next morning we visited the fair again. It was not so crowded and we had more opportunity to see the exhibits in the booths and the animals in their pens. Brother T. and I had paused to watch a very young colt with its mother. Sophy had wandered ahead. She came hurriedly back.

"Come quickly," she told us, "there's something you must see." We followed her around a corner. We saw an exhibition booth, for want of a better word, as large as a barn, divided into stalls, roofed over, but with the entire front open. In the center of the open space in front of the stalls a little boy sat on a magnificent black horse. The child could not have been more than five years old. He was dressed as we had seen the young riders the day before—the black hat cockily over one eye. A man in the uniform of the bull-keepers, scarlet jacket, with green stocking cap, stood at the head of the animal, his hand on the bridle. He was the personal attendant of the young prince. Evidently the child was the son of one of the great breeders judging from the magnificence of the exhibit. The child was probably going to take part in a procession. His right arm was in a cast; such a misadventure as a broken arm was not going to keep him from participating. The arrogant lift of his head, the look of assurance on his face were straight out of a portrait of one of the Infantes of the sixteenth century. I would happily have waited more than a week for that picture in my memory.

We returned to the hotel, had a bite of lunch, packed, filled the car. Our long-awaited visit to Santarém had come to an end.

We were pulling away when I heard a voice calling over the noise of the crowded streets. I knew I had heard the voice, and the words, somewhere before. I leaned out the car, looked around and, finally, up. High in the hotel my chambermaid was leaning well out the window over the street. She was waving a bright scarf and calling. When she saw I had found her, she waved even more vigorously, paused a moment to laugh, and then repeated the phrase I recognized. *"Não mexer, não mexer."* It was her good-by. I waved, calling the phrase back to her. As we turned the corner I looked again. She waved us out of sight.

On the way to Lisbon I thought about it. I hear it now when I think of Portugal. *Não mexer.* "Do not touch."

Now I say it to travelers going there, "Enjoy Portugal, be warmed by it, but leave it as it is. *Não mexer.* Do not touch."

ESTALAGEMS, HOTELS AND POUSADAS VISITED

Estalagem do Cruzeiro	Aljubarrota
Estalagem de Santa Iria	Tomar
Hotel Abidis	Santarém
Hotel Astoria	Coimbra
Hotel Bau	Alcobaça
Hotel Imperio	Lisbon
Hotel Infante de Sagres	Oporto
Hotel Palace	Bussaco
Hotel Seteais	Sintra
Hotel Tivoli	Lisbon
Pousada do Castelo	Óbidos
Pousada de Santa Luzia	Elvas
Pousada de Santo António	Sarem
Pousada de São Braz	Alportel
Pousada de São Tiago do Cacém	Cacém

Prices for *Pousadas* and *Estalagems* vary between $3 and $5 per day per person, while prices in the Hotels will generally be between $7 and $10 (meals included in both cases).

RECOMMENDED RESTAURANTS

Café Central	Caldas de Monchique
Escondidinho	Oporto
Estella do Portinho	Arrábida
Foclore	Lisbon
Giraldo	Évora
Negresco	Lisbon
O Faia	Lisbon
Pique-Nique	Beja
José Ribeiro	Olhão
Tavares	Lisbon
Varerinha	Ovar
Vera Cruz	Lisbon
Verde	Olhão

The average cost for dinner was about $3 in a first-class restaurant, and $2 for lunch.

275

MISCELLANEOUS INFORMATION AND ADDRESSES

American Tourists Service, 61 Rua Castilho, Cave Dto., Lisbon
Europeia Travel Bureau, 231 Avenida da Liberdade, Lisbon
Marmores de Sousa Baptista, Lda., 29 Praga do Municipio, Lisbon
Sociedade Inglesa Decorações e Antiguidades, Lda. (Renaissance), 26 Rua da Emenda, Lisbon

Volkswagen Microbus which was used throughout Portugal cost us about $15 per day with delivery from Amsterdam and an allowance of 5,000 kilos.

Cotton dresses for a hot climate were a mistake in May. During the month I wore mine only two or three times. A knitted dress was just right for motoring, a suit for town.

Note: As is often the case with foreign place names, guidebooks and maps differ as to spelling. Hence the spelling used in this book may not agree with that in another.

RECOMMENDED READING
(aside from Brother T.'s pamphlets)

All the Best in Spain and Portugal	Sydney Clark
Blue Moon in Portugal	William and Elizabeth Younger
No Garlic in the Soup	Leonard Wibberley
Portugal	Gilbert Renault-Roulier
Portugal and Madeira	Sacheverell Sitwell
The Bible in Spain	George Borrow
South of Lisbon	Frank Huggett
This Delicious Land	Lady Marie Noële Kelly